INTERPRETATION, LAW AND THE CONSTRUCTION OF MEANING

INTERPRETATION, LAW AND THE CONSTRUCTION OF MEANING

Collected Papers on Legal Interpretation in Theory, Adjudication and Political Practice

by

ANNE WAGNER

Université du Littoral Côte d'Opale,
Boulogne-sur-Mer, France

WOUTER WERNER

Institute of Public International Law,
Vrije Universiteit,
Amsterdam,
The Netherlands

and

DEBORAH CAO

Griffith University, Australia

Springer

A C.I.P. Catalogue record for this book is available from the Library of Congress.

ISBN-10 1-4020-5319-3 (HB)
ISBN-13 978-1-4020-5319-1 (HB)
ISBN-10 1-4020-5320-7 (e-book)
ISBN-13 978-1-4020-5320-7 (e-book)

Published by Springer,
P.O. Box 17, 3300 AA Dordrecht, The Netherlands.

www.springer.com

Printed on acid-free paper

CONTENTS

BIOGRAPHICAL NOTES

Moshe AZAR is Professor of Hebrew language and linguistics at the University of Haifa, Israel; member of The Academy of the Hebrew Language; Ph.D. in Linguistics, University of Nancy, France. His writing includes books (*Language of Commitment in the Old Testament and the Mishna* (in Hebrew); *The Syntax of Mishnaic Hebrew* (in Hebrew)) and articles on Hebrew syntax, semantics, and pragmatics. In recent years, he became interested in pragmatic interpretation of legal texts.

Clive BALDWIN is Senior Lecturer in Dementia Studies at the University of Bradford. Having trained as a social worker and been employed in community development he completed his PhD at the Department of Sociological Studies, University of Sheffield in 2000. His thesis focused on the competing narratives of innocence and guilt in cases of alleged Munchausen syndrome by proxy. He has since presented at national and international conferences on the narrative disparity between professional and lay accounts in such cases, and how this disparity can lead to wrongful or unreliable investigations and court judgements.

Farid BENAVIDES is a Colombian Lawyer, specialist in Human Rights and International Humanitarian Law. He studied Sociology of Law at the University of Barcelona and currently he is a PhD Candidate in Political Science at the University of Massachusetts. His Dissertation is about indigenous peoples and indigenous rights in Colombia.

Dr Deborah CAO is a Senior Lecturer affiliated with the School of Languages and Linguistics and the Socio-Legal Research Centre of the Law School, Griffith University, Australia. She was educated in China and Australia in interpreting/translation, linguistics, and law. She has published in the areas of legal translation and philosophical and linguistic analysis of Chinese law and legal culture. Her books include *Chinese Law: A Language Perspective* (Ashgate, 2004) and the forthcoming *Translating Law*.

Ross CHARNOCK, after first degrees in Exeter (UK), took his doctorate in linguistic pragmatics in Paris during the early 80s, under O. Ducrot. He is now senior lecturer at the University of Paris, where he teaches language for specialists of other disciplines, with a particular interest in the language of the law. Within this field, he specialises in the rhetorical and semantic analysis of common law judgments. He also has research interests in pragmatics and argumentation as applied to language teaching and testing, and continues to publish regularly on classical music for strings.

Maarten HENKET received his law degree in 1972 at Amsterdam University. He has taught law, legal philosophy and legal writing at Utrecht University until his retirement in 2005. His main research areas within the wide field of legal semiotics are argumentation theory, including logic and rhetoric, and legal pragmatics.

Agnes SCHREINER is Lecturer at the Law Faculty, University of Amsterdam, studied law and lectures on several themes of the General Jurisprudence. She has specialized in a series of subjects associated with law: media, arts including rituals, semiotics and social sciences. See for instance *The Semiotics of Digital Law* (2004) and her 2003 free of charge web-edition *The Ritual Manifesto* (www.1001publishers.com/index_uk.html). She researches legal cultures of Australia and of Europe. Recent publications on these cultures include *Observing the differences* (2004) and *The Common Core of Trento. A Socio-Legal Analysis of a Research Project on European Private Law* (2004).

Anita SOBOLEVA graduated from the philological faculty of the Moscow State University in 1986 and from the Moscow Law Institute in 1991. She holds an LL.M. in comparative constitutional law from the Central European University (Budapest) and a Ph.D. in linguistics from the Moscow State University (Russia). She is the author of numerous articles on the philosophy of law, legal rhetoric, legal reasoning and linguistic rights of minorities in Russian legal journals. In 2002 she published a book *Topical Jurisprudence* (in Russian). She is a member of the Bar Association and currently works as an Executive and Legal Director of a not-for-profit organization "Lawyers for Constitutional Rights and Freedoms" and is involved in human rights, civil liberties and public interest law litigation.

Dr. Hanneke VAN SCHOOTEN is a senior researcher at the Centre for Legislative Studies of Tilburg University, the Netherlands. Among her books are *Regulering in de Rechtsstaat* (1998), *Semiotics and Legislation* (ed. 1999), *Recht naar binnen kijken. Een toekomstverkenning van huisrecht, lichamelijke integriteit en nieuwe opsporingstechnieken* (with B.J. Koops and M. Prins, 2004). Her articles include 'The Meaning of Law as Instrument' (1996), 'Freedom of Expression: Censorship and Sense Construction' (2003), 'On War, Peace and Armed Conflict' (2004), 'A New Conceptual Framework for Analysing a Case Study on ICT and the Sanctity of the Home' (2004), all published in the *International Journal for the Semiotics of Law*.

Dr. Pekka VIRTANEN is a social scientist (international relations and anthropology). He has worked extensively in Africa and recently also in Brazil, where he has participated in various research projects and development co-operation activities. His research interests include identity politics, legal pluralism, the role indigenous institutions in natural resource management, and international environmental regimes – especially market-based normative mechanisms.

Anne WAGNER is a Senior Lecturer in LSP affiliated with the Université du Littoral Côte d'Opale, France. She is the deputy Editor-in-Chief and the French Book Review Editor of the *International Journal for the Semiotics of Law* (Springer). She is the president of the International Roundtable for the Semiotics of Law (IRSL). Her main research interests include legal language, law and semiotics, legal translation, plain language, interpretation, contemporary legal theory, law and literature, legal history. She is the author of *La Langue de la Common Law* (L'Harmattan 2002), and has recentely co-edited *The Feminine in Legal Discourse* (special issue of *The International Journal for the Semiotics of Law* 19/2, 2006), as well as three books entitled *Contemporary Issues in the Semiotics of Law: Cultural and Symbolic Analyses in a Global Context* (Hart 2005), *Images in Law* (Ashgate 2006) and *Legal Language and the Search for Clarity: Practice and Tools* (Peter Lang 2006).

Wouter WERNER is Professor of public international law at the *Vrije Universiteit*, Amsterdam. His main fields of interest are the theory of international law and the legal regime regulating the use of force in international relations.

INTRODUCTION

ANNE WAGNER, WOUTER WERNER AND DEBORAH CAO

Semiotic theories have emphasized the contextual and dynamic nature of meaning and knowledge. As one of the founding fathers of semiotics has argued, all meaning emerges in a triadic structure, where a 'sign stands for an object, not in all respects, but in reference to a sort of idea ... the ground'.[1] This understanding of the construction of meaning rules out the possibility of a fixed foundation of knowledge. All knowledge is mediated by a sign, which can only be interpreted by reference to yet another sign, its ground. In the same fashion, legal semiotics has emphasized the dynamic character of legal concepts and stressed the importance of interpretation and the construction of meaning. In response to new problems, changing power structures, changing societal norms and new faces of injustice, established doctrines are reconsidered, reformulated and partly replaced by competing doctrines and hypotheses.[2]

The open and conjectural nature of legal knowledge raises some foundational questions regarding the nature and function of law. How is, for example, the openness of legal rules to be reconciled with the quest for final authority? Who has the power to define words and concepts in a concrete case? How is the construction of meaning in law affected by societal discourses? Such questions are closely related to the central topic of this volume: the problem of legal interpretation and the construction of meaning within and through law.

The contributions to this volume are based on a selected number of papers that were presented at the 2004 International Roundtable for the Semiotics of Law in Lyon. The contributions reflect the connectedness, as well as the diversity, of the community of legal semioticians. While all contributions deal with issues of interpretation and the construction of meaning, the fields of application as well as the theoretical underpinnings of the contributions are broad. We hope that this ′diversity in unity′ will contribute to a fruitful discussion on the foundations and application of semiotic theories of law.

---

[1] Charles Sanders Peirce, *Collected Papers* (Cambridge: Harvard University Press, 1931-1935), Vol. II, at 34.

[2] See for an analysis of the dynamics of law and legal interpretation Roberta Kevelson's seminal work, *The Law as a System of Signs* (New York: Plum Press, 1988).

Part I of this volume discusses the problem of legal interpretation from a more general, theoretical perspective. The four chapters in this part discuss the topic of legal interpretation from different, yet overlapping perspectives: institutionalism (van Schooten), contextualism (Charnock), legal rhetoric (Soboleva) and communicative rationality (Cao). All four chapters explicitly relate the problem of interpretation to the notion of intersubjectivity and emphasize that legal interpretation is embedded in wider social practice. Thus, van Schooten examines the importance of common societal beliefs that shape the law to law and structure the interplay between legal rules, the application of those rules and social interaction. In a similar fashion, Charnock criticizes the literal rule of construction and argues that the content of legal rules is established by consensus in the relevant community. Soboleva sets out how *topoi,* or commonplaces, guide legal reasoning and function as constraining and disciplining structures. Finally, Cao takes up the Habermassian notion of communicative rationality to explain legislative and judicial acts. By contrast to approaches to (legal) speech acts that derive meaning primarily from intention, Habermas stresses the importance of intersubjectivity and acceptability, thus echoing the Piercian reading of the relation between the construction of meaning, intersubjectivity and rationality.[3]

The notion of intersubjectivity also figures prominently in Part II of this volume that deals with the problem of interpretation in judicial reasoning. In Chapters Five, Six and Seven, Baldwin, Henket and Azar, discuss respectively one of the most delicate topics related to the application and interpretation of law: the construction of legally relevant facts in legal proceedings. In several respects, Baldwin and Henket take different positions towards the role and construction of facts in legal proceedings, as may be inferred from the respective titles of their contributions: 'Who needs fact when you got narrative?' (Baldwin) and 'Taking facts seriously' (Henket), whereas Azar, in his paper, approaches judicial reasoning from a different angle: in terms of ambiguity and indeterminacy[4] where law and language often intercept. Indeed, Azar

---

[3] See for example Habermas's discussion of Pierce in J. Habermas, *Texte und Kontexte*, Suhrkamp (Frankfurt: a.M., 1991).

[4] For more information, see L. Solan, 'Vagueness and Ambiguity in Legal Interpretation', 73-96, in J. Engberg, M. Gotti, V. Bhatia and D. Heller (eds.), *Vagueness in Normative Texts* (Bern: Peter Lang, coll. Linguistic Insights, 2005), vol. 23, A. Wagner, 'Semiotic Analysis of the Multistage Dynamic at the Core of Indeterminacy in Legal Language', 173-200, in J. Engberg, M. Gotti, V. Bhatia

insists that these are crucial features in legal discourse analysis where the role of 'de-vaguefying' or 'desambiguation' still remains crucial for the interpreters. Azar argues that judges tend to adopt an anti-pragmatic approach in such disputed cases treating them as cases of vagueness instead of what they actually are, that is, cases of ambiguity. In their contributions, Baldwin and Henket give concrete analyses to legal interpretation and both agree on two important points. First, judges and juries base their decisions on the most convincing narrative of facts - on narrative coherence rather than on 'correct representation' as such. Second, such a semiotic understanding of judicial practice does not rule out the possibility of critique. Notions such as due process, communicative rationality or accuracy do not lose their meaning in non-positivistic readings of judicial reasoning.

Part III of this volume takes up the interplay between law and globalization and the role of law in (international) politics and thus touches upon the question of who is able to define legal words and concepts in concrete circumstances. The power to define has played a crucial role in the formation of Latin-American States, as the contributions of Benavides Vanegas and Virtanen demonstrate.

Benavides Vanegas discusses how the fight for independence, as well as the conceptualization of 'the nation', in Colombia was shaped by the 'coloniality of power' and the dominant European legal and political concepts. The initial struggles for independence, Benavides Vanegas argues, should be interpreted as struggles for equality within the Spanish nation, while the later process of nation building was based on a logic of inclusion and exclusion that can only be understood in terms of predominant racial definitions and hierarchies. Without a proper understanding of the coloniality of power, current discussions on nationalism in the era of globalization start from the wrong place. The chapter by Virtanen shows how in the Brazilian Amazon, economic globalization and integration in an authoritarian central State have reshaped local cultures and disciplined local populations. However, Virtanen's

---

and D. Heller (eds.), *Vagueness in Normative Texts* (Bern: Peter Lang, coll. Linguistic Insights, 2005), vol.23.

James B. White, *The Legal Imagination: Studies in the Nature of Legal Thought and Expression* (Boston/Toronto: Little Brown, 1973), Brian Bix, 'Can Theories of Meaning and Reference Solve the Problem of Legal Determinacy?' (2003) *Ratio Juris* 16: 281-295.

chapter also warns against simplistic, unidirectional interpretations of the process of globalization. Based on Lotman's semiotics of borders and identity, Virtanen argues that 'current international relations are characterized by interpenetration of different normative systems' and could in some areas – such as international certification – lead to 'interesting alternative(s) to the prevalent forms of unidirectional and homogenising globalization.' Agnes Schreiner, on the other hand, deals with the willingness of Aborigines to demonstrate the struggle for their rights and their 'traditional connection to the land' in Australia, analyzing their art of memory which is 'a big play of combinatorial exchanges'. She insists on, and grounds this argument, in the deep semiotic analyses of two particular landmarks, i.e., the Manggalili and the Djarrakpi.

PART I

LEGAL THEORY

CHAPTER 1

Law as Fact, Law as Fiction: A Tripartite Model of Legal Communication

Hanneke Van Schooten

Tilburg University, The Netherlands

1. Introduction

Regardless of the concept of law that is adopted – whether the viewpoint that law is '[t]he prophecies of what the courts do in fact ...',[1] or the viewpoint that law is a system of norms, a separate universe of normativity, apart from the factual effects in the real world[2] – enacting legislation is generally recognized as an act of communication. Even in the latter legal-positivist view, the working of the law (the effectiveness of the law) cannot be completely set aside. Kelsen's basic assumption is that the relationship between norm and fact, between rule and conduct, is logically irreducible in nature. From the fact that something *is*, it cannot be concluded that it *ought* to exist. The same is true for the opposite: if something *ought* to be, it cannot be concluded that it *is*.[3] This conclusion is the basis of the concept of law as a hierarchical system of *norms*, separate from factual considerations, i.e. *conduct*. However, the gap between norm and fact is not quite as unproblematic as Kelsen indicates. He states that the validly enacted norm needs to have a minimum degree of effect (working) in the real world in order to be a legitimate norm.[4] This implies that the conduct prescribed in the legal rule has to be 'realistic'. For example, the legal rule enacted in Tsarist Russia, which prescribed that every female prisoner had to give birth to a child of the male sex every year, is, in this sense, not a legitimate legal norm. The interdependence of the legitimate rule and its social effect illustrates the problematic character of strict separation.

For a long time, the processes that take place in the relationship between a rule and its materialization have been, to some extent, like a

---

[1]Oliver Wendell Holmes, 'The Path of the Law', *Harvard Law Review* 457 (1897), 461.
[2]Hans Kelsen, *Reine Rechtslehre* (Wien: Österreichische Staatsdruckerei, 1992), 5.
[3]*Supra* n. 2, at 5-9.
[4]*Supra* n. 2, at 10-14, 215-221.

A. Wagner et al. (eds.), Interpretation, Law and the Construction of Meaning, 3–20.

black box; rules enter on one side and norm-conforming conduct comes out on the other. Lack of insight into these processes resulted in the creation of several models of legal communication.[5] Although the legal effects differ, most models are in essence based upon linear causality of goal-oriented legislation. The legal 'message' is 'transported' in a one-sided 'flow model' of information, that is, from 'law-giver' to 'law-taker', from sender to receiver. This metaphor presupposes the possibility of transmittable legal information: the words obviously express a meaningful 'message'. This raises the question of what this 'message' is and how it is communicated.

Institutional legal theory has adopted a concept of law through which a reciprocal element can be added to the one-sided models of legal communication, i.e. by defining the meaning of legal information in a semiotic-pragmatic way. In Section 2, I will analyze institutional legal theory, its concept of law, the metaphors used, and the consequences for the ideas about meaning transmission and sense construction. In particular Ruiter's tripartite conceptual model will be analysed: the interplay between rule, rule application, and social practices. In Section 3, a case study of Article 11 of the Dutch Constitution - the protection of personal integrity - is presented. Finally, in Section 4 the case study will be analysed by means of Ruiter's institutional model.

2. Institutional Legal Theory: Reciprocal Dimensions?

2.1 Legal language

What has been described as the 'linguistic turn' in science, at the beginning of the 20th century, has pushed the question of language and communication processes more and more to the centre of theorizing; it emphasized the centrality of symbols and meaning to social life. A dichotomy frequently cited in this respect is the dual character of language. On the one hand, descriptive language is a representation of the real, factual world – the real world constitutes the touchstone, the test, for the truth or untruth of the spoken or written words. If the words constitute untruth, the *words* have to be adapted to the brute facts of the real world. On the other

---

[5]For an elaboration and description of several models of legal communication, see my 'Instrumental Legislation and Communication Theories', in Hanneke van Schooten (ed.), *Semiotics and Legislation: Jurisprudential, Institutional and Sociological Perspectives* (Liverpool: Deborah Charles Publications, 1999), 183-211.

hand, with the use of language 'speech acts' can be performed.[6] An example of a classic speech act can be found in the Bible. In Genesis, the words of God took effect according to their literal sense: 'Let there be light, and there was light.'[7] The light came into being because He so commanded; and everything else on earth was created in the same way: by commands of God. In this example, the effects of the commands (or imperatives) were physical. The almighty Creator was supposed to be capable of bringing about light, herbs, animals, etc., through his words. However, the effects of imperatives in legal language are not physical: they bring about 'legal effects'; rights, duties, and legal qualities. In legal language, the legal norm is the touchstone, the test for the correctness or incorrectness of the actual or factual behaviour. The legal rule expresses reality, or some part thereof, in words. The words of the legal rule cast realizations ahead; they determine behaviour before it has taken place; they express future behaviour and events. The latter function of language provides the opposite image of the former: the real world has to be adapted to the words, not the reverse. Legal language aims at creating a new world.

This brings us to the second characteristic of legal language, i.e. the observation that its terminology has no physical counterpart or reference in the world of fact, while terms like 'chair', 'tree', and 'house' do. The terms 'right', 'duty', and 'legal quality' cannot be pointed out as 'facts'. Herbert Hart called this phenomenon 'the anomaly of legal language'.[8]

Nevertheless, legal terminology plays an important role in social life. Often without a proper understanding of the phenomenon, 'property' is obtained, 'contracts' are signed, 'states' are created, 'rights' are granted, 'borders' are fixed, and 'marriage ceremonies' are performed. Relatively uniform ideas of ownership, states, and all kinds of rights and their corresponding duties and legal qualities are disseminated among the general public. The regular use of these terms, if correctly applied, is connected to uniform ideas about corresponding behaviour. Here, we recognize 'institutional facts' – the opposite of 'brute facts' – i.e. acts that exist by virtue of rules, like playing chess exists by virtue of the rules of

---

[6]John R. Searle, *Speech Acts*: *An Essay in the Philosophy of Language* (Cambridge: Cambridge University Press, 1970).

[7]Genesis 1:3-4.

[8]H.L.A. Hart, *Essays in Jurisprudence and Philosophy* (Oxford: Clarendon Press, 1983), 22-23.

chess. What is the importance of these observations? This question is analysed in the next section.

2.2 Legal rules as 'thought objects'

The observation that legal language refers to 'supersensible'[9] mental entities is considered to be one of the essential elements of law. Law as a linguistic phenomenon and its relationship with social practices can be divided into three subsystems:

> the legitimate legal rule (the formal dimension), which comprises a message (the material dimension);
>
> the acts of the application of the rule by an official (and, in the case of a conflict, a judge), and
>
> a degree of rule-conforming patterns of behaviour in social practices.[10]

Considering the relationship between words and reality described above, it has been concluded that within these three categories only subsystems (ii) and (iii) are *discernible*:[11] i.e. the acts of the official applying the rule are *perceptible* (and, in the case of a conflict, the decision of the judge (see ii)) and the rule-conforming patterns of behaviour are *observable* in social practices (see iii). The legal rule itself is an indiscernible construct; it is *thought* to be the basis of the two other subsystems. The words of the legal rule project an image: an image that is aimed at actualization in the real world.[12] This means that the substantive message of the legal rule is a mental construct (a thought object): an ideal entity to be distinguished from physical things.[13] The message of the rule projects an imaginary reality; people should *think* of as being real. In the words of Jeremy Bentham: 'we are under the necessity of talking about them [fictions, HvS] in terms which pre-suppose their existence'.[14] And

---

[9]This terminology is used by Karl Olivecrona in his book *Law as Fact* (London: Stevens and Sons, 1971), 223.

[10]Dick W.P. Ruiter, *Legal Institutions* (Dordrecht: Kluwer Academic Publishers, 2001), 24-25.

[11]Among others, Ruiter, *supra* n. 10, at 25.

[12]Olivecrona suggests that the original explanation of the sense of a legal command may have been magical; *supra* n. 9, at 98, 226 and 231.

[13]Olivecrona states that the notion of legal rules should be viewed as a reality only like an idea in people's mind, a 'fantasy'; *supra* n. 9, at 223.

[14]C.K. Ogden, *Bentham's Theory of Fictions* (New York: Harcourt, Brace and Company, 1942), Iii.

'the existence of a fictitious entity is feigned by the imagination' and 'is spoken of as a real one'.[15]

The imaginary reality of a rule's message can only be distinguished in its perceptible application by officials (or, in the case of a conflict, by the judge), on the one hand, and in observable social practices, on the other. In this view, the message of legal language can only be observed through *acts*. Only *by acting* does the written legal message obtain its meaning. Wittgenstein's frequently quoted 'meaning is use' also seems to be relevant in this context.

Unlike the Institutional Legal Theory (ILT) developed by MacCormick and Weinberger – which starts from the viewpoint that law consists of *two dimensions*, i.e. normative institutions (a set of rules) and real institutions (a set of patterns of behaviour)[16] – Ruiter creates *three dimensions*: (i) a set of rules, (ii) the acts of application of the rules by officials, and, in the case of a conflict, the acts of the judiciary, and (iii) patterns of behaviour in social practices.[17]

With respect to the relationship between the legal rule and its materialization, the following categories can be posited.

> (a) *Ideally*, the projected image of a legitimate legal rule is entirely materialized in corresponding patterns of social behaviour.
>
> (b) An imaginary reality that is projected by a legitimate legal rule, but is not the object of a common belief underlying the legal practice, is *ineffective*.
>
> (c)An imaginary reality that is the object of a common belief underlying a legal practice but is not projected by a legitimate legal rule is '*illegal*'.

In the second category, the substantive sense of the projected picture partly fails to materialize. In the third category, an imaginary reality emerges from observable social practices without the existence of any legal rule. In both categories, *common belief* or *shared beliefs* in the existence of the imaginary reality of the legal message are absent.[18] The phenomena

---

[15]*Supra* n. 14, at Iiii.

[16]Neil MacCormick and Ota Weinberger, *An Institutional Theory of Law: New Approaches to Legal Positivism* (Dordrecht: Kluwer Academic Publishers, 1986), 1-27.

[17]*Supra* n. 10, at 24-25.

[18]Eerik Lagerspetz, The Opposite Mirrors: An Essay on the Conventionalist Theory of Institutions (Dordrecht: Kluwer Academic Publishers, 1995), 14.

called mutual or shared beliefs, and common belief or common knowledge are not well established. These terms are used in different senses; for example, in the sense that images of legal rules are the object of mutual beliefs causing patterns of behaviour in conformity with these beliefs.[19] This point of view differs from the sense that a variety of observable patterns of social conduct can be *interpreted* as resting on shared beliefs. The latter definition takes the observable patterns of social conduct as a basis. These patterns of conduct *suggest* the existence of particular common beliefs in society, *regardless* of what the members of society *really and actually believe.*[20] Patterns of social conduct, interpreted as resting on a common belief in an imaginary reality of a legal rule, show the existence of *reciprocity* in the relationship between rule and conduct. In categories (b) and (c), we recognize the partial absence of such a common belief in the imaginary reality,[21] expressed by observable behaviour in social reality.

2.3 A tripartite conceptual framework

From this viewpoint, the relationship between rule and conduct has reciprocal elements. The idea of the existence of linear causality between rule and social practices is partly put into perspective. Observable social practices express the existence of a particular common belief in the projected image of the legal rule, as well as social practices – actions – determining the meaning of the corresponding words of the legal rule. This interplay is not exclusively restricted to the relationship between normative and real institutions, as developed by MacCormick and Weinberger,[22] but takes place twice. First, it takes place when the rule is applied by officials. For instance, a police officer stops a woman cycling in a park by saying 'Vehicles are not allowed in the park' and imposing a fine on her for riding a bike in an area which is not open to vehicular traffic. When a conflict arises about the application of a legal rule, the Court has the competence to take a final decision. In the Court's interpretation, the law – in particular the legal rule – has to be reconstructed in every new case. Secondly, in social behaviour substantive legal rules can partly or wholly be realized, but patterns of behaviour may also be observed without the existence of any legal rule: the 'illegal' practices. Illegal practices indicate that particular behaviour is regulated by common belief but is not related to any

---

[19]*Supra* n. 10, at 9.
[20]*Supra* n. 10, at 22-23.
[21]For a definition of Ruiter's 'common belief', see Ruiter, *supra* n. 10, at 21-24.
[22]*Supra* n. 16.

legal rule. These processes make clear that social practices are not merely subject to unilateral legal steering, but have their own 'momentum' to create institutional facts. The tripartite conceptual framework offers a more sophisticated model to analyse the complexity of legal communication than the models of linear causality.

In earlier publications, I used this conceptual framework for the case study of a fundamental right in the Dutch Constitution, the sanctity of the home (Article 12).[23] The starting point was the legal rule, projecting an imaginary reality – the protection of the home – which becomes manifest and discernible in the application of Article 12 as well as in 'illegal' social patterns of conduct. Article 12, as we can understand from the characters printed on paper, concerns a thought object; there is no physical counterpart to the sanctity of the home, such as there is to the word 'cheese'. The protection of the home – as a thought object, as an imaginary reality – is expressed by and becomes manifest in acts. For instance, does a police officer who does not enter a house, but only puts his arm through the open door, violate the sanctity of the home? What about the police officer who uses heat sensors on the outside of a house to detect the cultivation of cannabis? Does he violate the sanctity of the home? Is the monitoring of conversations that take place inside, by means of microphones installed outside, a violation of the sanctity of the home? Whenever an executive officer acts and a judge reaches conclusions with respect to these issues, the words of the rule obtain a narrowed or broadened meaning. In this way, the extent and interpretation of Article 12 developed over the course of time while the text itself remained unchanged. 'Home', for instance, is not only a construction of walls and a roof, but also a tent, a home trailer, a boat and a hotel room. The 'occupant' is not necessarily the owner or the tenant of the house, but may also be a squatter. 'Entry' of the home does not only take place by *walking* into the home, but also when a police officer, standing outside the front door, grasps the occupant who is standing in the doorway, and pulls him outside with one arm. To scan a house by means of new technology is not defined as 'entry' because it lacks the physical aspect of entering.

In short, while the legal text remains unchanged, the substantive meaning of the words of the legal rule (projecting an image of a certain

---

[23]Hanneke van Schooten, 'A New Conceptual Framework for Analysing a Case Study on ICT and the Sanctity of the Home', *International Journal for the Semiotics of Law* (forthcoming, 2005).

behaviour) is changed fundamentally. The image projected by the legal rule becomes manifest in social practices; on the one hand, by the application of the image of the rule by officials and, in the case of a conflict about its application, by the judge; on the other hand, social and technical developments and changing patterns of behaviour can be observed in social practices: the use, for instance, of Information and Communication Technology (ICT) is not included in Article 12 and can be regarded as an 'ineffective legal practice', even as an 'illegal practice' which is not projected by any legal rule. Modern technology and ICT unsettle the sanctity of the home: the hitherto protecting walls of the home seem to be virtually transparent. In the case study of Article 12, the existence of a codified legal rule constituted the starting point; application thereof and judiciary interpretation, on the one hand, and technical developments in society, on the other, did their work. Article 12 is one of the oldest fundamental rights, already codified in the 18th century. Its meaning has developed over time. This has consequences for the application of the conceptual framework.

The question arises as to what the consequences will be when applying the conceptual framework to a new fundamental right, such as the protection of personal integrity (codified in Article 11 of the 1983 Dutch Constitution), in particular the period *before* the codification. The analysis of this period, i.e. the period in which a written constitutional rule protecting the right of personal integrity was absent, is emphasized in this paper. In the next section, the history of Article 11 of the Dutch Constitution will be described.

3. Personal Integrity: A Case Study

3.1 Discussion and case law before 1983

Unlike the sanctity of the home (Article 12), which was codified in the first Dutch Constitution in 1798 and shows a long history of development, the personal integrity right (Article 11) was codified relatively late (1983). Article 11 states:

> Everyone shall have the right to inviolability of his person, without prejudice to restrictions laid down by or pursuant to Act of Parliament.[24]

---

[24]This translation can be found at <http://www.oefre.unibe.ch/law/icl/nl100000_.html>. The original text of Article 11 reads: 'Ieder heeft, behoudens bij of krachtens de wet te stellen beperkingen, recht op onaantastbaarheid van zijn lichaam.'

A privacy right formulated in *general* terms – 'Everyone shall have the right to respect for his privacy, without prejudice to restrictions laid down by or pursuant to Act of Parliament'[25] – is laid down in Article 10 of the Constitution. Like Article 12, which is a differentiated form of the general privacy right, i.e. the protection of privacy within the walls of the home, Article 11 is a differentiated form of the general privacy right, i.e. the specific protection of the human body. This was one of the two arguments on which the government based its reservation about the Parliamentary proposal to provide for the protection of the human body in a separate Article: the government stated that personal integrity was already protected by the general privacy right of Article 10. The other argument was that with the realization of a separate right to personal integrity, the notion of the general right to privacy would be diminished.[26] This standpoint was in accordance with the negative advice given by the *Staatscommissie van advies inzake de Grondwet en de Kieswet* ['National Advisory Committee on the Constitution and the Election Act'].[27] The policy document in which the government standpoint was expressed includes an investigation into the necessity of the protection of personal integrity in German literature and German case law.[28] The aspects of personal integrity were listed as follows:

torture,

corporal punishment,

physical and mental maltreatment,

forced medical experiments,

forced medical treatment for venereal diseases,

electroshock administered to mentally disturbed persons,

forced feeding during a hunger strike,

stomach pumping,

---

[25]This is the wording in paragraph 1. Paragraphs 2 and 3 of Article 10 focus on the specific field of the protection of personal data, which are not relevant in this article.
[26]*Kamerstukken II* [Parliamentary Documents II], 1978/79, 15 463, nos. 2, 7-9.
[27]The National Advisory Committee on the Constitution and the Elections Act, (The Hague, 1968), 32.
[28]*Supra* n. 26.

encephalography,

blood samples,

vaccination,

X-ray examination,

injury,

operations,

body search,

medical treatment,

hair cutting.

Although the right to personal integrity was not codified until 1983, this fundamental right played a role in Dutch case law before that year. The cases involved, however, were concerned with a particular field of the law - penal law – and a particular situation, viz. the rules with respect to the treatment of the suspect or the accused: search and/or examination of the individual's body and clothes as laid down in Articles 56 and 195 of the Code of Criminal Procedure. Although the right to personal integrity was not incorporated in the Constitution at the time, the *Hoge Raad der Nederlanden* (the Supreme Court of the Netherlands) decided in the *Tweede bloedproef-arrest*[29] (*Second Blood Test* case) that taking a blood sample is a wrongful injury of the body if the individual involved did not consent. In this case, a drink-driver caused an accident and grievous bodily harm to another road user. In general, a suspect has to undergo examinations of the body and/or the clothes, as is laid down in Articles 56 and 195 of the Code of Criminal Procedure. The Court focussed on the question whether a blood test is included in the 'examination' as mentioned in Articles 56 and 195. The Supreme Court decided that this was not the case. The Articles are only to be interpreted in a strict and grammatical way. Taking blood without the subject's consent in order to determine the blood alcohol level and using the blood as evidence against the suspect is 'a wrongful violation of the suspect's bodily integrity' (*een onrechtmatige aantasting van de verdachtes lichamelijke integriteit*). It is beyond the scope of Articles 56 and 195; a blood test does not have a legal basis in

---

[29]HR 26 June 1962, *NJ* 1962, 470.

other Acts either.[30] In this *Second Blood Test* case, the Supreme Court referred to a fundamental right, the *bodily integrity* of the suspect, which was not incorporated in the Constitution.

Twelve years later, in a case concerning forced medical treatment, the Supreme Court formulated a general rule concerning a right to self-determination with respect to the body, however, without calling it the right to personal integrity.[31] In this case, the accused was detained under unconditional hospital order for life. The suspect was described as a severely mentally disturbed and very dangerous person. The forced treatment included psychotherapy, psychiatric medication, and potentially a lobotomy. The accused explicitly refused the operation. The Supreme Court formulated the general rule that 'a surgeon is not authorized to operate on a patient without his consent'. Although exceptions are possible, this unwritten rule was the basis for the Court's final decision that compulsory treatment in the form of an operation on the brain is not 'automatically' allowed when the accused is detained under hospital order for life. This viewpoint expresses the idea that even an accused under such circumstances as described above is not a person completely without rights.

A year later, the same Court arrived at the same conclusion in a more or less similar case.[32] Here, the main question concerned the psychotherapeutic treatment of an individual having been detained under hospital order for five years.[33] Here too, the consent of the individual involved was lacking and, here too, the Court concluded that psychotherapeutic treatment was not allowed against the will of the accused. Here too, compulsory psycho-therapeutic treatment was obviously not a part of the detainment under hospital order. The accused is protected under the fundamental right to self-determination with respect to the body.

The cases above concern judicial conclusions within the field of criminal law. The famous case that triggered the discussion about the desirability of codifying the right to personal integrity and, in the end, resulted in the codification of the right was the *Fluoriderings-arrest*

---

[30]The *Besluit alcoholonderzoeken* (Alcohol Testing Decree) and the *Regeling bloed- en urineonderzoek* (Blood and Urine Analysis Regulation) came into force at a later date, in July 1997.

[31]HR 14 June 1974, *NJ* 1974, 436.

[32]HR 15 April 1975, *NJ* 1975, 288.

[33]HR 15 April 1975, *NJ* 1975, 288.

(*Fluoridation* case).[34] This case concerned the adding of fluoride to drinking water by an Amsterdam water supply company, in order to prevent dental caries. This raised the question of to what extent water fluoridation amounts to a violation of the body. The plaintiffs, a group of citizens who were against adding fluoride to drinking water, invoked Article 8 of the ECHR. According to this Article, interference of a public authority with the right to privacy is only permitted if it is 'in accordance with the law', viz. interference is only permitted when it is based upon an Act of Parliament. The Supreme Court decided that in this case the legal ground was lacking since the *Waterleidingwet* (Water Supply Act) prescribed the supply of *good drinking water*. Adding fluoride to drinking water goes *beyond* this legal purpose. By adding fluoride to drinking water, the water is used as a means of transport, but for purposes other than those prescribed by the Act. Here, the basis of the Court's argumentation is not a legal rule, nor an unwritten rule, but a *legal principle*: the principle that the exercise of state power is only permitted on the basis of previous and generally binding legislation adopted by the people's representatives: Acts of Parliament.

3.2 Developments after 1983

The right to personal integrity was – after fierce debates in Parliament – finally codified in 1983.[35] From the discussions on the topic in Parliament it has become clear that the right to personal integrity can fulfil an important role in many situations and in various social fields. In general, the right can be categorized according to two essential dimensions:

1. The right to remain free from violation of the body by other persons (a defensive right);
2. The right to have control of one's own body (a self-determinative right).[36]

The scope of the personal integrity right is usually restricted to the areas listed above. Death does not end the latter dimension: organs may not be taken from the body without the consent of the deceased given during

---

[34]HR 22 June 1973, *NJ* 1973, 386.

[35]However, before the incorporation of personal integrity into the Constitution, the human body was protected by Acts of Parliament concerning specific situations in the field of criminal law, especially the Code of Criminal Procedure, Book II, Titles XX and XXI.

[36]Both elements can be distinguished in the case law described in subsection 3.1.

his/her life.[37] Issues such as environmental pollution, traffic security, or the use of harmful materials on the work floor, however, remain unclear. Are they included in the right to personal integrity? Does the government have a special responsibility in these fields? Another question is the relationship between personal integrity, abortion, and euthanasia. Although the government recognizes this problematic relationship, the debates do not make clear what the consequences will or may be. These moral questions will have to be answered in case law.

The right to personal integrity as it is laid down in Article 11 of the Constitution has been the subject of court decisions since 1983. The ongoing development of new medical technology raised questions with respect to the inviolability of the body; for instance, the famous *Wangslijm-arrest* [*Buccal mucous membrane* case] concerning DNA testing.[38] In this case, a suspect was accused of a criminal offence under the Opium Act; in particular, the selling of one of the products listed in the Act.[39] The suspect was also accused of a criminal offence under the Penal Code: armed robbery. Without the suspect's consent, body material had been removed - mucous membrane from the mouth – in order to determine his DNA profile and, secondly, he had been sniffed by a police dog that was trained to detect a person's identity by scent, also without the consent of the suspect. Before turning to its decision, the Court summed up several methods of examining a suspect. With respect to a *blood test* (to examine an individual's blood alcohol level), the Court had decided in the *Second Blood Test* case[40] that, in order to obtain blood, the body has to be injured. For this reason, a blood test – carried out without the suspect's consent – was considered a breach of bodily integrity. In the *Buccal mucous membrane* case, taking cell samples from the inside of the cheek by means of swabs without the suspect's consent was also considered to be a breach of Article 11, even though the body need not to be injured. The criterion used by the Court was that taking tissue from the mouth implies removing cellular material from the body. The difference with the sniffing test was explained by the argument that sniffing does not involve removing cellular material, and for that reason is not protected under the personal integrity right. Besides, the removal of body material in order to determine a suspect's DNA has far-reaching consequences: it reveals a huge amount of

[37]In general, fundamental rights apply from a citizen's birth until his or her death.
[38]HR 2 July 1990, *NJ* 1990, 751.
[39]Except for soft drugs, e.g. cannabis, which are allowed in limited quantities.
[40]HR 26 June 1962, *NJ* 1962, 470.

information about an individual. The sniffing test – recognizing a person or a person's objects by means of scent – only reveals a person's identity. Although a suspect is to a certain extent the object of legal examinations, the line that marks the breach of the protection of the body is here drawn at the removal of body material for DNA testing even though the body need not be injured. Here, a remarkable distinction can be noticed. A legal police examination of a suspect's clothes and body, as laid down in Articles 56 and 195 of the Code of Criminal Procedure, is a legal restriction to personal integrity as included in Article 11 of the Constitution. It includes rectal and vaginal examination. According to the Court's decision in the *Buccal mucous membrane* case, these examinations are considered less far-reaching than the removal of cells from the mouth by means of swabs, which is a breach of Article 11. The breach of the intimacy of the body is more drastic in the case of rectal or vaginal examination, however, than during the removal of cells from the mouth.

Another interesting judiciary decision was the *Aidstest-arrest* (*Aids Test* case).[41] Unlike the *Buccal mucous membrane* case – which concerned the hierarchical relationship between the Public Prosecutions Service and the suspect – the *Aids Test* case concerned a legal battle between two citizens. A woman, Q, had been raped twice by X, under the threat of a gun. X was sentenced for his crime. The victim, who was afraid that she had been infected with HIV during the rape, stated that the consequences of the rape should be reduced as much as possible and demanded a blood test to be taken from X to determine the presence of the virus. X refused to cooperate. He referred to Article 11 of the Constitution: his personal integrity was at stake. The Court considered X's refusal to cooperate a wrongful act under Article 1401 of the old Civil Code, which includes the norms of decency that have to be observed by citizens in social life. The victim herself underwent a medical examination, with a negative result; but the examination had to be repeated after six months, in order to be sure about the absence of infection. This period of waiting and insecurity put a heavy emotional stress on the victim. Since the Supreme Court concluded that X's refusal to cooperate in a blood test was a wrongful act, Article 11 of the Constitution played a role, not only – as usual – in the hierarchical, vertical relationships of criminal law, i.e. the relationship between the lawful authorities and the citizens, but also in the equal and horizontal relationships between citizens in civil law.

---

[41] HR 18 June 1993, *NJ* 1994, 347.

3.3 A futurologist view

At present, discussions are taking place about which technical developments should be considered violations of personal integrity. Increasingly, objects are equipped with chips or tags that bear unique codes. A reader can detect the signals sent by the chips, and identify the object. Until now, such chips have been used in machines that are often stolen, such as cars and motorbikes. However, in the near future all kinds of everyday objects will be equipped with chips. Such RFID (Radio Frequency Identification) chips have the size of a grain of sand. Their signals can be detected at a range of 30 centimetres to several metres. Clothing can be equipped with chips, not only to prevent theft, but also for the washing machine to recognize the garment. The European Central Bank aims at equipping euros with such chips, from 2005 onwards, in order to prevent counterfeiting, but also for an other interesting use: with the aid of RFID at customs offices and airports suitcases with 'black money'[42] can be detected. To what extent the signals of such chips can be detected by generally available readers will depend on the protection of these chips. Pickpockets, for example, should not be able to 'see' whether a potential victim has many euros in his wallet. Moreover, it is socially undesirable to be able to examine someone's actions and dealings on the basis of the signalling of a chip in his tie. It is not unthinkable that in the future a police officer will be able to read from a few metres' distance whether someone wears a brand-new Armani suit and rather old Marks & Spencer underpants or whether one carries two tins of Coke, two packets of Marlboro, and the latest Playgirl magazine in one's bag and 500 euros in one's wallet, all without body search and unnoticed.

Another technological possibility is implanting chips in the human body. Implanting in animals is done regularly nowadays. For instance, pedigree dogs are implanted with chips, instead of being tattooed. Implanting chips in the human body is still in its experimental phase. However, for medical reasons implanting chips will become more widely used. In May 2002, in the US 'medichips' were implanted in eight test subjects. The chips are equipped with unique codes. These codes give access to a database with medical information on the patient, so in the case of emergencies their medical information can be read at once. Furthermore, chips are implanted in order to regulate the ingestion of medicines. These

[42]Money gained through questionable transactions, such as the trade in weapons and drugs.

chips detect chemical signals in the body and release drugs in response to such signals, keeping the concentration of the drug in the body at the therapeutic level desired. Recently, such systems have been developed and trialled in test subjects.[43]

One of the researchers who is fascinated by the changes of new technology, Kevin Warwick, Professor of Cybernetics at the University of Reading, UK, had chips implanted twice in his arm, 'just to find out what it would be like'. The chips were charged by a radio signal across the doorway, causing them to transmit their unique identifying signals. As a result, Warwick was welcomed by the computer when he entered, and elsewhere in the department the network was able to track him, logging at what time he entered rooms and at what time he left. Doors opened automatically, lights were switched on, and the computer checked how many new email messages he had received. To his surprise, he noticed that very quickly he came to regard the implant as a part of his body.

Although most of the possibilities provided by new technology, such as chips implanted in objects and in the human body, are only in an experimental phase, the question arises whether all these possibilities would fall under the protection of personal integrity in Article 11.

4. Applying the Conceptual Framework

As stated above, the general and fundamental right to bodily integrity did not exist – as a codified legal rule – in the Dutch Constitution before 1983. So, a legal rule, that, in terms of the model, projects its image of bodily protection, did not exist, except for rules that are indirectly connected with this issue, viz. the examination of the body and its limits – including rectal and vaginal examination – for a relatively small and specific group (the accused) under specific law (criminal law). In the court cases, judges came to their decisions on the basis of Articles 56 and 195 of the Code of Criminal Procedure and drew the limits of these Articles on the basis of unwritten rules: taking blood from an accused is 'a wrongful violation of the suspect's bodily integrity'. Operating on the brains of an accused without his consent is not allowed, for 'a doctor is not authorized to treat a

---

[43]For an elaborate description of future technologies, see B.J Koops, H. van Schooten and M. Prins, *Recht naar binnen kijken. Een toekomstverkenning van huisrecht, lichamelijke integriteit en nieuwe opsporingstechnieken* [Looking Right In: A Prospective Study of the Sanctity of the Home, Bodily Integrity and New Investigation Techniques] (Den Haag: Sdu Uitgevers, 2004).

patient without his consent', not even if the patient is a mentally disturbed accused person and detained under a hospital order for life. In a similar case (NJ1975/288), judges decided that forced psychotherapeutic treatment was not allowed without the consent of the accused, because of the 'right of self-determination with respect to the body', even for those who are detained under a hospital order.

However, the famous civil law case, the *Fluoridation* case (1973), affected *all citizens* because it involved the distribution of one of the primary necessities of life: water. The court decision was formulated on the basis of the *legal principle* that the exercise of state power needs previous and democratic legislation. The Supreme Court concluded that the decision to add fluoride to drinking water is 'so far-reaching in character' that it cannot be taken without the legal basis of an Act of Parliament.

Unlike the conceptual model, where the meaning of the legal rule becomes clear and manifest by its use – in the official's application (and the judge's decision) as well as in patterns of behaviour – here, in the case study, we find the order reversed: in social practices, official's acts and the acts of judges, institutional facts are created, not related to any codified legal rule, but formulated on the basis of *unwritten rules* and on the basis of a *legal principle*, viz. the 'rule of law'. Moreover, on the basis of unwritten rules and principles and the underlying common sense – used in the argumentation of judges – an imaginary reality of 'bodily integrity' was created, which was later codified as a fundamental right in the Constitution. This phenomenon expresses the *reciprocity* between rule and conduct and, in reverse, between conduct and rule in its ultimate form. It is social practice that generates a rule, not only in a court decision, but also in the patterns of behaviour in society: the technical developments within medical science, within medication or neurosurgery, and within scientific research on the effect of chemicals on the human body, for instance.

With respect to the period *after* the codification of the right of personal integrity (1983), the tripartite model can be used as usual. From that moment on, the analysis of Article 11 follows a course similar to that of Article 12 (see section 2.3). Firstly, by applying the projected picture of Article 11 by the officials – or, in the case of a conflict, by the judges – the meaning of the right will be constructed and/or transformed. Secondly, patterns of behaviour concerning the use of modern technology and its amazing possibilities are not protected under Article 11 and can be regarded, in terms of the model, as 'ineffective legal practice' and even as 'illegal practice', not projected by any legal norm at all. Modern technology unsettles personal integrity: the body becomes almost transparent; the secret character of the body's detection makes protection even more difficult.

5. Final Remarks

The processes described express a strong 'bottom-up' influence on the determination of a rule. More precisely, the processes express the meaning construction of a new rule, in an even stronger way than the model itself indicates. In the analysis of the right to bodily integrity, *before* its codification in 1983, the *reciprocity* in the relationship between the rule and its actualization in society, expressed by the model, turns into its opposite: owing to the absence of a legal rule, it is in society, by the development of medical technology and the judge's use of unwritten rules and a legal principle, that the meaning of the fundamental right is determined. From this analysis it can be concluded that the primacy of the legislature has to be put into perspective. The projected meaning of a legal rule not only becomes manifest in social practices and 'illegal' patterns of behaviour, but also generates social practices and 'illegal' patterns of behaviour rules (and principles). The idea of linear causality models of legal communication – i.e. the 'top-down' idea that the legal rule determines social practice, that the legal rule creates a new world – which was already put into perspective by the tripartite model by way of adding *reciprocal* elements to this relationship – here turns into its opposite: we can observe the meaning construction of institutional facts stemming from social practices and acts, under the pressure of particular circumstances: the 'bottom-up' perspective. In general, it can be concluded that the 'top-down' view of instrumental rules and its effect is overestimated in the Continental theoretical notion of the *primacy of the legislature*.

CHAPTER 2

Lexical Indeterminacy: Contextualism and Rule-Following in Common Law Adjudication

Ross Charnock

Université Paris Dauphine (France)

In spite of claims to be giving effect to the intention of the legislature, English judges are expected to follow a literal rule of construction. However, strict observation of this rule can lead to absurdity. In other cases, the literal meaning may appear indeterminate, as predicted by the semantic theory of contextualism, according to which 'what is said' is necessarily occasion-sensitive. It follows that the content of legal rules must be considered not as being objectively fixed, but as being established by consensus within the relevant community. Although philosophers of law tend to reject this version of rule-scepticism, certain aspects of legal judgments in well known cases shows that it corresponds well to the conventions of common law adjudication.

1. Intentional and literal meaning

Common law interpretation frequently involves an apparent tension between 'what was said' in the written instrument, and what seems to have been intended. At first sight this distinction appears to correspond to that made in linguistic pragmatics between literal meaning and speaker's intentional meaning. In the semantic model associated with Grice, the (acontextual) literal meaning is associated with the sentence or sentence-type, while the intentional meaning is associated pragmatically with the utterance as observed in a particular context.[1] However, this distinction does not appear relevant to legal interpretation.

There are two principal reasons for the rejection of pragmatic interpretation. The first is the absence of shared knowledge of the discourse situation. Pragmatic understanding depends on an awareness on the part of the interlocutors of the relevant details of the context, and this in not

---

[1] H. P. Grice, 'Utterer's meaning and intention' (1969), in Grice, *Studies in the way of words* (collected papers) (Harvard University Press: Cambridge, Mass. 1989).

A. Wagner et al. (eds.), Interpretation, Law and the Construction of Meaning, 21–47.

available in the context of statute construction. Firstly, as it is tendentious to speak of the legislature or any other group having a collective intention, there cannot [CUT therefore] be said to be a clearly identifiable speaker. Clearly, some participants may not have considered the implications of the proposed legislation; while others may have voted for purely political reasons.[2]

Further, the legal text is not addressed to any particular interlocutor, whose interpretation may be considered as privileged. Texts are to be interpreted in their ordinary, natural meaning, as they would be understood in the wider community, this sense (usually) being decided by a community of judges. [CUT Again,] The members of the relevant group will not always agree.

Finally, there is no well defined context. It is a defining characteristic of legal rules that they are made to be applied in new, hitherto unenvisaged situations. It has frequently been pointed out that where a situation has never previously been envisaged, and where no consideration has been given to the point, the legislature cannot be said to have expressed any particular intention. A construction involving intentional meaning will therefore depend on speculation, as was pointed out for example by Lord Watson in *Salomon*:

> 'Intention of the legislature' is a common but very slippery phrase, which, popularly understood, may signify anything from intention embodied in positive enactment to speculative opinion as to what the Legislature probably would have meant, although there has been an omission to enact it.[3]

The second reason for the inadequacy of pragmatic interpretation in legal adjudication is that intentional meaning is subjective, depending as it does on personal understanding. Further, it is necessarily context dependent, the same expression being understood in different ways on different occasions. Such a flexible approach to interpretation would allow the judges an unacceptable level of discretion. Indeed, if the content of the rule were allowed to vary according to circumstances, they would find themselves adjudicating on a case-by-case basis. They could no longer be said to be following a rule at all. In the context of legal adjudication, therefore, pragmatic interpretation tends to be rejected in favour of a fixed, literal meaning. Even where there is an evident conflict between the

---

[2] English judges often prefer to speak of the intention of the draftsman.

[3] *Salomon v Salomon & Co Ltd* [1897], AC 22 (HL) *per* Lord Watson.

apparent intention and what was said, English judges prefer to base their decisions on the literal meaning of the text.[4] Indeed, it has often been judicially stated that the aim of legal interpretation is not to discover and give effect to the (presumed) intention of the legislature, but rather to establish the 'correct' meaning of the words used. The intention is assumed to correspond directly to what is said. This was the conclusion proposed in *Salomon*:

> In a Court of Law or Equity, what the Legislature intended to be done or not to be done can only be legitimately be ascertained from that which it has chosen to enact, either in express words or by reasonable and necessary implication.[5]

More recent judgments continue to express an explicit preference for literal over intentional meaning, for example in *Black-Clawson*:

> We often say that we are looking for the intention of Parliament, but that is not quite accurate. We are seeking not what Parliament meant but the true meaning of what they said.[6]

In order to resolve the case in favour of one party or the other judges are obliged to decide on a single, 'correct' meaning ('the true construction'). Further, this sense must be thought of as fixed and invariable, so that it can be applied consistently, not just in the particular case but also in new, unenvisaged situations. However, the reliance on so-called literal, rather than intentional meaning raises new problems.

2. Literal meaning and indeterminacy

Where the meaning appears clear, literal interpretation can frequently lead to absurdity. In *Salomon*, for example, there appeared to be a particularly flagrant contradiction between the supposed intention of the legislature and the statute to be interpreted, the *Companies Act* 1862. No one could seriously suppose that in approving the concept of limited responsibility, Parliament intended to allow cobblers (here Salomon, 'a pauper') to set up

---

[4] According to the 'literal rule' English judges are expected to adhere as far as possible to 'the grammatical and ordinary sense of the words' (*Grey v Pearson* [1857] All ER 21 (HL), *per* Lord Wensleydale), 'giving the words their ordinary signification' (*River Wear Commissioners v Anderson* [1877] All ER 1 (HL) *per* Lord Blackburn).]

[5] *Salomon* [1897], *per* Lord Watson.

[6] Black-Clawson International Ltd v Papierwerke Waldhof-Ascaffenburg AG [1975] All ER 810 (HL) per Lord Reid.

convenient financial arrangements in order to avoid paying their debts. On a literal reading of the text, this would, however, be the inevitable result. Lord Watson nevertheless held that the judgment should be based on the text alone.

Another celebrated example of absurdity is observed in *Whiteley v Chappell* 1868-9. In this case, the defendant was accused of 'personification', defined in statute as the impersonation of 'any person entitled to vote' at an election. He had in fact impersonated someone who would have been entitled to vote if he had not died shortly before the date of the election. Although he had cast a vote to which he was not entitled, he was acquitted on the grounds that dead men are not entitled to vote.

A more complex problem arose in *Magor and St Mellons* 1951, which involved the merger of two local councils. The *Newport Extension Act* 1934 failed to provide for the fact that the two Rural District Councils would no longer be in existence after the reorganisation, and could no longer make any financial claims. The new council could only claim as 'successor to its predecessors', and, as they could make no claims, it could recover nothing. Although this situation appeared never to have been 'present to the minds of those responsible for the *Local Government Act* 1933' (*per* Lord Tucker), and in spite of Denning LJ's vigorous attempt to discover the intention of the legislature, it was considered that the only remedy lay in an Amending Act.[7]

In 1957, the House of Lords was obliged to recognise, contrary to good sense, that a foreign Prince was entitled to British nationality. According to a 1705 statute, passed during the reign of Queen Anne, British nationality was granted to Princess Sophia, Electress of Hanover, and also to her descendants, in perpetuity ('[to the end that] the said Princess ... and the issue of her body, and all persons lineally descending from her, born or hereafter to be born, be and shall be deemed natural born subjects of this Kingdom'). The judges could find no ambiguity in the text which would allow them to depart from the literal interpretation. Numerous members of European Royal families were therefore to be considered as de

---

[7] *Magor and St Mellons RDC v Newport Corporation* [1951] 2 All ER 839. 'We sit here to find out the intention of Parliament and of Ministers and carry it out, and we do this better by filling in the gaps and making sense of the enactment than by opening it up to destructive analysis.'(per Denning LJ). Lord Denning's approach was rejected by Lord Simonds in the Lords as 'a naked usurpation of the legislative function under the thin disguise of interpretation'.]

facto subjects of Her British Majesty. Viscount Simonds referred to the 'absurdity' of the situation but nevertheless considered that it was not absurd enough to justify a departure from the literal rule:

> However absurd we today may think an interpretation which would lead to most of the Royal families of Europe being British subjects, I cannot say that in 1705 there was such manifest absurdity as to entitle one to reject it.[8]

Quite apart from the risk of absurdity, a further problem associated with literal interpretation is that the ordinary or natural meaning is not always clear.

In cases of doubt, the judges follow the relevant precedents wherever possible. However, precedent is not always a sufficient guide, as the particular points raised in new cases may not have been discussed in prior cases.

Where the meaning of a statute has not been authoritatively decided, judges refer to the meanings clauses, which form an integral part of English statutes. However, these clauses do not usually supply detailed definitions. On the contrary, they tend to refer only to prototypical cases in the sense of Rosch[9], thus permitting the elimination of certain improbable, peripheral interpretations. Furthermore, they are often hedged with phrases to the effect that the judge may supply a different definition if he sees fit. Typical examples of such phrases are: 'unless the contrary intention appears' or 'except insofar as the context otherwise requires'. In cases of linguistic indeterminacy, meanings clauses are rarely useful as an aid to adjudication.

Where there are no relevant precedents and the meanings clause is of no help, judges are obliged to rely on their own personal intuition as competent speakers of the English language. In *R v Ireland*, the accused was said to have caused psychiatric illness by making silent telephone calls. As 'stalking' had not yet been defined in statute, he was charged under the *Offences Against the Person Act* 1861, s 20, the question to be decided being whether 'causing' psychiatric illness could be assimilated to 'inflicting' grievous bodily harm:

---

[8] AG v Prince Ernest Augustus of Hanover [1957] 1All ER 49, per Viscount Simonds.

[9] E. Rosch, 'Prototype classification and logical classification -the two systems', in T. Moore (ed.), *New trends in cognitive representation.* (Hillsdale NJ, Erlbaum, 1983), 111-44.

> The problem is one of construction. Although the words 'cause' and 'inflict' were not exactly synonymous, in the context of the Act of 1861, one could nowadays quite naturally speak of inflicting psychiatric injury [10]

Such an approach amounts to adjudication by introspection. The judge assumes that his intuition, possibly corroborated by that of his colleagues on the bench, will be accepted as valid for the relevant linguistic community. In *Wagamama v City Centre Restaurants* 1995 Laddie J, called upon to assess likelihood of confusion in a Trade Mark case, stated explicitly that in coming to his opinion, the judge should be guided by common usage:

> A judge brings to the assessment of marks his own, perhaps idiosyncratic, pronunciation and view or understanding of them. Although the issue of infringement is eventually one for the judge alone, in assessing the marks he must bear in mind the impact the goods make or are likely to make on the minds of persons who are likely to be customers for the goods or services under the marks.[11]

In this case, the evidence of a telephone poll of likely customers was ruled admissible.

Where all else fails, judges occasionally cite dictionary definitions either as support for a particular interpretation or in cases of genuine doubt. They do this with reluctance, first because the use of a dictionary seems to imply the substitution of a technical definition for the preferred "natural" meaning, and secondly because dictionaries do not provide a single, "correct" solution, but rather a variety of possible meanings as be observed in different contexts. Problems arise in cases of vagueness, where the sense is ambiguous, where the reference is imprecise, or where the meaning appears indeterminate.

Statutory meaning is said to be vague where a broad term is used, the details of the application being left to the discretion of the judge. Words like 'reasonable', 'fair' or 'safe', are often used in this way by statutory draftsmen. According to Bennion,[12] this may also have been the intention of the draftsman in using the expression 'a proper proportion', assumed to be ambiguous in *Pepper v Hart* 1993.[13] Although vagueness has been

---

[10] *R v Ireland* [1998] AC 147, *per* Lord Steyn.

[11] *Wagamama v City Centre Restaurants* [1995] F.S.R. 713 Ch.D, *per* Laddie J.

[12] F. Bennion, 'Hansard -help or hindrance? -A Draftsman's View of *Pepper v Hart* (1993) *Statute Law Review* 1.

[13] *Pepper v Hart* [1993] 1 All ER 42 (HL)

shown to be an ineradicable property of law,[14] it need not be thought of as a semantic problem, as such imprecision can always be remedied to the extent necessary by giving more accurate rules.[15]

The sense is said to be ambiguous where there are two possible interpretations, both of which are clear. In such cases the court has no alternative but to consider the context in order to resolve the ambiguity. Legal debate centres on the extent to which external evidence from the surrounding circumstances is admissible as an aid to construction. Examples may be given from contract law.

In *Raffles v Wichelhaus* 1864, the parties were at cross purposes because there were two ships both named "Peerless", both sailing from Bombay, one in October, one in December. The defendant was held to be entitled to refuse delivery in December, as he could show that he intended the October sailing. The contract was said obiter to be void for mistake. Knowledge of the context would have enabled the parties to supply the appropriate references and thus avoid the ambiguity.

The question of the admissibility of external evidence as an aid to (literal) construction was discussed explicitly in *Prenn v Simmonds* 1971. According to his contract, an employee had the right to purchase shares in his company at a fixed price, on condition that 'aggregate profits' were above a certain sum. He claimed that the contractual references to 'profits' were to the consolidated profits of the group, while the employer claimed that they referred on the contrary to the profits of the holding company. In the latter case, the amounts declared would depend on simple accounting decisions, at the discretion of the employer. Lord Wilberforce stated that in construing a written agreement the court is entitled to take account of the surrounding circumstances with reference to which the words of the agreement were used, but was not entitled to look at the pre-contractual negotiations. It was held that, even on a purely linguistic construction, the employee's interpretation was correct.

In other cases, the reference may be imprecise, the question being whether a particular usage can be derived by extension from a primary, or principal meaning. In *Attorney-General's Reference (No 5 of 1980)*[16], the

---

[14] T.A.O. Endicott, *Vagueness in Law* (Oxford, OUP, 2000).

[15] See, especially, Waismann, 'Verifiability' in A. Flew, (ed.), *Logic and Language* (1st series). Cambridge, Blackwell, 1951) at 120.

[16] [1981] 1 WLR 88

Court had to decide whether the articles defined in the *Obscene Publications Act* 1959, could be said to include video-cassettes, even though these were a relatively modern invention, and could not have been in the contemplation of Parliament at the time the Act was passed. The meanings clause of this Act gives the following definition: 'In this Act, "article" means any description of article (*sic*) containing or embodying matter to be read or looked at or both, any sound record or other record of a picture or pictures.' The material in question was described as being 'shown, played or projected'. According to the *ejusdem que* rule of construction, the words 'any other record' had to be restricted to articles of the same kind as in the preceding list of examples. It was pointed out that, contrary to film, video-cassettes do not contain pictures but only electrical impulses, which are not projected onto a screen. Further, video-cassettes cannot be said to be 'played' in the same way as sound recordings. Nevertheless, in the opinion of Lawton LJ, who referred in his judgment to 'ordinary parlance', the statutory words were 'sufficiently wide to cover what happens when pictures are produced by way of a video-cassette'.

A more extreme example of imprecision regarding the variable extension of a word is found in *Garner v Burr* 1951, which concerned the meaning of the word 'vehicle'. Contrary to the *Road Traffic Act* 1930, which forbade the use of vehicles without rubber tyres on the public highway, a farmer strapped wheels to his chicken coop and towed it along the road behind his tractor. When prosecuted, he claimed, reasonably, that his chicken coop could not be said to be a vehicle, and that the absence of tyres was therefore immaterial. The intention of Parliament was presumably to prevent damage to public roads, whether by the inappropriate use of a vehicle or otherwise. However, on appeal, Lord Goddard CJ preferred to prevent this mischief while respecting the text of the statute, by redefining the word 'vehicle' so as to include chicken coops and poultry sheds:

> The regulations are designed for a variety of reasons, among them the protection of road surfaces; and, as this vehicle had ordinary iron tyres, not pneumatic tyres, it was liable to damage the roads. [The magistrates] have put what is in my opinion too narrow an interpretation on the word 'vehicle' for the purposes of this Act. It is true that, according to the dictionary definition, a 'vehicle' is primarily to be regarded as a means of conveyance provided with wheels or runners and used for the carriage of persons or goods. It is true that the [magistrates] do not find that anything was carried in the vehicle at the time; but I think that the Act is clearly aimed at anything which will run on wheels which is being drawn by a tractor or another motor vehicle. Accordingly, an offence was committed here. It

> follows that [the magistrates] ought to have found that this poultry shed was a vehicle within the meaning of s 1 of the *Road Traffic Act* of 1930.[17]

Where the literal meaning appears indeterminate, the question to be decided is no longer whether a particular understanding can be derived from a principal or prototypical meaning, but rather how the literal meaning itself is to be defined. As the judge is usually called upon to decide between two competing interpretations, the problem is often presented in legal judgments in terms of ambiguity. However, the analysis itself is more likely to illustrate the concept of polysemy. Examples are numerous.

Alexander v Railway Executive 1951 involved the interpretation of the word 'misdelivery' in a contractual exclusion clause. The ticket supplied to a stage conjurer who had deposited various theatrical effects in a left luggage office included a clause limiting responsibility for loss or damage *inter alia* in case of 'misdelivery'. The goods were claimed by and delivered to the conjuror's assistant, who subsequently disposed of them for his own purposes. The defendants relied on the dictionary meaning, which appeared to cover any delivery to the wrong person. However, Devlin J considered obiter that '"misdelivery" in its natural and ordinary meaning conveys to the ordinary man that there has been some mistake or inadvertence.[18] [CUT Here,] Either meaning could have been intended, with no modification of contextual reference. The judge decided that, as the delivery to the conjurer's assistant was the result of a deliberate decision, the term did not apply in the present context. The conjuror was therefore entitled to compensation. Devlin J could not be said here to be pointing out an established fact of the matter, but appears to have made a personal decision concerning the application of the word in hitherto unenvisaged circumstances.

In *Antonelli v Secretary of State for Trade and Industry* 1997, the judge exercised his discretion concerning the interpretation of the word "violence" in the context of the *Estate Agents Act* 1979. Under this Act the Director General of Fair Trading had the right to prevent anyone 'convicted of [...] an offence involving fraud or other dishonesty or violence' from practising as an estate agent. Prior to the passing of the Act, Antonelli, an American citizen, had been found guilty in Detroit, USA, in 1973, of 'burning real estate other than a dwelling house' contrary to the Michigan Criminal Law Act. The question to be decided in the English court was

---

[17] *Garner v Burr* [1951] 2 All ER 683, *per* Goddard CJ.
[18] Alexander v Railway Executive [1951] 2 All ER 442.

whether "burning real estate" should be considered as an offence "involving violence". At trial the judge relied on the dictionary definition of the word and decided in the affirmative. This decision was confirmed on appeal:

> [T]he judge relied on the definition of violence cited to him from the Oxford Dictionary as: "The exercise of physical force so as to inflict injury or to cause damage to persons or property." He said: "Once it is agreed that violence can be directed against property, as well as against the person, I can see no reason for saying that setting fire to property is not an act of violence towards it.[19]

Although it is possible to cause damage to property by acting violently, the idea of an act of violence towards property appears counter-intuitive. The property, even if damaged, is unlikely to be considered as a victim.

R v Bournewood Community and Mental Health NHS Trust, ex parte L 1999 depended on the meaning attributed to the word 'detention' in the context of the *Mental Health Act* 1983. This case concerned a patient [L], of 48 years of age, who was mentally deficient, incapable of speech and who understood very little. He had been resident at a psychiatric hospital for over 30 years. He was judged incapable of expressing his consent to or indeed his refusal of hospital treatment, but as he had made no attempt to leave the hospital premises, the authorities had not gone through the administrative formalities of compulsory detention. After disagreement with paid carers, the hospital was accused of false imprisonment.

In the High Court, Owen J consulted the dictionary to discover whether a person could be said to be 'detained' even though he was unaware that he would not be allowed to leave, and remained blissfully unaware that he would not be allowed to do so. The judge cited the first definition given in the *OED* as 'keeping in custody or confinement'. He took this to correspond to the ordinary or natural sense of the word, and held accordingly that, as [L]'s administrative status was that of a voluntary patient, he could not be said to be in custody or confinement and was therefore not 'detained'. However, on appeal, Lord Woolf MR cited authority for the proposition that, in law, it was possible to be 'imprisoned' without knowing it: 'So a man might, to my mind, be imprisoned by having

---

[19] Antonelli v Secretary of State for Trade and Industry [1998] 1 All ER 997, per Beldam LJ.

the key of a door turned against him so that he is imprisoned in a room although he does not know that the key has been turned.'[20]

Lord Woolf's judgment again raises the question of whether the judge should be considered as pointing out a pre-existing literal meaning of the word, of which the linguistic community may have been hitherto unaware, or deciding on his own initiative how the word should be interpreted in this new, previously unenvisaged context. Those who consider that a word cannot have a meaning unknown to the linguistic community must consider that the judgment depended on a decision rather than on empirical observation.

There was genuine disagreement concerning the sense of the word 'appropriates' in relation to the definition of theft in English law. According to the *Theft Act* 1968 s 1(1): 'A person is guilty of theft if he dishonestly appropriates property belonging to another with the intention of permanently depriving the other of it'. This text was taken from the *Larceny Act* 1916 s 1(1), which included the words 'without the consent of the owner' after the verb 'appropriates'. It was not at first clear whether or not the omission of these words was deliberate or the result of some mistake. Nor was it clear whether 'appropriates' should itself be understood as implying the absence of consent. The first question was authoritatively decided in *Lawrence v Metropolitan Police Commissioner* 1972. A Mr Occhi, an Italian tourist, arrived at Victoria station and attempted to take a taxi to Ladbroke Grove. He offered to pay in advance, and held out his open wallet to the taxi driver, inviting him to take the correct sum. The driver took £6, whereas the correct fare should have been around 10s 6d. In his defence, the driver, Lawrence, claimed that he could not be guilty of theft, as his client had consented to the taking of the notes. The question was certified for the Lords, where Viscount Dilhorne took the opportunity to clarify the law:

> I see no ground for concluding that the omission of the words "without the consent of the owner" was inadvertent and not deliberate. Parliament has relieved the prosecution of the burden of establishing that the taking was

[20] *R v Bournewood Community and Mental Health NHS Trust, ex parte L* [1999] 3 All ER 289 The Court of Appeal therefore found that the hospital was acting outside the law. This decision applied equally to all the other psychiatric hospitals in the country. The judgment was later reversed by the Lords, at least partly for reasons of policy.

> without the owner's consent. That is no longer an ingredient of the offence.[21]

Viscount Dilhorne was simply applying the literal rule of construction, which limits interpretation to the text itself. However, the question of the meaning of the word 'appropriates' remained open. This was examined in *R v Morris* 1984, another case of "theft with consent". The accused had switched labels on the products displayed on supermarket shelves, in order to pay less than the full price. In his defence, he claimed that he could not be guilty of theft, as he had paid the price requested at the check-out. In view of the competing interpretations, The problem was stated by Lord Lane in terms of ambiguity, although, as a knowledge of the context was not sufficient to resolve the ambiguity, it might more properly be said that the meaning was indeterminate:

> There are two schools of thought. The first contends that the word 'appropriate' has built into it a connotation that it is some action inconsistent with the owner's rights, something hostile to the interests of the owner or contrary to his wishes and intention or without his authority. The second contends that the word in this context means no more than to take possession of an article and that there is no requirement that the taking or appropriation should be in any way antagonistic to the rights of the owner.[22]

The Court of Appeal considered that the true construction corresponded to the second of the two interpretations suggested, and accordingly confirmed the guilty verdict. However, in the Lords, in a concurring judgment, Lord Roskill appeared to redefine the verb 'appropriates', as involving an "adverse interference" with the rights of the owner."[23]

The correct interpretation of the word 'appropriates' was decided in *DPP v Gomez* 1993. The defendant, assistant manager in a shop, had persuaded his manager to agree to accept a cheque from an accomplice. He (the defendant) was aware that his accomplice was using a stolen cheque, but claimed in his defence that as the manager had authorised the transaction, there was still no 'appropriation'. The majority in the Lords confirmed that consent was no longer an ingredient of the offence.

---

[21] *Lawrence v Metropolitan Police Commissioner* 1972, [1971] 2 All ER 1253 (HL), *per* Viscount Dilhorne.
[22] *R v Morris*, [1984] AC 320, *per* Lane CJ.
[23] *Morris* [1984], *per* Lord Roskill).

However, Lord Lowry, dissenting, referred to the dictionary meaning of the word 'appropriate':

> The ordinary and natural meaning of 'appropriate' is to take for oneself, or to treat as one's own, property which belongs to someone else. The primary dictionary meaning is "take possession of, or take to oneself, especially without authority", and that is in my opinion the meaning which the word bears in s1(1). Reading sections 1-6 as a whole, the ordinary and natural meaning of 'appropriates' is confirmed.[24]

Lord Lowry seems to have considered that the 'primary definition' must be accepted as the 'correct', legal meaning. He also appears to have ignored the word 'especially', which would seem to imply that appropriation may occur on occasion with authority. He makes no mention of alternative definitions. Yet his reading of the Criminal Law Revision Committee 1966, whose propositions were adopted substantially unchanged by Parliament, shows that his understanding corresponded to the intention of the legislature. The majority seems to have felt obliged to follow authority as decided by Viscount Dilhorne in 1972. As the question had already been decided, there was no legal justification for the introduction of external evidence in the form of a judicial committee report.[25]

Fundamental disagreement concerning the legal definition of [CUT literal] meaning emerged in *Smith v United States* (USSC) 1993. This case concerned the meaning of the word 'used' in the context of a Federal statute imposing severe mandatory sentences on drug offenders if a firearm was used 'during and relation to' a drug trafficking offence. Having 'used' his machine-gun, not by shooting it, but by negotiating with an undercover agent with a view to exchanging it for two ounces of cocaine, Smith was sentenced to the mandatory 30-year period. In the Supreme Court, Justice O'Connor consulted *Webster's Dictionary* to confirm the ordinary, natural sense of the word 'use'.

> Surely petitioner's treatment of his MAC-10 can be described as 'use' within the everyday meaning of that term. *Webster's* defines 'to use' as 'to convert to one's service' or 'to employ'. [...] In petitioner's view, § 924(c)(1) should require proof not only that the defendant used the firearm,

---

[24] *DPP v Gomez*, [1993] 1 All ER 1(HL), *per* Lord Lowry, dissenting.)

[25] It seems probable, therefore, that the authoritative legal interpretation does not correspond to the intention of Parliament. The result is that it is possible in English law to be accused of theft for having (dishonestly) accepted a gift.

> but also that he used it as a weapon. But the words "as a weapon" appear nowhere in the statute. Rather, § 924(c)(1)'s language sweeps broadly, punishing any 'use' of a firearm, so long as the use is 'during and in relation to' a drug trafficking offense.[26]

Justice O'Connor thus considered that, given a suitable occasion, almost any usage could be considered ordinary and natural. On this view, even though one meaning may seem more natural than another, it does not follow that other possible meanings should be rejected. In particular, the sense of 'use for barter' could not be excluded. Thus, the relevant meaning, as legally defined, was assumed to be available across the range of possible discourse situations.

> It is one thing to say that the ordinary meaning of 'uses a firearm' includes using a firearm as a weapon, since that is the intended purpose of a firearm and the example of 'use' that most immediately comes to mind. But it is quite another to conclude that, as a result, the phrase also excludes any other use. Certainly that conclusion does not follow from the phrase 'uses a firearm' itself. As the dictionary definitions and experience make clear, one can use a firearm in a number of ways. That one example of 'use' is the first to come to mind when the phrase 'uses a firearm' is uttered does not preclude us from recognizing that there are other 'uses' that qualify as well.[27]

On the authority of *Webster's Dictionary*, the majority therefore declared that Smith had indeed 'used' his machine gun when offering to swap it for a few ounces of cocaine, and that the mandatory minimum sentence should therefore be applied.[28]

Justice Scalia found himself in the minority in defending the contextual, rather than the literal, interpretation. He considered that in the context of the statute, the word 'use' would ordinarily be understood as involving shooting.

---

[26] *Smith v United States* [1993] 508 USSC 223, *per* Justice O'Connor.

[27] *Smith* [1993], *per* Justice O'Connor.

[28] Smith was sentenced to the minimum period of thirty years' imprisonment. It seems legitimate to suspect the majority of having based their decision not just on the meaning of the relevant statute, but also at least partly on the fact that the accused was known to be a dangerous drug-dealer. See also *Bailey v US* 516 U.S. 137 (1995) on 'use', *Muscarello v US* 524 U.S. 125 (1998) on 'carry a firearm', and the commentary in Cunningham and Fillmore, "Using Common Sense: A Linguistic Perspective on Judicial Interpretation of 'Use a Firearm'", 73 *Washington. U. LQ*. 1159 (1995)

The Court does not appear to grasp the distinction between how a word can be used and how it ordinarily is used. [...] Given our rule that ordinary meaning governs, and given the ordinary meaning of 'uses a firearm', it seems to me inconsequential that the words 'as a weapon' appear nowhere in the statute; they are reasonably implicit.[29]

3. Contextualism and occasion-sensitivity

Hart showed that all substantive terms are subject to what he called a "penumbra of uncertainty". He gave the example of a motor car as an uncontroversial, prototypical example of a 'vehicle', proposing 'bicycles, airplanes, roller skates' as less clear cases subsisting in the penumbra of the general term.[30] Because of the what he called the open-textured quality of natural language, judges will always be required to exercise their discretion in interpreting rules prohibiting for example the use of vehicles in the park.

This approach may appear to account satisfactorily for cases where there are doubts concerning the extent to which a central term may be used to refer to related concepts, as in *Attorney-General's Reference (No 5 of 1980)*,[31] where the court decided that the video-tape could legitimately be considered as sufficiently like a film to come within the terms of the *Obscene Publications Act* 1959. However, the theory of open texture does not solve the problems of construction encountered where the central terms themselves appear indeterminate. The senses given to words like 'violence' in *Antonelli*,[32] 'misdelivery' in *Alexander*,[33] 'detention' in *Bournewood*[34] or 'appropriates' in *Gomez*[35] do not seem to be derived from some more prototypical usage. In the case of 'vehicle' in *Garner*[36], it is difficult to include 'poultry shed' as part of the periphery associated with the term.

In his famous endnotes, Hart refers explicitly[37] to Waismann's earlier, more radical definition of open texture,[38] which appears more

---

[29] *Smith*, [1993] *per* Justice Scalia, dissenting.
[30] H.L.A. Hart, The concept of law (1961) (Oxford, Clarendon, 1994) at 126.
[31] [1981] 1 WLR 88.
[32] [1998] 1 All ER 997.
[33] [1951] 2 All ER 442.
[34] [1999] 3 All ER 289.
[35] [1993] 1 All ER 1.
[36] [1951] 2 All ER 683.
[37] Concept of law at 297.
[38] 'Verifiability' at 119.

relevant to the problem of lexical indeterminacy as observed in legal interpretation. Waismann points out that all concepts are associated with an indefinite number of semantic features, some of which have not yet been noticed and perhaps never will be noticed by anyone. Descriptions are therefore inevitably incomplete. An indefinite number of features will remain implicit as part of the 'hidden background'. On this view, a doubt will always remain, even regarding prototypical usage.

Hart supposed that '[t]here will indeed be plain cases, constantly recurring in similar contexts, to which general expressions are clearly applicable'[39]. He assumed that the problems associated with open texture would be exceptional. However, if, following Waismann, the concepts themselves are defined according to the current state of knowledge in the relevant linguistic community, then meaning remains provisory, and cannot be fixed independently of context.

Given open texture in the sense of Waismann, whether a word or phrase is applicable in new circumstances becomes an empirical question, depending on background assumptions and hitherto unnoticed contextual features. In the words of Recanati: 'The applicability of a term to novel situations depends on its similarity to the source situations. The target situation must be similar to the source situations not only with respect to the "explicit" definition of the term, but also with respect to the hidden background. If the two situations diverge, it will be unclear whether the term will be applicable.'[40]

Other semantic arguments have since been independently proposed to show the impossibility of an acontextual, literal meaning. In discussing the meaning of natural kind words, Putnam points out that what people mean by their words must be limited by their knowledge. For most speakers, in most circumstances, 'gold' refers to a metal which is shiny and yellow; and 'water' to a liquid which is wet, tasteless and colourless. Experts may use atomic weight or molecular structure as a criterion for determining whether a particular metal is gold, or a whether particular liquid is water, but ordinary people are usually unaware of such scientific details, and cannot be said to have had such a definition in mind. [41]

---

[39] Concept of law at 126.

[40] F. Recanati, *Literal meaning* (Cambridge, CUP, 2004) at 143.

[41] H. Putnam, 'The meaning of "meaning"' in *Mind, language and reality* (vol. 2) (Cambridge, CUP, 1975).

Putnam's solution is to present the concept as a kind of 'stereotype', corresponding to shared, possibly imperfect knowledge in the linguistic community. The stereotype established by consensus will usually function unproblematically. However, problems appear where there is only a partial resemblance between the referent and the socially established stereotype, for example where the referent could just as easily be taken for an apple as for a lemon. In such a case, speakers no longer know what to say, and, the applicability of the term will appear again as an empirical question, depending on usage in the community.

Searle also showed that, even for the simplest sentences, meaning must depend to some extent on background assumptions, even where there are no contextual ambiguities. His argument can be summarised as follows (Searle 1979: 37). After references have been assigned, the sentence 'the cat is on the mat' may be assumed to have a literal meaning in which the mat is horizontal in relation to the cat. However, if the scene is placed in outer space, in a zero gravitational force, there is no longer any way of knowing which way is 'up'. Here, the mat may well be vertical in relation to the cat. Searle's conclusion is that all utterances must be interpreted in relation to some default context. In the absence of any plausible context, there can be no precise literal meaning. The meaning is therefore under-determined by the words and the (pragmatic) context must play a necessary role in establishing what is said. There can no longer be said to be a literal meaning independent of context.[42]

Travis has gone further, showing how the truth values of perfectly mundane sentences vary according to the purpose of the utterance, even where the words used have the same, unambiguous, referents. To take just one of his many examples, a sentence like 'the water's blue today' would be true for someone admiring the view of a lake in midsummer; yet the same sentence, spoken on the same day, and referring to the water in the very same lake, may well be evaluated differently by someone concerned with pollution levels.[43] Note that the occasion-sensitive interpretation is not pragmatically implied in the sense of Grice.[44] However, in a more

---

[42] J.R.. Searle, 'Literal meaning' in *Expression and meaning*. (Cambridge, CUP, 1979).

[43] C. Travis, The uses of sense: Wittgenstein's philosophy of language. Oxford, Clarendon:1989).

[44] H.P. Grice, 'Logic and Conversation' (1975) in *Studies in the way of words*, 1989.

particular sense, the semantics of what is said may be used to convey certain pragmatic implicatures. On one reading, the mention of blue water may for example imply a suggestion to go bathing; while on the other, the implication may consist of a warning to keep well away from the beach.

In the example given, a purely literal interpretation would be rejected as self-contradictory, since it is well known that water is not in fact blue, but colourless. The understanding must therefore be occasion-sensitive. It must therefore be accepted that even the most mundane examples depend to some extent on the context. This is close to the approach taken by Justice Scalia in *Smith.*[45]

In his extended discussion of the debate between the linguistic 'literalists' and 'contextualists', Recanati proposes a form of what he calls 'Meaning Eliminativism'. He rejects the notion of literal meaning, and speaks instead of the 'semantic potential' of expressions, allowing the content of 'what is said' to depend on certain aspects of the context. The sense in question is not fixed, but may be actualised in different ways according to context.[46] This corresponds well to the approach of English judges, who habitually use common but paradoxically obscure phrases to the effect that a given expression is 'wide enough' to include a certain interpretation, or that a given interpretation should be considered to be 'within the meaning' of the relevant expression.

The importance of context in ascertaining not just the intentional meaning, but also the meaning of "what is said" is confirmed for example by Viscount Simonds, who speaks of the 'colour' of words as understood in context: "Words, and in particular general words, cannot be read in isolation, their colour and content are derived from their context."[47] More recently, Bennion, writing as an experienced parliamentary draftsman, points out that, according to the 'informed interpretation rule', 'the interpreter is to infer that the legislator, when settling the wording of an enactment, intended it to be given a fully informed, rather than a purely literal, interpretation (though the two usually produce the same result)'.[48]

---

[45] [1993] 508 USSC 223.
[46] *Literal meaning* 2004, 146 ff)
[47] *Prince Ernest Augustus* [1957] *per* Viscount Simonds. The notion of 'colour', as a grammatical concept, is also introduced in *Bourne v Norwich Crematorium* [1967] 1 All ER 576 *per* Stamp J) and *Bromley LBC v GLC* [1983] All ER 768 (*per* Lord Scarman).
[48] 'Hansard -help or hindrance?', at 2.

In the most recent judicial pronouncement on the subject at the time of writing, in *Kirin-Amgen* 2004, Lord Hoffman seems to be proposing an occasion-sensitive approach to legal interpretation. He considered the meaning of 'what is said' to be:

> [H]ighly sensitive to the context of and background to the particular utterance. It depends not only upon the words the author has chosen but also upon the identity of the audience he is taken to have been addressing and the knowledge and assumptions which one attributes to that audience.[49]

In his judgment in this case, Lord Hoffman went so far as to express doubt as to whether the literal approach to statute construction was ever strictly observed, allowing only that such principles 'used to be applied in legal interpretation (at any rate in theory)'.

If the legal construction of 'what is said' depends to some extent on the domain of discourse, then it seems necessary to accept that the so-called literal meaning, as well as the pragmatic intentional meaning, will vary according to circumstances. To the extent that this is so, it does not appear possible to avoid case-by-case adjudication. However, the rejection of a fixed literal meaning should not be taken as a justification for pragmatic interpretation of speaker's intentional meaning in the sense of Grice.[50] On the contrary, if there is no fixed literal meaning, then there is nothing to which the machinery of pragmatic implicature can be applied in order to yield the desired intentional meaning. The absence of any pre-existing, objective meaning appears rather to confirm the analysis of Austin, who considered that explicit performatives, and illocutionary acts generally, were fundamentally conventional, deriving their meaning not from their semantics, but from contextual use.[51] However, if contextual use is itself constitutive of meaning, it will be necessary to accept, with Austin, that the law does not consist of factual propositions: 'Of all people, jurists should be best aware of the true state of affairs. Perhaps some now are. Yet they will succumb to their own timorous fiction, that a statement of "the law" is a statement of fact.'[52]

---

[49] Kirin-Amgen Inc v Hoechst Marion Roussel [2004] UKHL, 21/10/04, per Lord Hoffman.

[50] 'Logic and Conversation' (1975) in H.P. Grice, *Studies in the way of words*, 1989.

[51] J.L. Austin, 1958. *How to do things with words* (Oxford, Clarendon, 1962).

[52] *How to do things with words*, 1962 at 4, fn 2. Austin was no doubt thinking of his Oxford colleague, HLA Hart.

4. Consensual interpretation and rule-following

The fact that rules are expressed in words, leads to the inevitable conclusion that where the application of terms in novel situations cannot be decided in advance, the rules expressed will also appear indeterminate. In his 'exegesis' of Wittgenstein, Kripke gave strong arguments for this conclusion.[53]

Kripke (1982) takes Wittgenstein's remarks on rule-following[54] as leading up to the private language argument. As he explicates it, the argument is based on the possibility of divergent understandings of rules. Kripke's basic, and now well known example is that of the arithmetic rule of addition, involving the function *plus*, which would conventionally give, for example $68 + 57 = 125$. A different, somewhat more complex rule, (called 'quaddition', involving the notional function *quus*), would give the same results up to $x, y < 57$, but thereafter 5. Kripke imagines a 'bizarre sceptic' who gives the answer 5 when asked to add 68 and 57. When questioned, this sceptic claims that he is following the rule (of 'quaddition') he has always followed, and that he is now simply going on in the same way. From his point of view, it is those who are now performing 'addition' (involving the function *plus*) who are now misinterpreting their own previous usage (Kripke 1982: 9).[55]

By hypothesis, it cannot be known in advance which of the two rules was previously being followed, either by the sceptic or by the wider community, as the answers given, until the anomaly unexpectedly emerged, were identical. Nor can the rule be identified by introspection, as, again by hypothesis, that particular calculation has not been performed or envisaged previously. On this view, as the content of the rule as applied in novel circumstances cannot be known in advance, an individual, divorced from

---

[53] S.A. Kripke, *Wittgenstein on rules and private language* (Blackwell, Oxford, 1982).

[54] L. Wittgenstein, *Philosophical Invenstigations* (Oxford, Blackwell, 1953).

[55] Wittgenstein himself used an even simpler example to illustrate the same point. He imagines a pupil being asked to follow the teacher's example by continuing a mathematical series by adding 2 to each number. The pupil successfully continues the series up to 1,000, but then writes: 1000, 1004, 1008, 1012 ....' (*Philosophical Invenstigations,* 1953, §85) The pupil may have understood the rule as something like: 'Add 2 up to 1000, 4 up to 2000, 6 up to 3000 and so on'.

society, could not be said to know his own mind regarding the meanings he attaches to words.[56]

Note that the philosophical problem cannot be avoided by giving more precise rules of interpretation, as these will also be susceptible to reinterpretation. The sceptical argument thus leads to Wittgenstein's paradox: 'This was our paradox: no course of action could be determined by a rule, because every course of action can be made to accord with the rule.'[57] It follows, contrary to popular assumptions, that rules do not constrain behaviour.

As applied to simple arithmetic, the thesis appears fantastic, as Kripke himself readily admits. However, the problem appears relevant to the problems of legal interpretation, and should not be ignored by jurists.

Kripke's proposed solution to Wittgenstein's paradox depends on the notion of consensus within the appropriate community. According to this solution, rules are not objectively fixed, independently of context, any more than words are attached to a fixed, literal meaning. The content of rules, like the meaning of words, depends on shared knowledge within the relevant community. This model corresponds well to contextualist definitions of meaning, depending on the current state of knowledge and the occasion of use.

However, Kripke's solution has repeatedly been rejected, often without argument, by philosophers of law. Marmor denounces it as absurd: 'This is evidently absurd, not a philosophical conclusion which has to be taken seriously.'[58] Smith similarly rejects the proposed solution as implausible: 'But the sceptical solution regarding mathematical addition is not only implausible in an intuitive sense (in making mathematical functions more contingent or a matter of choice, than we think they are), it seems impossible on Kripke's own account. It is no solution at all.'[59]

In the same way, Bix rejects the consensual view of rule-following on the dubious grounds that: 'It is very hard to find a Wittgenstein scholar

---

[56] Hence Kripke's mention of an 'eerie feeling' when contemplating this situation. (*Rule-following* 1982 at 21).
[57] Philosophical Invenstigations, 1953 § 201.
[58] A. Marmor, 'No easy cases?' in D.M.Patterson (ed) *Wittgenstein and legal theory* (Boulder CO, Westview., 1992) at 189, fn 46.
[59] G.A. Smith, 'Wittgenstein and the sceptical fallacy' in Patterson (ed) 1992 at 180.

who is in substantial agreement with Kripke's reading.'[60] He further claims that: 'There are ample reasons to believe that we cannot simply apply directly Wittgenstein's ideas meant for easy cases, to hard cases.'[61] He fails to see that Wittgenstein's consistent strategy is to take the simplest cases as the strongest possible argument for the point he is making, that is that even the simplest rules stand in need of interpretation. If the argument is valid for the rule "add two", then a fortiori it will remain valid for all rules. The converse is not true.

Schauer claims that the problem of interpretation will dissolve if the instructions for example for the rule 'add 2' are given in writing, but fails to account for the fact that these instructions are also susceptible to re-interpretation.[62] Contrary to Schauer's claim, it is by showing the pupil what to do in particular cases that the teacher hoped to dissolve the problem in cases of doubt over the interpretation of a given rule. Schauer himself admits that his putative solution does not appear convincing: 'Before you, the reader, tear up this paper in disgust, I know that at first it appears that what I have said just misses the point entirely.'[63]

Endicott follows Hart in supposing that '[t]here is indeterminacy (if any) only in borderline cases',[64] and simply denies the possibility of a consensual solution: 'This seems to say that no action can follow a rule unless there is a community that says that it does. That sceptical view of the social nature of rules cannot be right.'[65]

It is clearly possible to marshal stronger arguments against the consensual view of rule-following. Even if it is accepted that the content of rule cannot be defined on the individual level, it remains unclear how we are supposed to discover the meaning ascribed to the rule by the community. The difficulty is compounded if it is considered that a collectivity cannot be said to have any precise intention. Further, if, following the private language argument, it emerges that an individual has

---

[60] B. Bix, 'The application (and mis-application) of Wittgenstein's rule-following considerations to legal theory' , in Patterson (ed) 1992 at 210, fn 10.
[61] *Ibid* at 217)
[62] F. Schauer, *Playing by the rules* (Oxford, Clarendon, 1991) at 66.
[63] *Ibid* at 66.
[64] Vagueness in Law at 9)
[65] *Ibid* at 25.

no way of verifying his own previous usage, then language itself will appear meaningless, and the debate therefore futile.[66]

It should nevertheless be noted that the sceptical solution is not intended to show that rules do not exist or that linguistic communication is impossible. The aim is rather to show how difficult it is, given the impossibility of private language, to account for successful rule-following. Kripke's suggestion should thus be seen as an account of accepted practice, not as a denial of basic intuitions.[67]

It is interesting to note the extent to which the consensual approach corresponds to normal practice as observed in legal judgments relating to interpretation, the rule of precedent and the conventions of overruling.

That 'every action according to a rule is an interpretation'[68] may seem tendentious, yet the fact that legal rules stand permanently in need of interpretation is uncontested. This is true even in those 'easy' cases where only one interpretation appears plausible. Even Hart, who considered arguments for rule-scepticism as 'incoherent'[69] was forced to admit that the plain cases, 'where the general terms seem to need no interpretation', are simply the most familiar ones, constantly recurring in similar contexts.[70] The fact that a particular context is familiar does not imply that it has no role to play in interpretation.

Rules of interpretation have been developed within the common law, and to some extent consolidated in the *Interpretation Act* 1978, but

---

[66] Wittgenstein himself may have rejected aspects of the proposed solution, insofar as it makes truth appear relative and fails to account for certainty. He says, contrary to Kripke: 'If I have exhausted the justifications I have reached bedrock and my spade is turned' (*Philosophical investigations*, 1953, § 217), and speaks of a series as 'a visible section of rails invisibly laid to infinity' (*Philosophical investigations*, 1953, § 218). He claims further that there is 'a way of grasping a rule which is not an interpretation.' (*Philosophical investigations*, 1953, § 202) As Kripke does not claim to represent Wittgenstein's own, considered view, his reading is often referred to as the 'Kripgenstein problem'.

[67] Kripke himself points out (1982 at 69) that his "sceptical' solution is only so-called because it attempts to explain the existence of rules without refuting the sceptical argument. This corresponds to Wittgenstein's own approach: 'This merely shews what goes to make up what we call 'obeying a rule' in everyday life' (*Philosophical investigations*, 1953, §235).

[68] Wittgenstein, *Philosophical Investigations*, 1953, §202.

[69] *Concept of Law*, 1961 at 136.

[70] *Ibid* at126.

these 'metarules' of interpretation, like the written instructions suggested by Schauer, remain themselves susceptible to changing interpretations.

The claim that the rule is what the (appropriate) community says it is corresponds closely to the common law rule of *stare decisis*. Just as it may not be clear in advance whether a term is applicable in a novel situation, it may be unclear whether a precedent is binding.[71] To distinguish a case involves making new semantic distinctions on the basis of hitherto unnoticed, background features. It is equivalent to interpreting the rule in a new way, by bringing out a new element of the situation. It amounts to a claim that the rule we were following, now adapted to allow for exceptional circumstances, is more complex than we thought it was. It is no longer the same rule.

The question of whether a new interpretation is equivalent to a change in the law is discussed expressly in *Perrin v Morgan* 1943. The court considered the rule of construction regarding the interpretation of the word 'money' in an English will, which had apparently been regarded by the courts as binding since 1725. Viscount Simon proposed to abandon the rule altogether:

> I protest against the idea that, in interpreting the language of a will, there can be some fixed meaning of the word 'money', which the courts must adopt as being the 'legal' meaning as opposed to the 'popular' meaning. [...] It is far more important to promote the correct construction of future wills in this respect than to preserve consistency in misinterpretation.[72]

Lord Thankerton, however, considered that the question to be decided was 'whether the rule, as applied by the courts in the decisions referred to, is a wrong rule altogether, or is a sound rule, which has been wrongly applied.' He was not prepared to abolish a rule of such long standing, but nevertheless considered that it should be applied differently:

> I have always understood the rule as one which yielded to a sufficient context. With this understanding I do not see why the rule, properly applied, should fail to work justice. The blot, if any, is not the rule, but its misapplication [73]

To modify the application of a rule is to change its content in order to obtain a different result, whilst appearing to preserve the rule itself. Even

---

[71] Compare Recanati, *Literal meaning*, 2004 at 143.
[72] *Perrin v Morgan* [1943] 1 All ER 187 (HL), *per* Viscount Simon).
[73] *Perrin v Morgan, per* Lord Thankerton).

while making his distinction, in order to avoid being bound, the judge claims to be respecting the basic principles of the earlier rule, and to be going on as before. A similar point was discussed in *Kleinwort Benson v Lincoln City Council* 1998, concerning the right to recover money paid under a mistake of law.

> What is in issue at the heart of this case is the continued existence of a long standing rule of law, which has been maintained in existence for nearly two centuries in what has been seen to be the public interest. It is therefore incumbent on your Lordships to consider whether it is indeed in the public interest that the rule should be maintained, or alternatively that it should be abrogated altogether or reformulated.[74]

The difference between modifying a rule and simply overruling it appears here as a matter of degree.

In certain circumstances, English judges find themselves obliged to depart from the rule of *stare decisis* to the extent of overruling a line of earlier decisions. This power is used only rarely, and usually marks a significant turning point in the development of the law. However, even (or perhaps especially) in these particularly important cases, the judges avoid stating openly that they are changing the law. Instead, by convention, they declare themselves to be correcting earlier mistakes and misapprehensions. Again, even when establishing new rules, they still claim to be following the law as they have always understood it.

In *Kleinwort Benson*, Lord Browne-Wilkinson referred to the words of Lord Reid, who had notoriously described the 'declaratory theory', according to which the common law is supposed to have remained fixed and unchanging since time immemorial, as a 'fairy-tale':

> The theoretical position has been that judges do not make or change law: they discover and declare the law, which is throughout the same. According to this theory, when an earlier decision is overruled the law is not changed: its true nature is disclosed, having existed in that form all along. This theoretical position is, as Lord Reid said, a fairy tale in which no-one any longer believes [75]

An extreme example is found in *R v R* 1992, which overruled the longstanding rule concerning marital rape. The law on this subject was originally defined by Hale, where he states: 'But the husband cannot be

---

[74] Kleinwort Benson v Lincoln City Council, [1998] 4 All ER 513 (HL), per Lord Goff)

[75] *Kleinwort Benson,* 1998, *per* Lord Browne-Wilkinson.

guilty of a rape committed by himself upon his lawful wife, for by their mutual matrimonial consent and contract the wife hath given up herself in this kind unto her husband which she cannot retract.'[76] Lord Lane nevertheless felt entitled to take account of the social developments, which had already given rise to a considerable number of exceptions to the rule. He adopted what he called a 'radical' solution in declaring in effect that Hale's rule of constructive consent had never been the law:

> This is not the creation of a new offence, it is the removal of a common law fiction which has become anachronistic and offensive and we consider that it is our duty having reached that conclusion to act upon it.[77]

The judicial convention regarding overruling again allows the judges to claim, like Kripke's bizarre sceptic, to be going on as before, following the rule they have always followed, even while obtaining different results.

5. Conclusion

In the account of rule-following under discussion, the content of a rule, like the meaning of words, depends not on individual knowledge or intuition, but on consensus within the appropriate community. The same is true of the law, which is also established by consensus within the legal community. Individual judges can still dissent, just as they can disagree about whether the rule is just, but they accept the decision of the community as to what the rule actually is, after authoritative decision. It is implicit in Hart's 'rule of recognition' that members of the general public are also prepared to follow the primary rules of obligation.[78] If it were not so, the legal system would fail. The fact that the law evolves over time, to take account of emerging social needs and values, shows that it is not fixed independently of the participants, but is indeed responsive to the changing consensus.

Judgments on questions of interpretation have been seen to make frequent reference to common usage in the wider community. In *Wagamama* 1995, Laddie J stated that it was right to bear in mind the views of likely customers.[79] Lawton LJ, referred in *Attorney-General's Reference (No 5 of 1980)* to 'ordinary parlance'.[80] In *R v Ireland* 1998,

---

[76] Hale, Sir Matthew, *History of the Pleas of the Crown* (1736) at 629.
[77] *R v R*, [1991] 4 All ER 481, *per* Lord Lane)
[78] *Concept of law*, 1961 at 100)
[79] [1995] F.S.R. 713 Ch.D per Laddie J.
[80] [1981] 1 WLR 88.

Lord Steyn justified his personal linguistic intuition by referring not to his personal idiolect, but to how 'one could nowadays speak'.[81]

As a philosophical theory, however, the consensual solution to the rule-following paradox faces formidable obstacles. A model in which individuals are not expected to know their own minds is unlikely to provide a satisfactory account of knowledge and certainty. Clearly, to make the validity of mathematical results depend on the agreement of the community at large would be wrong. Serious objections may also be made to the appeal to consensus as final arbiter regarding ethical questions. Nevertheless, in other fields agreement does depend on social, rather than objective facts. Grammatical usage is indeed discovered by the observation of practice, rather than being imposed by external authority. Within a particular linguistic community, words and phrases do mean what that community thinks they mean. To that extent, the consensual approach seems intuitively acceptable. Thus, even though it may be inadequate as a theory of truth, the social solution may still be considered plausible as an explanation of meaning, and more particularly as an account of the practice of rule-following.[82]).

Legal adjudication is also a collegial activity, depending fundamentally on meaning and interpretation. Yet it also makes claims to certainty, whilst not ignoring ethical questions. It must therefore remain unclear whether the social view of rule-following is appropriate as a theory of law. The question is discussed by Bjarup in his review of Kripke.[83] (1982). He fails to come to a clear conclusion:

> If the community all started saying that 57 + 68 = 5, to use Kripke's example, then this 'brute empirical fact' does not make me wrong when I insist that the correct answer is 125. What is the case with legal decisions is more difficult to answer.

In view of the indeterminacy of linguistic meaning, the question must be considered relevant to any account of common law adjudication.

---

[81] [1998] AC 147.

[82] The extent to which it is sensible to debate theories of truth independently of meaning remains a challenge to philosophers.

[83] J. Bjarup, 'Kripke's case' (1988) 19 *Rechtstheorie* 49.

CHAPTER 3

Topical Jurisprudence: Reconciliation of Law and Rhetoric

Anita Soboleva

Jurists for Constitutional Rights and Freedoms, Moscow

1. Introduction

Topical jurisprudence is an attempt to apply the methodology of rhetoric to the investigation of legal texts and legal reasoning. According to ancient tradition, rhetoric is defined as the art of persuasion, and rhetorical *topica* as the art of finding – or 'inventing' – arguments in order to persuade, to formulate these arguments, to counter-balance them and, thus, more broadly, to find the best solution for the problem. The understanding of rhetoric as a methodology for problem-solving was initially thoroughly investigated by Theodor Viehweg in his famous *Topics and Law*.[1]

Rhetorical *Topica* (Topics) as an ancient technique for generating thoughts about problems providing handy recipes for finding different approaches to the problem by suggesting arguments *pro* and *contra*. In relation to problem-solving in law, in its turn, cannot be separated from interpretation, *topoi* for inventing legal arguments can be also considered as the commonplaces for interpretation of legal texts.

2. The nature of *topoi*

The Greek term *tópoς*[2] means 'place' or 'region'. Aristotle used it for designating an 'area', or a 'place' in the mind of a person, where the arguments were stored and retrieved. He distinguished between two types of *topoi:* common for all fields of knowledge, and common for a particular discipline or type of oratory. He did not, however, made any attempts to draft a list of specific *topoi* belonging to any particular science.

---

[1] Theodor Viehweg *Topics and Law*, (Frankfurt am Mein: Peter Lang, 1993).

[2] The term *tópoi* (ancient Greek), or *loci* (Latin) literally means 'seats of arguments', 'places of arguments', 'regions of arguments', and is more frequently understood as headings under which arguments can be classified.

A. Wagner et al. (eds.), Interpretation, Law and the Construction of Meaning, 49–63.

Cicero used the topical approach as a way to find arguments 'by a rational system without wandering about'.[3] He wrote:

> It is easy to find things that are hidden if the hiding place is pointed out and marked; similarly if we wish to track down some argument we ought to know the places or topics: for that is the name given by Aristotle to the 'regions', as it were, from which arguments are drawn.[4]

Perelman and Olbrechts-Tyteca applied the notion of 'topics', or *loci*, to 'premises of a very general nature that can serve as the bases for values and hierarchies'.[5] As implied values, they participate in the justification of most of the choices we make. However, when some of these commonplaces have been used by an arguing party, another party may required to justify them. Each *topos* (locus, commonplace) understood as a value can be challenged by one that is contrary to it, and, thus any society can be characterized by the particular values it prizes most and by the intensity of its adherence to one or the other of a pair of counterbalanced values. This approach – commonplaces understood as values – enables use of the topical doctrine not just as a device to make a handy list of sources of arguments, but to use it as a methodology of research into legal reasoning and decision-making, because it enables the arrangement of arguments into hierarchies, their counterbalancing them and making a value judgment; all crucial for any legal dispute. Judicial decisions, even in cases when they cannot be considered as necessary conclusions drawn by formal logic from existing legal provisions, might nevertheless be justifiable in rhetorical terms, because rhetorical context includes wider relations of the text of law both to justice and social facts.

Theodor Viehweg in *Topics and Law*[6] investigated in detail the correlation between the topical system of reasoning and legal prudence, and showed quite convincingly, that the topical approach served perfectly the task of searching for premises, which could be shared by disputing parties as generally accepted, relevant, permissible, acceptable, and defensible. He was also one of the first who noticed that the topical approach enables an adjustment of the 'natural', or 'ordinary' language of legal statutes – by means of interpretations and reinterpretations – to legal practice.

---

[3] Cicero *Topica* I,2, in Cicero (Loeb Classical Library Edition, 1976), at 2:382-83.
[4] Cicero *Topica,* I,6-8. *Ibid*, at 2:386-87.
[5] Chaim Perelman and Luac Olbrechts-tyteca, *The New Rhetoric: A Treatise on Argumentation* (Notre-Dame/London, 1969), at 83-84.
[6] Theodor Viehweg, *Topics and Law* (Frankfurt am Mein: Peter Lang, 1993).

Julius Stone in *Legal System and Lawyers' Reasoning*, while sharing Viehweg's viewpoint that 'the kind of reasoning from *topoi* is an open (though oriented) universe of discourse',[7] and admitting that rhetorical *Topica* represents a kind of reasoning to which moral, social and political problems may prove more tractable, remained, however, quite sceptical about the real possibility of identifying the *topoi* on which legal reasoning may rest. For Stone *topoi,* or commonplaces, remained one of many kinds of illusory categories that certainly affect the process of good judgment, but remain intangible and inarticulate.

We can agree to some extent with the 'intangible' nature of commonplaces, but this 'intangibility' does not mean that they do not exist. It is explained by the variety of senses, in which commonplaces are understood, and, consequently, by the absence of clear criteria by which they can be singled out. So far, no special attempts have been made to create any list of *topoi* (commonplaces) for law, and it is impossible to think of any single or final list of this kind. First of all, commonplaces can be singled out and grouped on different grounds depending on our understanding of their nature: as (1) commonly shared values, (2) generally accepted views, (3) previously stipulated premises, (4) any propositions that we take for granted without discussion, or (5) landmarks in topography of argumentation. In this respect, a law thesaurus can be also considered as a hierarchical sequence of commonplaces (*topoi*), where each term of a more general nature designates a 'box', which has inside legal definitions of a lower hierarchy. Or, we can create a system of commonplaces for any particular field of law, namely for civil law, criminal law or human rights law. Secondly, this list can be more or less detailed. In this article, I adduce as an example the list of *topoi* for constitutional law, that I drafted, based on my research of judicial decisions of the US Supreme Court and Constitutional Courts of Germany and Russia.[8] I believe that the types of arguments used in judicial decisions involving interpretation of constitutional texts are more general, more flexible, and less restrictive from the point of view of freedom of the interpreter.

The purpose of such as investigation was to look for those starting points in the process of legal reasoning, which were common for the higher

---

[7] Julius Stone, *Legal System and Lawyers' Reasoning* (London, 1964), at 331.

[8] А.К. Соболева Топическая юриспруденция: аргументация и толкование в праве, (Москва: Добросвет, 2002). (A.Soboleva. Topicheskaya yurispudentsiya: argumentatsiya i tolkovaniye v prave. Moscow: Dobrosvet, 2002).

courts belonging to different legal systems and legal cultures, and to try to answer the question, whether *topoi* are indeed a kind of illusory categories, or they can rather be considered as 'disciplinary rules' (Owen Fiss),[9] a 'structure of constraints' (Stanley Fish),[10] or 'safe rules to guide us on dangerous path' (Francis Lieber),[11] that is, constraints imposed on the interpreter, for which many scholars have searched. Which of these *topoi* are considered by judges to be more reliable sources (or 'storages') of arguments? What are the objective criteria (if any) of admissibility and validity of arguments in legal reasoning? What can rhetoric add to the everlasting dispute about objectivity of interpretation in law?

3. *Topoi* in legal reasoning and interpretation

I came to the conclusion that, from rhetorical point of view, we can consider as commonplaces (*topoi*) of legal reasoning and legal interpretation, the well-known sources from which most arguments are drawn, namely:

1. Maxims of law
2. Texts of legal statutes (literal construction)
   -ordinary meaning
   -terminological meaning
3. Former interpretation (precedent)
4. Legislative Intent
   -travaux préparatoires
   -parts of the text
5. Aim of the statute
6. Best consequences (pragmatic arguments)
7. Social changes as basis for changes in interpretation

---

[9] Owen M.Fiss, 'Objectivity and Interpretation,' in Aulis Aarnio and D.Neil Maccormic (ed.), *Legal Reasoning*, vol. II (Aldershot: Darthmouth Publishing Company, 1992), at 302.

[10] Stanley Fish, 'Working on the Chain Gang: Interpretation in Law and Literature,' in Aulis Aarnio, D.Neil Maccormic (ed.), *Legal Reasoning*, vol. II (Aldershot: Darthmouth Publishing Company, 1992), at 290.

[11] Francis Lieber, Legal and Political Hermeneutics or Principles of Interpretation and Construction in Law and Politics with Remarks on Precedents and Authorities, 3rd ed. (St.Lous.: F.H.Thomas, 1880), at 53.

8. Principles, concepts and doctrines of constitutional law
    -principles, concepts and doctrines created by courts (judicial tests)
    -legal doctrines and theories

9. Social values

10. Scientific data

11. Social theories

12. Statistics

13. Common sense.

This list can be used in different ways. First of all, it is convenient for teaching law students how to analyze cases. Secondly, it is convenient for judges when they need to find arguments to justify the decision made. Thirdly, it is convenient for practicing lawyers, for any case you can find at least some arguments in favour of your client. More generally, it enables tracing of how the process of legal reasoning moves. Moreover, the adherence of the courts to certain commonplaces and their reluctance to employ some others may lead to some interesting inferences about legal culture, political situations, state of the rule of law, understanding of justice and morality in a particular country or jurisdiction.

In rhetorical terms, maxims of law can be considered as what Russian rhetorical school after professor Yuri Rozhdestvenskiy calls 'external rules of speech' (*vneshnije pravila slovesnosti*),[12] that is, the rules established by special agencies (state, administration, corporation, and so on) for regulating speech – its time, place, subject, preservation, etc. These regulations, as distinct from grammar rules or rhetorical rules, lie 'outside' speech *per se*, but create conditions for its generation, circulation and storage, and make communication acts possible. In our case, these are procedural requirements which should be met prior the process of interpretation and application of a certain legal provision may begin. The rule of *ultra vires* may serve as an example. Disputes about jurisdiction and competence concerns the formal requirements that should be met before we can further discuss the interpretation of words and legal definitions. Thus, we do not need to search for arguments in order to resolve a dispute about compliance of a particular rule of the regional act with the federal

---

[12] Ю.В.Рождественский. *Общая филология* (Москва: Фонд «Новое тысячелетие», 1996) at 12-13. Yuri Rozhdestvenskiy. *Obshchaya philologia.* (Moscow: Novoye Tysyacheletiye Fund, 1996), at 12-13).

Constitution, if this act was issued beyond powers confirmed upon the regional legislature.

The first argument concerning the legal text itself is a linguistic argument, by which I understand the argument in support of interpretation following the words of the law, that is a literal, strict, or formal interpretation, and by linguistic meaning of the word – its ordinary meaning and/or the meaning prescribed by the legal definition. I also call the 'linguistic argument' an argument based on the meaning of a word derived from a linguistic context, namely, from the text of the analyzed legal act as a whole (the so-called 'contextually harmonizing argument'). The logic of the legal analysis requires starting the search for meaning with the linguistic context, further involving the broader social context and, finally, to a counter-balancing of all the arguments received.[13] Thus, a literal construction seems to be a starting point of interpretation.

The linguistic arguments rule practically all the decisions of the Russian courts of general jurisdiction, though are rarely used by the Constitutional Court. For instance, Russian courts, based on strict literal interpretation of the statute, which granted compensations and benefits to persons 'evacuated (transferred) or voluntarily moved from polluted settlements' after the accident in 'Mayak' enterprise in 1957, rejected the claims of people who suffered from radiation as a result of this accident, but were evacuated (transferred) to another, newly built, street of the same village. The district court of Chelyabinsk refused to grant this benefit, because a plaintiff 'did not move *from* the polluted settlement', but was accommodated within the same place. The Constitutional court disagreed with this argument and used a broad interpretation, which enabled defense of the rights of all individuals who suffered during this event. At the same time, the Constitutional Court did not find the statutory provision unconstitutional, confining itself to making a statement about the unconstitutional nature of the existing practice of its application by law implementing bodies.

---

[13] For the purposes of the legal research, considering the whole of the reality as a context would not be justified, since this sort of broad interpretation of the 'context' does not allow to identify starting points of legal arguments. It does not give the researcher an opportunity to see how a word changes its meaning depending on specific factors, what these factors are, and, most importantly, what weight of each of them has. Whereas for a linguist all the contexts are equal, for a lawyer they have strict hierarchy and different obligatory power.

4. *Topoi* in jurisprudence of the Russian Constitutional Court

It is common knowledge that the literal interpretation is too often incompatible with the concept of justice which underlies any democratic legal system, and that therefore, in addressing a legal controversy one should also take into account other criteria. The jurisprudence of the Russian Constitutional Court is no exception. At the same time, the distinctive feature of the Russian Constitutional Court's approach consists in its unwillingness to declare unconstitutional the provisions whose plain meaning is *prima facie* inconsistent with the Constitution. It prefers to make a statement that the provision should be assigned a new meaning and that it must be read differently while preserving the old wording.

The Court's decision in the following case will exemplify this approach. Art. 336 sec.2 of the old Code of Criminal Procedure said:

> The Supreme Court ... sends a notification of the date of the appellate hearing to those parties of the case who requested such notification in their written appeals or in their objections to appeals and complaints.

For all other courts, such as the district and regional, notification to all the parties who submitted their appellate complaints, of the date and place of the hearing was, according to section one of the same article, mandatory. One applicant, who was a convicted person kept in detention, did not attend the session of the appellate court since neither he nor his lawyer petitioned for that and, therefore, they were not notified of the date and place of the hearing. He challenged the provision as unconstitutional. The Constitutional Court, in its previous rulings concerning other articles of the above mentioned Code, had already clearly formulated its legal position by saying that the right to defense implies the possibility for the parties to participate in court proceedings, to familiarize themselves with the positions of other participants, to have access to additional materials, to give explanations and to be notified of the time and place of the hearing. Having this in mind, in the case under consideration, the Constitutional Court refused to declare section 2 of article 336 unconstitutional because it decided, that such a ruling would have been excessive and unnecessary. The Court issued a ruling while refusing to consider the claim, stating in this ruling that there was no need for any judicial decision, because the provisions of the article discussed, in the light of previous decisions, cannot provide a ground for failure to notify the parties about the date of the hearings in the appellate court at any level. 'Any other interpretation of the above provisions in the judicial practice to be excluded', wrote the Court.[14]

It remained unclear, however, why the Court simply did not find this text unconstitutional. Unsurprisingly, in practice the law implementing bodies do not feel bound by the rulings of the Constitutional Court, especially by their opinions, containing the so called 'refusals'. The practice of the Constitutional Court includes issuing rulings about inadmissibility of the complaint on procedural grounds with legal arguments in favour of the applicant, which must be taken into account by ordinary courts while adjudicating the case. Partly this practice can be accounted for by the heritage of the Soviet judicial system, based on the presumption, that the interests of the state always prevail over those of the individual, and the interests of those in power over the interests of civil society. This leads to the situation when the Constitution is quite often violated by the practice of interpreting and implementing statutes in favour of the state agencies rather than on the basis of the mere language of these statutes. The Constitutional Court tries to 'correct' this practice and to intervene, even when procedural grounds for such intervention are weak. Partly this practice is accounted for by the Court's desire to escape a legal vacuum, that is, creating a situation when the provision declared null and void in which it would have been replaced by another by the legislator. It should be pointed out that, notwithstanding these considerations, this practice of the Constitutional Court is very dangerous, because in many cases it enables it to avoid real judgements against the executive and its policies. The Court spells out its legal position as if defending individual rights, while allowing the state agencies to proceed with their unconstitutional practice in all other cases, because there is no mechanism for implementation of the 'constitutional legal meaning', as distinct from implementation of the Court's decisions.

The search for 'constitutional legal meaning' outside the words of the Constitution itself involves a certain risk: the 'constitutional legal meaning' like the 'revolutionary legal sense' applied elsewhere in Soviet times may justify any decision, because it does not rest upon the consideration of all arguments drawn from different commonplaces. When it is applied as a primary and basic (rather than an auxiliary and additional)

---

[14] *N. Chipurda Case*, Ruling of the Constitutional Court of October 17, 2001// Определение КС РФ по делу Н.Н.Чипурды (Вестник Конституционного Суда, 2002, № 2).

criterion, the legal provision loses any relation to its wording, and this means that there is no criterion left to judge the objectivity of the interpretation. The Constitutional Court becomes the sole keeper of a kind of sacred knowledge about the sense and meaning of constitutional provisions, and one can only wish that in considering the complaints it is guided by the ideas of protection of human rights and the limitation of powers rather than otherwise.

When a court in its reasoning adduces only arguments in favour of the decision made and intentionally ignores all other possible arguments, that is all other possible viewpoints relevant for democratic and just decision-making, we can suspect that it is biased or not independent enough. The decision of the Russian Constitutional Court 'On the interpretation of Section 4 Article 1 of the Constitution of the Russian Federation'[15] in this respect poses many questions and subjects to critique.

Section 4 of Article 111 of the Russian Constitution provides:

> ... after the State Duma thrice rejects candidates for Chairman of the Government of the Russian Federation, the President of the Russian Federation shall appoint the Chairman ... dissolve the State Duma and call a new election.

A request for interpretation of this provision was filed by the State Duma after President Boris Yeltsin nominated the same person for the second time as a candidate for the position of Prime Minister. The deputies asked the Constitutional Court to answer a question, whether the President was entitled to nominate once more the candidate who had already been rejected by the State Duma, and, further, what the legal consequences of triple rejection by the State Duma of this same person would be.

The Constitutional Court wrote in its decision, that, according to the literal meaning of the provision, the word combination 'thrice rejects candidates' may mean both: nomination of the same person three times in a row or nomination of a new candidate every time. The Court held that the language of the article by itself did not exclude or preclude either of these two interpretations. Further, using as context the provisions of other articles of the Constitution, namely, the provision that the President appoints the Chairman of the Government with the consent of the State Duma (Article

---

[15] Decision of December 11, 1998 //Постановление Конституционного Суда РФ от 11 декабря 1998 г. (Конституционный Суд Российской Федерации: Постановления, определения. 1997-1998. Москва: Юристъ, 2000), at 22-25.

83 par. 'a'), that the President dissolves the State Duma in cases prescribed by the Constitution (Article 84 par. 'b') and that giving consent to the appointment of the Prime Minister, nominated by the President, is within the competence of the State Duma (Article 103 par. 'a'), the Court concluded that the selection of a candidate for the position of Prime Minister is the President's prerogative and that the Constitution allows the President to choose the specific manner of exercising this right himself, namely, to propose the same candidate twice or thrice or to nominate a new candidate each time. Another interpretation, in the Court's opinion, would jeopardize the stability of the constitutional system and the maintenance of civil peace and concord. In this context, if the State Duma thrice rejects the person nominated by the President, whether this is the same person three times in a row or different persons each time, the President then appoints the Chairman, dissolves the State Duma and calls a new election.

Thus, by its interpretation the Court in effect negated the powers of the State Duma relating to the appointment of the head of government, allowing the President to manipulate the Duma.

In many cases the linguistic argument cannot serve as a reliable ground for decision-making, because it is hard to reveal the 'plain meaning' of seemingly 'plain words'. The Russian Constitutional Court in 1995 had to define the meaning of the words 'the overall number of deputies': whether it was the number prescribed by the Russian Constitution, that was 450 persons, or whether it was the number of existing deputies, which was somewhat lowers, because some deputies had died or otherwise left their position and had not yet been replaced. The Constitutional Court came to the conclusion that this phrase meant 450 persons.[16] Interestingly enough, 4 years earlier, in 1991, the Congress of Peoples' Deputies adopted a Resolution in relation to the interpretation of the notion 'the overall number of deputies of the RSFSR', which clearly stated that 'overall number of deputies' should mean the number of peoples' deputies that were actually elected/in office.

5. Choice between arguments: how *topoi* may help.

The adduced examples convincingly show that we can consider the 'ordinary meaning' or 'legal definition' simply as headings under which

---

[16] Decision of April 12, 1995 // Постановление Конституционного Суда РФ от 12 апреля 1995 г. (Вестник Конституционного Суда, 1995, № 2-3).

different arguments can be found. The choice between any two possible interpretations lies outside linguistics.

The courts may also look for definitions of terms belonging to different areas of science and knowledge: medicine, technology, accounting, and so on. Terms and definitions of art and science can also serve as a source of arguments. They cannot dictate the choice of the 'right' or 'wrong' interpretation, but they can be useful for clarifying the meaning of the statutory words.

In most cases the judicial decision rests on several *topoi.* Arguments, consistently adduced in the judicial decision, enable us to trace the process of legal reasoning made by the judges elaborations on the case. We can use this type of reasoning as a model of how to deal with a legal dispute. After the question of competence and jurisdiction has been decided positively, we can start the analysis of legal text with its literal construction and continue to move along the path of interpretation involving linguistic and non-linguistic factors, putting the case into broader and broader context.

Within each of the most general *'tópoi'* several different types of arguments are possible (e.g. by comparison, by incompatibility, by reason, by transition, etc.). When we have adduced as many arguments as we can, we need to make a choice between different *tópoi* and different arguments, that is, to balance them. We also need to choose between different rules, equally applicable in the situation. This can only be done by making a value judgment that rests upon the epideictic system and hierarchy of values of a particular legal and social culture. The difference between the American, Russian and German approach to controversial problems lies not so much in the system of argumentation and types of arguments, but rather in the adherence of judges to certain types of commonplaces (*topoi*) and the hierarchy of values which affect the final decision of the court. For instance, Russian courts do not recognize statistics as an argument; this is why we do not find discrimination cases in courts, even though legislation enables to prosecute for discrimination in employment or health care cases. Thus it is not possible to bring a discrimination claim, because in most cases it can only be proven with statistical evidence, evidence that has no value in the courts in Russia. In the German Constitutional Court the judges frequently base their decisions on legal doctrines, social theories, principles of law and values enshrined in the German Constitution, and rest their decisions on considerations of morality and a hierarchy of values.

Here we come across the second type of list of *topoi,* namely *topoi* understood as values. This list includes at least six *topoi*, common to the US, Russia and Germany: law, morals, politics, science, historical experience, and religion. Of course, we can extend this list by adding democracy, order, justice, freedom and so on, because the length of the list depends on how detailed we wish to make it. I did not include the latter in the hierarchy for each of these countries (this is work for the future), but the differences between legal cultures will certainly be clear exactly from such inclusive hierarchies. For instance, if a priest can be required to testify in court, then obviously religion in this society will be of lower value than law and order; if religion affects the decisions of the court in abortion cases (explicitly or implicitly), then religion is of higher value than science and individual freedom; if deputies enjoy immunity in criminal cases (as they do in Russia) one cannot count on a strict application of the rule-of-law principle in other cases.

When we speak of *topoi* as 'seats of arguments', we imply that at this point they have equal value for the audience (readers of the judicial decisions). For *topica,* literal construction in discrimination cases is of just the same argumentative value as statistics. All interpretations found as a result of the process of legal thinking are just points of view that should be taken into account in order to make an informative choice. The second type of *topoi*, that is *topoi* understood as values, affects choice. If we know that politics drives the choice of judges, or religion drives the choice, or customary law drives the choice, we can make the court's decisions more predictable.

6. Conclusion: how rhetoric may contribute to legal thought

A rhetorical approach enables consideration of the process of invention of a new text (that is, the text of judicial decision) from the existing text (the text of a statute), to reveal regular features in this process, to trace the interconnections between linguistic and non-linguistic factors, and to investigate the process of understanding and interpretation of a written text in compliance with the purpose of the interpreter. The written text of law can change its original meaning in the process of interpretation and re-interpretation, and still preserve its wording. This means that the process of interpretation in law cannot be reduced solely to the clarification of meaning of words used in a legal sense, but must be considered also as a means of manipulation with different outcomes and meanings in accordance with the task of interpreter (judge, lawyer for the defence, attorney for the state, etc.) and the expectations of the audience (parties to a lawsuit, general public, legal scholars, politicians, judges of the appellate court, legislators, etc.)

Legal hermeneutics, while looking for 'safe rules to guide us on the dangerous path',[17] failed to resolve the problem of what can be considered as an 'objective', 'true' or 'right' interpretation of a legal text, while the topical approach, elaborated in ancient Greece and revitalized in the middle of the 20th century by Theodor Viehweg, enables to overcome this problem.

The application of topical methodology to law enables not only the creation of a kind of a handy recipe book for the use of legal students analyzing a case, but more generally helps us to better understand how law is functioning, how lawyers think, how legal and other social norms interact, how law and language, law and politics, law and philosophy influence one another.

In accordance with rhetorical thought, the structure of legal reasoning looks as follows: first we define the main issue in the legal conflict (*status* in terms of Quintilianus); [18] then each party analyses a case according to its own strategy, employing those *tópoi* which assist it in finding arguments in its favour; then the court, by counter-balancing the adduced arguments and reconciling the competing values, makes a decision, which serves as a means to resolve a conflict.

The topical approach in law requires consideration of as many *tópoi* as possible, for the more view-points we are able to discuss, the more informed and just decision we can make. This in turn allows the decision-maker to argue for adherence of the parties to the decision made. Thus, legal interpretation, involving arguments from all the *tópoi* is more perfect and more exact than other methods, as it enables some elements of axiology to be taken into account and it enriches the law with certain elements of ethics.

Every *tópos* constitutes a 'seat of argument' from which any lawyer can begin his search for the most appropriate and desirable construction of a legal text before him in order to adjust it to his client's

---

[17] Francis Lieber, Legal and Political Hermeneutics or Principles of Interpretation and Construction in Law and Politics with Remarks on Precedents and Authorities, 3rd ed. (St.Lous.: F.H.Thomas, 1880), at 53.

[18] Marcus Fabius Quintilianus, *The Institutio Oratoria of Quintilian* (London, 1951), vol. I, at 408-63.

needs. That is why one can claim that the topical approach is a kind of manipulative mode, enabling the text to be read in the way one might wish without any constraints. However, in rhetoric the constraints on interpretation are imposed by ethical rules, by general feelings of what is just and unjust, by moral values, and by a hierarchy of values which exists in the community at the time. Initial strict constraints are provided by *tópoi* such as maxims of law. Further constraints are imposed by *tópoi* connected with the strict interpretation of the text. The most severe constraints are imposed by *tópoi* such as values. Altogether, they make possible the unification of a flexibility of interpretation with its relative predictability.

A lawyer interprets not only the text, but also the reality connected or not connected to this text. Disputes about the validity or admissibility of these or those arguments are, in fact, disputes about right and wrong, appropriate and non-appropriate understandings of the statutory text. As distinct from a literary critic, a lawyer interprets the text bearing in mind a third actor – a judge, who will draw a line under the dispute by deciding which interpretation should from now on be considered as right, as the only possible and thus obligatory outcome. Disputes about interpretation in law, as distinct from disputes in literature, always have their end. That is why the everlasting question about the objectivity or 'rightness' of interpretation is not relevant for the legal texts. Interpretation of any statutory text is not aimed at a *search* for meaning or understanding – it is aimed at *prescribing* a certain meaning or understanding to a particular text and situation, regulated by this text. Therefore, the interpretation in law is *conventional* (i.e. agreed upon by convention).

Rhetorical *Topica* is characterized by its tolerance to a plurality of the results of argumentation and interpretation. However, as it is necessary to make a final judgment and to decide of favour of one of them, it is necessary to use the hierarchy of *topoi* that rules this choice.

It is not possible to understand legal texts without rhetorical context, that is, without taking into consideration the reason why the text was created, the argumentative situation and the composition of the audience perceiving the text.

Interpretation of legal texts may contradict the original intent of its author, if this interpretation better serves the idea of justice. Rhetoric, as distinct from hermeneutics, enables the judging of the results of interpretation not in terms of 'right' or 'true', but in terms of what constitutes an 'adequate' interpretation, that is, one based upon generally accepted views and shared values.

Thus, *Topica* can be understood as: 1) a means to analyze the problem; 2) a theory of argumentation; and 3) a theory of interpretation. Reasoning from *'tópoi'* is a kind of reasoning to which moral, social and political problems are more tractable. It helps to reconcile the ideas of justice into the formal text of legal definitions. Application of the topical approach to law is a way to fill the gap between legal theory and other humanities, including political science, linguistics, cultural studies, moral philosophy, ethics and logic. It also helps us to bridge the gap between theory and practice.

CHAPTER 4

Legal Speech Acts as Intersubjective Communicative Action

Deborah Cao

Griffith University, Australia

1. Introduction

Law relies on language and particularly, it relies on the performative nature of language use. Legal effects and legal consequences are commonly obtained merely by uttering certain words, for instance, 'You are guilty', or 'You are sentenced to ten years's imprisonment' as regularly pronounced in court. By uttering words, one accepts public and private legal responsibilities and assumes legal roles and qualities; one transfers one's legal rights and imposes legal obligations onto others.[1] Thus, legal performative utterances are said to be constitutive of their effects. However, despite the frequent reference to legal usage in the development of speech act theories by such authors as Austin and Searle, it seems that more and in-depth discussions and analysis is needed to explore the intricacies of speech acts in legal context, which will benefit linguistics, pragmatics and legal theory.

This chapter examines performative utterances and speech acts in the legal context. It first discusses and reviews the general speech acts theories originally proposed by Austin and further developed by Searle. It then turns to discuss legal speech acts including legislative and judicial speech acts and attempts to characterise the general and basic features and the illocutionary force of such speech acts. In particular, the focus is on legislative speech acts with reference to Habermas's speech act theory. This approach to legal speech acts differs from Austin and Searle's traditional theories in that speech acts in this theory entail the notion of communication as social action. Such speech acts have an intersubjective rather than individual basis in communication and establish relationships between the various participants in legal contexts. This is regarded as particularly important in the study of legal speech acts.

---

[1] M. Jori, 'Legal Performative', *The Encyclopedia of Language and Linguistics*, Volume 4 (Oxford: Pergamon Press, 1994), at 2092.

A. Wagner et al. (eds.), Interpretation, Law and the Construction of Meaning, 65–82.

2. Speech Acts

The notion of speech acts starts with the assumption that the minimal unit of human communication is the performance of utterances such as asserting a proposition, asking a question, making a command, or expressing a desire, among other things. Words are not just used to say things, and Austin calls this 'constative',[2] we also use them to do things, the 'performative'. Austin distinguishes two kinds of utterances: constatives, which are statements or assertions and which describe or report things and events; and utterances which perform actions merely by virtue of the utterances being made. The second type of utterances are called 'performatives' by Austin to recognise their actional nature, what they do, as opposed to constative utterances which simply say.[3] For performative utterances, we do something rather than merely say that something is or is not the case. Uttering a performative is to constitute the performing of a further act in addition to the linguistic act itself. To say 'I promise that...' is performing the very act of promising that can only be accomplished by saying the right words. These words do not describe the fact of a person promising; they are the act itself. Such types of acts are illocutionary acts. An illocutionary act is the minimal complete unit of human linguistic communication.[4]

In the attempt to understand speech acts, in Searle's analysis, we need to distinguish the content of the act and the type of act it is.[5] According to Searle, utterances can in general be analysed into their propositional content and illocutionary force. Take for example, in the utterances: 'I assert that *p*', 'I promise *p*', 'I command that *p*', the same propositional content *p*, appears with varying illocutionary force as indicated by 'assert', 'promise' and 'command' respectively. Thus, the structure of illocutionary acts can be represented as F(*p*), where F stands for illocutionary force and *p* for propositional content. The part of the speech act that constitutes the illocutionary type or illocutionary force and the part that constitutes its propositional content represent the standard double

---

[2] J.L. Austin, *How to do Things With Words* (Cambridge: Harvard University Press, 1962).

[3] Austin, *supra* n.2.

[4] John R. Searle, *Speech Acts: An Essay in the Philosophy of Language* (Cambridge: Cambridge University Press, 1969); John R. Searle, *Expression and Meaning: Essays in the Theory of Speech Acts* (Cambridge: Cambridge University Press, 1979); John R Searle, *Mind, Language and Society: Philosophy in the Real World* (New York: Basic Books, 1998).

[5] Searle, *supra* n.4.

structure of speech acts. According to Habermas, these two components, the illocutionary and the propositional, can vary independently of one another, and we can hold a propositional content invariant vis-à-vis the different types of speech acts in which it occurs.[6] The propositional content can be infinitely diverse as the same propositional content can occur in different types of illocutionary acts. The dominating sentence (the main clause: I ...) establishes the illocutionary force of the utterance and the mode of communication between the speaker and hearer, thus the pragmatic situation of the dependent sentence (the predicative clause: that ...). The dependent sentence, consisting in general of an identifying (referring) phrase and a predicate phrase, establishes the connection of the communication with the world of objects and events.

Then, what are the different types of speech acts? Various attempts at a taxonomy of illocutionary acts have been offered over the years. The most influential are Austin's and Searle's. Austin distinguishes five basic types of performative verbs, that is, exercitives, verdicatives, commissives, behavitives and expositives. But as Searle points out, there are no clear principles by which Austin collects them into his classes.[7] Searle expands Austin's theory and classifies five categories of illocutionary force as representatives, commissives, expressives, declaratives and directives.[8] Furthermore, for speech acts to be performed, there are certain conditions, felicity conditions for Austin, and conditions of satisfaction for Searle, (as opposed to Habermas's conditions, see later) that must obtain. These conditions must be fulfilled for performative utterances to be successful or valid.

In this study, speech acts, apart from the presumptions in the traditional Austin and Searle's theories, also entail the notion of communication as social action from Habermas's speech act theory. In this thinking, speech act has an intersubjective rather than an individual basis. I regard this to be particularly important to legal speech acts.

Habermas's speech act theory forms the core of his universal or formal pragmatics, the theoretical underpinning for his communicative action theory, which in turn is a crucial element in his theories of society and of law. According to Habermas, communicative action is an action

---

6 Jürgen Habermas, *On the Pragmatics of Communication* (Cambridge: the MIT Press, 1989), at 63.
7 Searle, 1969, 1976.
8 Searle, 1969, 1976

whose success depends on the hearer's responding to the validity claims raised by the speaker.[9] In Habermas's theory, there are three basic types of validity claims that can be raised by a speaker in his/her speech acts: (1) a claim to the truth of what is said or presupposed, (2) a claim to the normative rightness of the speech act in the given context of the underlying norm, and (3) a claim to the truthfulness of the speaker.[10] In using linguistic expressions communicatively, the speaker raises all three claims simultaneously.[11] But typically, just one of the claims is raised explicitly, and the other two remain implicit presuppositions for understanding the utterance. These three universal validity claims provide a basis for classifying speech acts. In Habermas's view, communicative utterances can be divided into three broad categories according to the explicit claims they raise: (1) *constative* speech acts are connected with truth claims; (2) *regulative* speech acts with claims to normative rightness; and (3) *expressive* speech acts with claims to truthfulness.[12]

In contrast to Searle's classification cited earlier which is based on the illocutionary aims or intentions of the speaker, Habermas's system of validity of speech acts oriented toward reaching understanding underlies the differentiation of types of speech acts.[13] He argues that, if we start from the fact that the illocutionary aims of speech acts are achieved through the intersubjective recognition of claims to power and validity, and if we introduce normative rightness and subjective truthfulness and truth as validity claims, and interpret them in terms of actor/world relations, then, the classification of speech acts into the constatives, regulatives and expressives that are communicative use (as opposed to strategic use, as with imperatives) can be justified.[14] Moreover, communicatives also exist as a sub-class of regulatives, and operatives that designate the application of constructive rules. So, commissives and declaratives (as in Searle) as

---

[9] Habermas, *supra* n.6.

[10] Habermas, *supra* n.6.

[11] Habermas distinguishes between communicative and non-communicative (strategic) use of language. Communicative actions aimed at reaching understanding are primary and fundamental while strategic form of communication such as lying, misleading, deceiving, manipulating etc is derivative and parasitic on speech oriented towards reaching understanding, see Habermas, *supra* n.6.

[12] Habermas, *supra* n.6.

[13] Habermas, *supra* n.6.

[14] Habermas, *supra* n.6.

well as institutionally bound speech acts and satisfactives are all subsumed under the same class of regulatives.[15]

According to Maeve Cooke, Habermas's speech act theory has two important characteristics: first, speech acts are cooperative relationships of commitment and responsibility: participants in communicative interaction undertake to behave in certain ways, and the success of the interaction depends on the cooperation of both parties involved; and secondly, the relationships of mutual recognition characteristic of communicative action have an inherent rational dimension: the communicative actor undertakes an obligation to provide reasons for the validity of the claims he or she raises with his/her utterances while the counterpart in action may either accept the proffered reasons or challenge them on the basis of better reasons.[16] Habermas's theory stresses the connection between the meaning of utterances and social practices, drawing attention to the institutions and conventions of the forms of life in which communicative activity is always embedded.[17]

Habermas developed his speech act theory on the basis of Austin's and Searle's, placing an emphasis on utterances rather than sentences as the central unit of analysis, going beyond the traditional focus of linguistics. But Habermas's conception of illocutionary force goes beyond Austin's and Searle's.[18] Habermas objects to Austin's distinction between *force* and *meaning* as this, Habermas believes, overlooks the fact that utterances have a meaning distinct from the meaning of the sentences they employ; and he also objects to Austin's classification of speech acts into constative and performative.[19] Habermas's theory of utterance meaning brings together meaning and force, and extends the notion of illocutionary force to all utterances that are used communicatively. His theory gives an account of the meaning of utterances as inseparable from the act of uttering them, and defines utterances as acts of raising validity claims.[20]

When illocutionary acts succeed, they will result in bringing about an interpersonal relation. What, then, is illocutionary force (IF)? According

---

[15] Habermas, *supra* n.6, at 154-164.

[16] Maeve Cooke, 1998, 'Introduction', *On the Pragmatics of Communication*, Maeve Cooke (ed.) (Cambridge: The MIT Press, 1998), at 2.

[17] *Ibid.*

[18] Cooke, *supra* n.16, at 7-8.

[19] For Habermas's analysis of Austin and his objections, see Universal Pragmatics.

[20] Cooke, *supra* n.16, at 7-8.

to Habermas, IF has a rational foundation.[21] The illocutionary force of an acceptable speech act consists in the fact that it can move a hearer to reply to the speech-act-typical obligations of the speaker, that is, it can motivate the hearer to base his/her action on the premise that the speaker seriously intends the commitment he or she indicates.[22] IF is bound up with the speaker's assumption of a warranty to provide reasons in support of the validity of the claims he or she raises. IF is a rational force, for in performing a speech act, the speaker undertakes to support what he/she says with reasons, if necessary. According to Habermas, we understand the meaning of an utterance when we know what makes it acceptable. We know what makes a speech act acceptable when we know the kind of reasons that a speaker can offer, if challenged, in order to reach understanding with a hearer concerning the validity of the disputed claim.[23] Habermas argues that, if the speaker and hearer are to reach an understanding, they must communicate simultaneously at two levels: (a) the level of intersubjectivity on which the speaker and hearer, through illocutionary acts, establish the relations that permit them to come to an understanding with one another; and (b) the level of propositional content about which they wish to reach understanding in the communicative function specified in (a).[24] Thus, Habermas's theory of speech acts and his theory of communicative action are based on an intersubjective, rather than an individual, paradigm of communication and understanding.

Finally, in Habermas's view, to understand an utterance is always to understand it as an utterance in a given situation which in turn may be part of multiple, extended contexts.[25] He draws attention to different kinds of often implicit background knowledge. This background knowledge of the lifeworld forms the indispensable context of the communicative use of language. Thus, according to Habermas, various types of speech act are linked to specific social institutions. For example, norm-conformative action (i.e., a regulative speech act) is founded on institutional norms of moral behaviour with which social actors must comply. Each type of action has its own rationality – its own notion of truth. Habermas's ideal speech situation oriented to rationally motivated critique and understanding treats

---

[21] Habermas, *supra* n.6, at 81-88.
[22] Habermas, *supra* n.6, at 85.
[23] Cooke, *supra* n.16, at 7-8.
[24] Habermas, *supra* n.6, at 64.
[25] Habermas, *supra* n.6,

agreement as the telos of speech and as something that speaker and hearer arrive at through uncoerced consensus. [26]

Thus, Habermas's speech act theory incorporates and extends the classical speech act theories of Austin and Searle, and takes them to another level in the understanding and description of human communication and social interaction through language. I believe that this is particularly crucial for discussion of legal speech acts, in particular in terms of the intersubjective and non-intentionalist paradigm and communication oriented toward mutual understanding and consensus as applied to law and law making.

3. Legal Speech Acts

As said earlier, law relies on speech acts. What, then, makes legal speech acts different from ordinary speech acts? How can we characterise illocutionary force in the legal context?

In relation to legal discourse, Danet classifies speech acts based on Searle's classification in the following way:[27]

> (1) representatives which are utterances that commit the speaker to something being the case or assert the truth of a proposition, including testifying, swearing, asserting, claiming and stating;
>
> (2) commissives which commit the speaker to do something in the future, such as in contracts, marriage ceremonies and wills where both the relevant parties engage in commissive acts;
>
> (3) expressives which express the speakers' psychological state about or attitude to a proposition, including apologising, excusing, condemning, deploring, forgiving and blaming;
>
> (4) declaratives whose successful performance brings about a correspondence between their propositional content and reality, including marriage ceremonies, bills of sale, receipts, appointments, and nominations; and the legislative stipulation of rights and of definitions of concepts; lawyers' objections, sentences, and appellate opinions, indictments, confessions, pleas of guilty/not guilty, and verdicts; and there is a subcategory of representative declarations for certain institutional situations, e.g., a judge making factual claims, requiring claims to be issued with the force of declaration, and also require the speaker to have certain authority,

---

[26] Habermas, *supra* n.6,

[27] Brenda Danet, 'Language in the Legal Process', (1980) *Law and Society*, 14(3): 447-63.

representative declarations share with representatives a sincerity condition. This would cover a marriage ceremony, bills of sale appointment or nominations, legislative stipulation of rights and definitions of concepts, indictments, confessions, pleas of guilty/not guilty, verdicts etc.; and

(5) directives which are future-oriented speech acts, seeking to change the world, to get someone to do something, most prominent in legislation that imposes obligations.

As we can see, Danet's classifications are based on the types of illocutionary force of legal usage. However, within each category of speech act as described by Danet, there are significant differences, e.g., within the category of declaratives, the declarative of marriage ceremonies is very different from another type of declarative, that of legislation; the declaratives of lawyers' objections, confessions or indictments are very different from the declaratives of bills of sale, and so forth. Therefore, I believe that it is necessary to distinguish, within the legal setting, different types of speech acts according to different types of language use and purposes of use. There are significant differences in legal speech acts in different legal contexts.

Thus, if we are guided by the type of legal settings in which our speech occur, we can divide legal speech acts into three broad categories of (1) legislative speech acts, consisting of statutes in written language; (2) judicial speech acts, including oral and written utterances during court proceedings such as oral and written evidence, oral and written judiciary pronouncements, oral arguments and other presentations from lawyers, plea, swearing, verdicts and other court room speech acts; and (3) other legal utterances in oral and written forms and this may include private legal documents such as contracts, wills, and other legally binding oral and written texts. These speech acts all involve the law and they share similarities as well as differences.

We can follow Habermas's classification and divide legal speech acts on the basis of validity claims (instead of illocutionary force as in Danet) into (1) *constative* speech acts connected to truth claims; (2) *regulative* speech acts connected to claims to normative rightness; and (3) *expressive* speech acts connected to claims to truthfulness. Within each of these types of speech act, the legal utterances or texts (both written and oral) can have different illocutionary force e.g., legislation may contain both regulative and constative speech acts; judicial speech acts such as lawyers' objections, sentences, and appellate opinions, indictments, confessions, pleas of guilty/not guilty, and verdicts, may be expressive, constative and regulative speech acts.

For their similarities, legal speech acts, legislative, judicial and others, are institutional speech acts as opposed to ordinary everyday speech acts between two private communicators. Institutional speech acts are different from ordinary speech activities for everyday communicative purposes. Legal speech act performance is closely tied to or presumes the existence and functioning of the relevant legal institutions and conventions, and the relevant legal system, whether it is in the court room or in parliament. They are institutionally bound speech acts.

Legal speech acts in different legal settings also manifest differences. Firstly, in terms of addresser and addressee, for instance, one of the major differences is found in the status of and relationships between the Speaker (addresser) and Hearer (addressee) in these three different settings and classes. For legislative speech acts, the speaker is the legislature and the hearer is the public, and they are both collective entities (see later). For private legal documents, for instance in the case of a contract, there are normally two identifiable contracting individuals or parties, addressing each other. Another difference between legislative and judicial speech acts is that the medium of communication is different. Legislation is coded, in contrast to oral evidence given in court. Furthermore, oral testimony in court may be between a legal counsel and the witness, between two individuals, and it may also involve the judge, and jury and court officers. For court room speech acts, all the utterances must follow certain procedures and conventions. For instance, the order of speaking by the various parties, the linguistic form that must be used, e.g., 'Guilty' or 'Not guilty' as verdicts must be uttered by the judge or the foreman of the jury at the appropriate stage of the court proceedings and words must be uttered in a certain linguistic form (e.g., 'We find the defendant guilty'). Contracts, wills, and legislation in different jurisdictions must also follow certain styles and forms.

Within each of the three categories of legal speech acts, the illocutionary force is also different. For instance, for legislation, individual provisions in a statute may be declaratory acts and directives in Searle's terminology. For a contract, the illocutionary force is mostly that of a commissive from both parties. A judicial speech act in the form of a verdict may entail a representative declarative. If we use Habermas's classification, some legislative speech acts may involve regulative speech acts while judicial speech acts may also involve imperatives and expressives.

In this regard, legal speech acts as institutional speech acts are different from other types of institutional speech acts such as speech related to religion or to regulation of sporting matches. This difference is found first in the specific context, i.e., the differences between the institutions involved. There are also conventional procedures and conventions attached to different contexts. To understand the meaning of an utterance, we must refer to its social context, be it 'The court is in now session', or 'You are out' in a sporting competition. Context is consequently a vital constituent of any attempt to comprehend an utterance's performative strength. Secondly, legal speech acts are norm-conformative actions and they are founded on legal norms of behaviour with which social actors must comply. Thirdly, just as we create institutional facts by performative utterances, legal speech acts create legal facts. In law, constitutive rules, either derived from a constitution or convention, establish the legislature and its Acts as institutional facts. Legal speech acts create or bring about institutional acts merely by declaring them through legal instruments. In these cases, performance does not depend on purely linguistic competence, but on socio-linguistic, political and legal facts about the world.

4. Characterising Legislative Speech Acts

Of the three types of legal speech acts, I will now turn to legislative speech acts. If we characterise statutes as speech acts, then legislative speech acts are mostly regulatives, involving the domain of our world and society in the context of a social reality that the law tries to regulate. They display a basic norm-conformative attitude on the part of the language users, i.e., the legislature. The thematic validity claim is that of normative rightness and the general function of legislation is the establishment of legitimate interpersonal relations and the regulation of society and behaviour. The mode of communication is interactive between the lawmaker and the general public. The type of action is normatively regulated action and the action is oriented toward reaching understanding.

In terms of the linguistic form in legislative speech acts, it must follow the relevant legal institutional conventions. Statutes are written in a different structure from that of ordinary performatives. In ordinary speech acts, usually, the first person pronoun is used followed by the simple present form of the verb, e.g., 'I promise...', or 'I bet...'. However, legislative provisions are not written in the first person, but they may be paraphrased in such a form. For instance, 'We hereby declare that ...' or 'We hereby enact that ....'. The part of the statute that contains the explicit performative verb is known as the enacting formula, and it is usually found at the beginning of each statute. In Britain and the U.S.A., the enacting formula usually has the form of 'Be it enacted that …'. The explicit use of a performative verb in legislative texts is found only in common law countries.[28] In Chinese legislation, and some jurisdictions in the continental system, there is no such formula. Kurzon calls such cases 'implicit performatives' since it is only the occasion – the promulgation of a law – not the linguistic form, that allows for a performative interpretation.[29] In Chinese statutes, normally, below the title of an act are words in brackets indicating that the law was passed at such and such a date by the legislature (or a government department with lawmaking powers) at such and such a session, reporting the fact that the legislature has passed the law. It uses similar wording for amended laws except using the word 'amended' instead of 'passed'. For subordinate legislation, usually the words 'at such a date the regulation was announced by such and such a government body' are used. In the main text, the first article of an act is usually the object clause that states that for such and such a purpose, this particular act is hereby enacted. Sometimes it also names the particular law that gives the authorisation for making the law, for instance the Constitution or a basic law.

Within a statutory text, specific provisions do not normally follow particular formulae. However, statutory language normally follows special formal legal style and register. In different countries and jurisdictions there are often different linguistic conventions for legislative drafting.

Secondly, for a legislative illocutionary act to be successful, apart from meeting the verbal requirements of what the convention requires, it must also be issued by the right person under the right circumstances, meeting the specifications of the relevant convention. Conditions for statutory validity include the capacity and authority of the persons making the law and the appropriateness of the occasion of enacting and promulgation. Besides, if we see communication as primary as Habermas does, and if we see legislation as communicative in nature, then, who is communicating with whom in the constitutional speech act? Who are the addressor and addressee?

Specifically, the lawmaker is the speaker, the author or addresser of legislation, i.e., the legislature, the body which has the legislative authority

---

[28] Dennis Kurzon, *It is Hereby Performed ... Explorations in Legal Speech Acts* (Amsterdam, John Benjamins Publishing Company, 1986), at 9-15.
[29] Kurzon, *supra* n. 28.

to enact law. Furthermore, the hearer is the audience, the general public the law is directed at. The hearer is the receiver or addressee of the legislation, and this may also include the judiciary. Some commentators (see Bowers and Kurzon) seem to regard the addressee as consisting of only the judiciary for the purpose of statutory interpretation. This may not be an entirely accurate description. The judiciary can be regarded as one addressee of the collective addressees of legislation. But judges' interpretation of statutes as contained in decisions is a different type of speech act. In the pronouncements of the judiciary, the judge then is the addresser, talking to the litigating parties and the public at large, performing different illocutionary acts. So, the main addressee of legislation is the public that legislation is directed at in order to guide behaviour. We may also include the executive government as another addressee. Although the executive's intention is usually embodied in legislation, and in this sense the executive is the de facto author, the executive government is also a receiver or addressee, in the sense that law is enforced by the executive, and in the sense that the executive needs to follow the legislative directives as much as the general public. A different way to look at this is offered by Kurzon.[30] He describes the addresser and addressee of legislation in Western legal systems as consisting of the author, the implied author and the instantial author on the one hand, and the reader, the implied reader and the instantial reader on the other.[31] He argues that they are in fact all lawyers.[32] Such a description is true to some extent and is technically the case, as lawyers are usually employed to draft laws, and they are also the people who read and understand laws to convey the meanings to the public when advising clients. Undoubtedly, lawyers play a very important role in lawmaking in any society, but this seems simplistic or cynical and not a true depiction of a constitution when political and other factors are considered. Besides, in democratic discursive lawmaking, the addressee may also become an addresser.[33]

With regard to the legal competence of the addresser of legislation, an important component and a distinctive feature of legislative speech acts as part of the legal convention requirement, is that the addresser, i.e., the lawmaker, must have the *authority* to make legislative utterances in

---

[30] Kurzon, *supra* n.28.
[31] Kurzon, *supra* n.28.
[32] Kurzon, *supra* n.28.
[33] For discussions of legislative addresser and addressee, see Deborah Cao, *Chinese Law: A Language Perspective* (Aldershot, Ashgate, 2004).

lawmaking. Normally, the legislative authority derives either from convention and long-standing custom as in the case of the UK or from a written Constitution as in the US. In Australia, a country with a written Constitution, the authority for all the statutes derives from the Constitution which delegates to the legislature the ultimate but limited legislative powers to make law over its jurisdiction. Thus, a statute is a document with the highest constitutional authority with legal effect within its jurisdiction.[34] However, if we take Habermas's view, legislative authority and the legitimacy of legislation emerges from communicative actions or deliberative democracy. The law employed by the state must be legitimated through a broader discourse of citizens and their representatives, and this process of legitimation must be included in the legal system.[35]

Finally, an act of making law must also be performed on the appropriate occasion recognised by convention or law to be the occasion on which such acts take place. A statute has to be enacted in a prescribed manner. For instance, in Australia as in the UK, this entails, *inter alia*, the passing of the statute through both Houses of Parliament and its receiving the royal assent in the required manner.[36] Analogous to this situation is the classical example of naming a ship. The Prime Minister, or a certain person who is authorised to name a ship, that is having the appropriate authority, on the occasion says: 'I name the ship Elizabeth'. This very utterance is an act that confers that name to the ship. If another person unauthorised, at the same ceremony, or a person sitting at home watching the launching ceremony on television, utters the same words, the ship is not so named.

As said earlier, an important feature of legislative speech acts is that they are institutional speech acts that involve institutional behaviours and institutional facts. The performance of legislative acts depends on institutional facts such as those in government and the legislature, and such

---

[34] See Frederick Bowers, *The Linguistic Aspects of Legislative Expression* (Vancouver: University of British Columbia, 1989).

[35] Jürgen Habermas, *Between Facts and Norms: Contributions to a Discourse Theory of Law and Democracy*, translated by William Rehg (Cambridge: the MIT Press, 1996), at 38.

[36] As Jori, *supra* n.1, at 2094, commented, when doing legal things with words, not only a specific verbal formula is required which one is not allowed to substitute with a different expressions of equivalent meaning. One may also even be required to accompany the uttering of words with a complex ritual, to wear special costume and to make use of symbolic objects. This is the case in the UK (for both the judicial and legislative processes) and Australia (for the judiciary only).

performative acts thereby create further institutional facts. For instance, when a parliament promulgates laws, the very act of promulgation presumes and depends on the existence of a parliament or a lawmaking institution and the relevant institutional rules and conventions. Furthermore, as conventional illocutionary acts, they effect changes in institutional states of affairs. In some cases, they affect the institutional position or social status of persons or things. In other cases, they create institutional rights and obligations, and prescribe behaviours and prohibitions. In still others, they are part of some institutional practice, process or procedure. For instance, when a parliament passes a law introducing a new tax, a new tax regime as reality and fact is thus created by the very declaration of the law, and obligations thus follow. In short, a law creates legal or institutional facts.

5. Intersubjective Understanding in Legislative Speech Acts

In addition to identifying the addresser and addressee of legislation, we also need to consider, more importantly, whether legislative speech acts are communicated successfully in reaching understanding and establishing relationships between the two communicating parties, that is, between the lawmaker and the public, and how legislative speech acts perform the functions between the addresser and addressee linguistically and non-linguistically reaching understanding and establishing relations.

In the traditional theory of speech acts as in Searle, the hearer's recognition of the intention of the speaker and conditions of satisfaction must be satisfied for happy or successful execution of illocutionary force in any speech act.[37] However, Habermas argues that this is not the case. According to Habermas, with a speech act, the speaker or addresser has to do more than provide hearer, the addressee, with the opportunity to become aware of his/her own intention.[38] The speaker cannot achieve his/her illocutionary aim of conveying a fact, giving an order, making a requirement or a promise or revealing a subjective experience if he/she does not at the same time make known the conditions under which his/her utterance could be accepted as valid, and he/she must do so in such a way that in claiming that these conditions are satisfied, he/she implicitly also

[37] See also Kent Bach, and Robert M. Harnish, *Linguistic Communication and Speech Acts* (Cambridge, The MIT Press, 1979).
[38] Habermas, *supra* n.6, at 269.

offers to provide reasons in support of his/her claim, if necessary.[39] A speaker can rationally motivate a hearer to accept his/her speech act offer because, on the basis of an internal connection between validity, validity claims and the redemption of a validity claim, he/she can assume the warranty for providing if necessary convincing reasons that would stand up to a hearer's criticism of the validity claim.[40] Habermas states that,

> The essential presupposition for the success of an illocutionary act consists in the speaker's taking on a specific commitment, so that the hearer can rely on him. An utterance can count as a promise, assertion, request, question, or avowal if and only if the speaker makes an offer that he is ready to make good insofar as it is accepted by the hearer. The speaker must commit himself, that is, indicate that in certain situations he will draw certain consequences for action. The type of obligation determines the content of the commitment, from which the sincerity of the commitment is to be distinguished.[41]

Thus, according to Habermas, the communicative use of language oriented to mutual understanding functions in such a way that the participants either agree on the validity claimed for their speech acts or identify points of disagreement which they conjointly take into consideration in the course of further interaction and practical discourse. Every speech act involves the raising of criticizable validity claims aimed at intersubjective recognition. The content of the speaker's commitment is determined by both the specific meaning of the interpersonal relation that is to be established, and a thematically stressed universal validity claim.[42] In Habermas's words,

> In the final analysis, the speaker can illocutionarily influence the hearer and vice versa, because speech-act-typical obligations are connected with cognitively testable validity claims - that is, because the reciprocal binding and bonding relationship has a rational basis. The speaker who commits herself normally connects the specific sense in which she would like to take up an interpersonal relationship with a thematically stressed validity claim and hereby chooses a specific mode of communication.[43]

If we examine this in terms of legislative speech acts, in regulative speech acts as in legislation, the thematic validity claim is that of rightness

---

[39] Habermas, *supra* n.6, at 269.
[40] Habermas, *supra* n.6, at 269
[41] Habermas, *supra* n.6, at 83-84.
[42] Habermas, *supra* n.6, at 86.
[43] Habermas, *supra* n.6, at 85-86.

and appropriateness and the theme is interpersonal relations. In regulative speech acts, the obligation to justify refers directly to the claim that the speech act performed fits an existing normative background. The claims to the rightness or appropriateness for norms or values, that in a given context justify an interpersonal relation that is to be established performatively. But in every instance of communicative action, the system of four validity claims (comprehensibility, rightness, truth and truthfulness) are raised simultaneously, and come into play, and they must be recognised as justified for the speech act to be acceptable and thus result in successful communication.[44]

Furthermore, according to Habermas, the illocutionary force of the legislative speech act consists in its capacity to move the public to act under the premise that the commitment signalled by the lawmaker is seriously meant. The lawmaker and the public can reciprocally move one another to recognise validity claims because the content of the lawmaker's commitment is determined by a specific reference to a thematically stressed validity claim, whereby the lawmaker, in a cognitively testable way, assumes with a rightness claim, obligations to justify regulatives, and, implicitly and secondarily, with a truth claim, assumes obligations to provide grounds and, finally, with a truthfulness claim, assumes obligations to confirm.

In addition, according to Habermas, to understand the directives or regulatives as embodied in statutes, the hearer must know not only the satisfaction conditions for the state of affairs represented in it, but also the conditions under which it can be regarded as legitimate or as binding.[45] Illocutionary acts owe their motivating force to the validity claims they carry, since these claims are capable of being intersubjectively recognised to the extent that they are based on reasons that counts as reasons for all parties involved.

The legislative speech acts tell us that the lawmaker (speaker) by raising a validity claim, concomitantly takes on a sufficiently credible guarantee to vindicate the claim with the right kind of reasons, should this be necessary.[46] They rely on reasons or potential reasons. Any speech act therewith refers to the ideally expanded audience of the unlimited interpretation community that would have to be convinced for the speech

---

[44] Habermas, *supra* n.6

[45] Habermas, *supra* n.6, 267.

[46] See Habermas, 1996, *supra* n.35, at 18.

act to be justified and hence rationally acceptable.[47] Often, we are told, enough law provides illegitimate power with the mere semblance of legitimacy.[48]

Now let us examine the Chinese Constitution as a speech act, to illustrate the way the addresser and the addressee of the law either succeed or fail in respect of intersubjective communication and contesting the truthfulness and truth claims in te Constitutional speech acts. Regarding truth claims, if we take a Peircean perspective, truth claims or meanings arise through language only when an idea or concept can be related to through something else already existing in the mind of an interpreter. In our present situation, for instance, the Chinese legislature says: We declare in the Constitution that Chinese citizens enjoy freedom of speech, of the press, of assembly, of association, of procession and of demonstration. To such a statement, what kind of response could be generated from a Chinese hearer living with the everyday realities of China? Possibly:

> You (lawmaker) are not serious in saying that.
>
> You must be lying and cannot be trusted.
>
> You have never meant or guaranteed that.

To be fair, people do enjoy a certain degree of freedom in today's China, much more than in the past, but only to some degree, a degree that the government deems permissible measured against its own interests. It is common knowledge that the Chinese press is not free, in particular with regard to political freedom of expression. They are not guaranteed freedoms but permitted only subject to heavy political qualifications. Hence, there are not many reasons that the Chinese lawmaker and the government can actually or potentially provide to move or convince the public of the claims in the Constitution, even if they are truthfully uttered and even if they satisfy the normative rightness claim. As Habermas points out, understanding and reaching understanding are not the same, and a valid utterance and one that is merely held to be valid are not the same.[49] Law, as Habermas conceives it, and its legitimacy, stems from its being at once self-imposed and binding.[50] Moreover, all persons subjected to law must be

---

[47] Habermas, 1996, *supra* n.35, at 19.
[48] Habermas, 1996, *supra* n.35, at 40.
[49] Habermas, 1996, *supra* n.35, at 269-230.
[50] Habermas, 1996, *supra* n.35.

treated as free and equal actors, and laws that are self-imposed and binding must successfully reconcile legal and factual equality.[51]

In conclusion, in this essay, I have discussed the different types of legal speech acts, in particular legislative speech acts with reference to Habermas's theory of speech acts and his discourse theory of law. When we consider legislative speech acts, positive laws (legislation) which are not just commands backed by the threat of sanction as is now commonly accepted, especially laws in a democratic country, should appeal to reason that citizens who are affected by the law should find acceptable. Citizens should be equal participants in lawmaking in reaching understanding and establishing interpersonal, legal and social relations for law to be felicitous and successfully communicated.

---

[51] Habermas, 1996, *supra* n.35.

PART II

JUDICIAL REASONING

CHAPTER 5

Who needs Fact when you've got Narrative? The Case of P,C&S vs. United Kingdom

Clive Baldwin

University of Bradford (UK)

1. Introduction

The official view of investigations and Family Court hearings in the UK into cases of alleged child abuse is that they are disinterested, inquisitorial and fair. Such proceedings are, ostensibly, designed to reveal and test the facts through due process with a judgement being made on the basis of 'facts' that have withstood the test of interrogation. The persuasiveness, and thus legitimacy, of judgements rest upon claims to represent 'what actually happened'. If this is so, it should therefore follow that judgements founded on proceedings lacking such a basis would lack facticity and as such the credibility and persuasiveness of the judgement would be undermined. In practice, however, this is not always the case and it is possible to tell a persuasive narrative in the absence of fact. This paper explores the development of a persuasive narrative of dangerousness in a case of alleged Munchausen syndrome by proxy (MSbP).[1]

The case, P,C&S v United Kingdom[2] is particularly revealing in this matter. The arguments put forward at the domestic hearings by the Local Authority, Rochdale Metropolitan Borough Council, under the directorship of Ian Davey, in support of their narrative of dangerousness were upheld by the Court of Appeal but substantially rejected by the European Court of Human Rights (ECHR). Criticising the Local Authority, for their unnecessary 'draconian action' in removing the child without 'relevant or sufficient reason', the ECHR were clearly concerned about both the investigation and the presentation of the case in the domestic courts. Although the ECHR did not detail any individual criticisms of the

---

[1] Munchausen syndrome by proxy is said to be a form of child abuse in which a carer (usually the mother) fabricates or induces illness in another (usually a child) in order to seek medical attention. See, R Meadow, 'Munchausen syndrome by proxy: The hinterland of child abuse' *(1977) II Lancet: 343.*

[2] P,C&S v The United Kingdom ECHR (2002) Application no. 56547/00.

A. Wagner et al. (eds.), Interpretation, Law and the Construction of Meaning, 85–108.

Local Authority's investigation and presentation of the case, the clear inference from the ruling is that the Local Authority had either failed to investigate the case properly and thus acted without the necessary evidence, or had presented the case in such a way that made the case seem far more robust and the mother more dangerous than the evidence warranted.

In this paper I will argue that in the case of P,C&S the persuasiveness of the narrative of P as a dangerous mother lay not in reliable evidence or fact, as was claimed, but in narrative techniques that advantaged the Local Authority's narrative of guilt and dangerousness and disadvantaged the mother's narrative of innocence.

2. A note about narrative

Over the last 15 years or so there has been an exponential rise in the interest shown in narrative as a theory and a method across the disciplines. Narrative is, however, a somewhat nebulous term and its use is neither always clear nor consistent. For some, narrative provides a unique insight into the world and our experience of it.[3] In this view, narratives are more or less accurate representations of 'what really happened' and our understandings of that reality (that is, data for subsequent analysis).[4] For others, narrative forms reality.[5] These different stances with regard to narrative, in essence, reflect the older debates surrounding positivism and social constructionism: are our narratives representational or constitutive?

This question has particular import for the performance of the Law. For some, narratives are clearly representational:

> This may be embarrassingly non-postmodern, but reality exists. Of this the law, at least, has no doubt. Something happened or will be found to have

---

[3] See, for example, P Astedt-Kurki and RL Heikkinen, 'Two approaches to the study of experiences of health and old age: The thematic interview and the narrative method', (1994) 20 *Journal of Advanced Nursing* 418.

[4] This is a view found key authors and proponents of narrative analysis. See, especially, M Cortazzi, *Narrative analysis* (London: The Falmer Press 1993) and CK Riessman, *Narrative analysis* (London: Sage, 1993).

[5] Authors in this vein would include J Bruner, 'Life as Narrative' (1987)54 *Social Research* 11 and 'The narrative construction of reality' (1991) 18 *Critical Inquiry* 1; T Barone (1995). 'Persuasive writings, vigilant readings, and reconstructed characters: the paradox of trust in educational storysharing', in JA Hatch and R Wisniewski (eds), *Life history and narrative* (London: The Falmer Press, 1995); and, DE Polkinghorne, 'Narrative configuration in qualitative analysis', in JA Hatch and R Wisniewski (eds), *Life history and narrative* (London: The Falmer Press, 1995).

> happened. You can still be tried for perjury even though there supposedly is no truth. You can still be sued for libel, so somewhere reality exists to be falsified.[6]

In this view of judicial proceedings, while narrativity may be useful or unavoidable, the judicial process is one that hears, tests and evaluates claims to factuality to determine what really happened:

> Prosecution and defence necessarily offer contrasting accounts of the same event in the advocacy system, and one side or the other will eventually lose its audience under the assumption that procedural integrity rewards the account closest to the truth.[7]

Miscarriages of justice can thus be explained as a function of errors of evidence or process: new evidence has come to light, previous evidence was shown to be erroneous, the process of testing the evidence was flawed and so on.

There is, however, a body of literature that challenges the positivist view, arguing that legal reality is not representational but constitutive. Few in the legal arena would seem to go down the extreme post-modern route of claiming that there is no reality save that which is constructed through narrative but the notion that events and narrative are blended together by lawyers to present a persuasive case is common.[8] In this blending, however there are boundaries outside of which narrative construction cannot stray:

> It is a staple of legal practice that where facts are disputed, lawyers narrate a version most conducive to their legal arguments without violating credibility or ignoring or negating those facts that are unequivocally established.[9]

---

[6] CA MacKinnon, Law's stories as reality and politics, in P Brooks and P Gerwitz (eds), *Law's stories: Narrative and rhetoric in the law* (New Haven: Yale University, 1996), p.235.

[7] RA Ferguson, 'Untold stories in the law', in P Brooks and P Gerwitz (eds), *Law's stories: Narrative and rhetoric in the law* (New Haven: Yale University, 1996), p.85.

[8] See, for example, WL Bennett and MS Feldman, *Reconstructing reality in the courtroom: Justice and judgment in American culture* (New Brunswick: Rutgers University Press, 1981) and R Sherwin, 'The narrative construction of legal reality' (1994), 18 *Vermont Law Review* 681.

[9] R Weisberg, 'Proclaiming trials as narratives: Premises and pretenses', in P Brooks and P Gerwitz (eds), *Law's stories: Narrative and rhetoric in the law* (New Haven: Yale University, 1996), p.66.

Bennett and Feldman argue that narrative structure is an inherent part of the persuasiveness of any given narrative and that

> ...the way in which a story is told will have considerable bearing on its perceived credibility regardless of the actual truth of the story.[10]

Going further, they also demonstrate that the

> ...structural characteristics of stories become more central to judgment if facts or documentary evidence are absent,

and

> ... the structure of stories becomes crucial to judgment in cases in which a collection of facts or evidence is subject to competing interpretations.[11]

It is my contention that the case of P,C&S is illustrative of the above: it was a highly contested case that centred around the interpretation of medical records and opinions; and, as I shall attempt to demonstrate in Section V, a case that was characterised by an absence of fact. I will then explore some of the non-evidentiary factors that enhanced the persuasiveness of the Local Authority's narrative of the dangerous mother. In so doing, I shall indicate that the analysis of the American criminal justice system by Bennett and Feldman has some relevance to an understanding of the Family Court process in the UK.

3. The case of P,C&S vs United Kingdom[12]

Proceedings in the Family Courts in the UK are shrouded in secrecy, ostensibly on the grounds that such secrecy is in the interests of the child. It

---

[10] Bennett and Feldman 1981supra n.8, p89

[11] ibid

[12] This case has been reported widely. See, for example, B Hewson, D Casey and N Mole, 'The appearance of fairness' (2002) 152 *New Law Journal* 1245; D Casey, B Hewson and N Mole, 'Effective participation and the European court' (2002) 32 *Family Law Journal 755*; N Mole (with assistance from D Casey and B Hewson) 'P, C and S v United Kingdom – The implications for domestic UK law' (2002) AIRE Centre Case Law Update: July – September, 3-8.. While in this paper I am primarily concerned with the domestic hearings I draw on the documentation submitted to the ECHR and so in the interests of consistency the European case citation will be used throughout.

has been persuasively argued,[13] however, that secrecy also benefits the professionals involved and does not facilitate the administration of justice.[14]

The secrecy that surrounds cases in the Family Courts makes it difficult to properly analyse the relationship of the judgement to the evidence presented. For example, much of the detail in this paper is not to be found in the original judgement. When one looks at what was omitted from that judgement one can see how Justice Wall's narrative of P,C&S appears less persuasive and, as with many legal narratives, pitched in a certain way.[15] As with Hyman's example of patient dumping[16] the narrative only persuades because 'it is partial, in every sense of the word'.

The case of P,C&S, however, is somewhat different from the majority of cases in the Family Court in that the hearing before the ECHR was conducted in public and the documentation before the ECHR was, for a time, available for consultation in Strasbourg. This publicly available material gives us insight into what is usually veiled in secrecy.

3.1 Background

The mother, P, was originally living in the US with her two sons. Following an acrimonious divorce her ex-husband made several attempts to gain custody of the younger son, of whom he was the biological father. During the fourth custody hearing the father raised accusations of MSbP abuse on the part of P, despite not having raised any such concerns in his previous three unsuccessful attempts. P was subsequently charged with a felony offence of child abuse but the jury who found her guilty only of a misdemeanour rejected this. P was still allowed contact with her son and her parental rights were not terminated, the court appointed psychiatrist being firmly of the opinion that she was essentially a good and loving mother and that contact would be beneficial for her and her son.

P later moved to the UK where she remarried and conceived a child, S. Following P's attempt to have her previous marriage annulled her former husband informed the authorities and the social services contacted the parents about their concerns.

---

[13] B Morgan, 'A study in secrecy' in *Report and recommendations of the child exploitation and the media forum*, 91-95. (Dover: Smallwood Publishing Group, 1997).

[14] B Hewson, 'The problem with family courts' (2004) 10 Feb *Spiked-Online.*

[15] See, for example, D Hyman, 'Lies, damned lies, and narrative (1997) 73 *Indiana Law Journal* 797.

[16] ibid

Acting on the advice of Dr Herbert Schreier, the US psychiatrist who had initially evaluated P as suffering from MSbP despite never having met her or her son, and who had no first hand knowledge of her current circumstances, Local Authority social workers, Carole McCrystal and Thelma Kennedy, removed S shortly after birth and placed her with foster parents. The parents were allowed regular contact with their daughter, contact that even the social services themselves described in contact sheets and court reports as 'exemplary' and 'the best they had ever seen.'

The parents attended a psychiatric evaluation with the Local Authority's chosen expert. The report, though critical of the parents, did not rule out further work and the possibility of the family staying together. The report was, however, hidden from the parents and their legal teams for almost six months and only disclosed when the parents had been pressurised into agreeing to evaluation by another psychiatrist. This second psychiatrist produced a far more negative report.

A UK paediatrician, Paul Davies, also conducted an assessment, without seeing either the mother or child, and although he was called upon to evaluate the US medical records of P's previous child he was not a specialist in the illnesses of that child. The paediatrician's report later formed the basis of the social services' application for a care order and freeing for adoption. P challenged both the facts and interpretation of the report.

At the beginning of the final hearing, the father said he would not contest the care proceedings because he was of the opinion that given the hostility towards the family there was little likelihood of success and that he did not want to put his family through unnecessary anguish. In so doing, he was seeking both to protect his family and open the door to keep the child within his family with the involvement of social services. He did, however, say that he would continue to oppose the freeing order for adoption that the Local Authority was seeking. P's legal counsel then withdrew, claiming that P was being unreasonable by wanting to continue with her defence. P asked for a two-week adjournment to seek new representation but Justice Wall denied this, claiming that it was not in the child's interests to have the hearing postponed. He further stated that legal counsel for the Local Authority would aid P in making her case thus establishing a conflict of interest at the heart of the hearings. In the event, no legal help was forthcoming and P was forced to conduct her case in person without any legal training against the two full and very experienced legal teams of the Local Authority and the Guardian ad Litem[17].

At various points up to the final hearing the Local Authority attempted to argue for estoppel and to have the mother's conviction in the US held as proof of their current allegations despite the facts that the felony charge against the mother had been rejected by the jury and there were no court findings of MSbP (according to the juvenile court) in the US. Justice Wall rejected the argument of the Local Authority, stating that he would hear the US evidence for himself. Justice Wall was, originally, of the opinion that Dr Garcia, as the consulting physician in the original US case, was important because only Garcia could answer some of the questions raised in the UK proceedings. Dr Garcia, however, without providing any evidence, stated that he feared for his safety and refused to attend the hearings or even give evidence via video-link.

Despite the seriousness of the allegations made by Dr Garcia in the US, Justice Wall changed his position regarding the importance of the doctor's attendance and accepted his non-attendance, admitting reports and statements into evidence. This effectively prevented the mother from questioning these crucial witnesses as to the contradictions and errors contained in their reports and medical records. Furthermore, no attempt was made by either the Local Authority or the courts to secure the testimony of Dr Schreier in person despite the Local Authority's reliance upon his opinion and reports for both the initial investigation and removal of the child.

From the outset, the Local Authority's case rested upon both the alleged abuse in the US and upon their claims that the mother, P, had attempted to harm the index child, S, in utero. A series of claims were made regarding S, ranging from the unnecessary administration of steroids due to the mother giving a false medical history to P endangering the child by acting against medical advice. Despite not being legally represented and thus decidedly disadvantaged, the mother successfully argued that the allegations made against her regarding the child S were unsubstantiated. Justice Wall agreed, stating that he could find nothing in her actions that

---

[17] A Guardian ad Litem is an independent adult acting on behalf of the child in legal proceedings, whose responsibility it is to make certain that the interests and legal rights of the child are given adequate consideration and are adequately protected in that process.

supported the MSbP expert's opinion and the Local Authority's argument in this matter.[18]

Once the allegations against the mother regarding S had been roundly rejected, the Local Authority and Guardian ad Litem, Deborah McCallum, were forced to argue the weaker position that, based on evidence from the US, P's prior behaviour constituted a risk to S. This argument, in the absence of the key witnesses, had to be made upon the interpretation of medical records by the UK MSbP expert even though he was not an expert in the illness of P's son (gastro-enterology) and had little, if any, first hand knowledge of the US medical system. Despite the lack of opportunity for the mother to cross examine key witnesses and the wrongful allegations and failings in expertise on the part of the MSbP expert, Justice Wall ruled that the mother had harmed her son in the US and constituted a risk to the child S. He thus ruled that S should be subject to a care order and freed for adoption.

P sought leave to appeal but was denied such permission by Justice Wall. A week after the care proceedings the judge granted a freeing order on the basis that the parents were acting unreasonably in withholding their consent to the adoption. Again the parents were not legally represented.

The parents applied to the Court of Appeal but leave to appeal was refused with Justices Thorpe and Roch holding to the view that Justice Wall "was throughout meticulous in ensuring fairness, and scrupulously careful to consider any points that went to the advantage of the mother."[19]

Application to the European Court of Human Rights (ECHR) was made in December 1999 and the Local Authority was informed. The authority, however, continued with the adoption without awaiting the outcome of the hearings in Strasbourg and S was adopted out.

The case was heard in public in March 2002. The arguments put forward by both parties were very similar to the ones put forward in the domestic hearings. The government re-iterated the position of the Local Authority that the mother represented a danger to the child, S and that their actions were justified in order to protect the child. Furthermore, they argued that the domestic hearings were fair because, as Justice Wall had stated, the mother had a good knowledge of the documents, had been legally represented up until the final hearing and all parties (except the mother) were of the opinion that it was a fair hearing. The parents' argument

---

[18] Re: B (Children) [1999] EWCA Civ 1772.
[19] ibid

repeated those made by the mother before Justice Wall, that she did not present a danger to her child, that the local authority were wrong to have acted as they did and that she had been disadvantaged in the domestic hearings due to lack of legal representation.

In July 2002, finding decisively in favour of the parents, the ECHR ruled that:

> the original hearings had violated Article 6 of the Human Rights Act (the right to a fair hearing) and "not only gave the appearance of unfairness but *prevented the applicants from putting forward their case in a proper and effective manner*" (my emphasis);
>
> given the "serious disadvantage" to the parents by not being legally represented it could not "be excluded that this might have had an effect on the decisions reached and eventual outcome for the family as a whole";
>
> the "draconian step of removing S. from her mother shortly after birth was not supported by relevant and sufficient reasons and [...] cannot be regarded as having been necessary in a democratic society for the purpose of safeguarding S'";
>
> not only were the human rights of the parents violated but also those of the child.[20] In other words, the professionals and institutions that were charged with safeguarding the interests of the child failed to protect her against their own violations of her right to family life under Article 8 of the Human Rights Act.[21]

The UK government was ordered to pay damages and costs but because the adoption had been peremptorily completed without waiting for the European hearing the child remains permanently removed from her birth family.

3.2 The absence of fact

In the case of P,C&S vs United Kingdom it is possible to identify three factors that undermine the claim that the original judgement was reliably rooted in fact[22]: a disregard for facts on the part of some of the

---

[20] P,C&S 2002 at 2.

[21] C Baldwin, 'Letter to the editor. Removal of a baby for adoption' (2002) 10 *British Journal of Midwifery* 668. See also 7 above regarding the responsibilities of the Guardian ad Litem.

[22] All narratives are incomplete and it is possible to tell a number of equally persuasive narratives about the same events (see C Baldwin, *Munchausen syndrome by proxy: Telling tales of illness* (Unpublished PhD thesis, University of Sheffield, 2000). In the narrative presented here I am not in any way claiming that

professionals involved in the case; a disregard of the due process designed to test the veracity and reliability of evidence and testimony; and, the disregard for facticity, the need for fact, in the conceptualisation and operationalisation of the theory of MSbP. Following this, I will argue that the glue holding together the narrative of dangerousness comprises not of the narrative's representational 'fit' but of narrative (and other) techniques, explored in Section VI.

3.2.1 A disregard for facts

The case of P,C&S vs United Kingdom is one in which some of the professionals involved demonstrated a significant disregard for facts in their investigation and presentation of their case. For example, the social worker primarily involved in the case, Carol McCrystal, made factual claims without properly investigating matters. In one report to the court the social worker claimed that P had lied about a house fire in the US that allegedly destroyed P's property. This claim was based on fourth-hand information (from the midwife who had heard it from another midwife who had allegedly heard it from the mother) but was admissible into court because the Family Courts in the UK do not exclude hearsay evidence. Because she failed to verify the nature or location of the fire with the mother, the social worker contacted a fire department in a different US state, some 600 miles away from the actual fire, about the wrong address. The fire department, unsurprisingly, had no record of such a fire but informed the social worker that there had been a fire near to the address given by the social worker. The social worker then reported this incident as evidence of the mother's lying and dramatic propensities.[23]

Similarly, in the same report, the social worker claimed that the mother had endangered her child by acting against medical advice by

---

the whole case against the mother was fabricated or motivated by malice, merely that the actions of investigating professionals, the lack of due process and the problems inherent in MSbP as a diagnostic category undermine the reliability and persuasiveness of the narrative of dangerousness and thus raise significant questions regarding the justice of the proceedings and outcome of the case.

[23] It is worth pointing out in this context that the false reporting of house fires is, according to some authors, a feature of Munchausen syndrome by proxy – see K Artingstall, *Practical aspects of Munchausen by proxy and Munchausen syndrome investigation* (London: CRC Press, 1999) - and thus the social worker's reporting of this is not simply an idiosyncratic attempt to discredit the mother but an attempt to present her within the profile of the MSbP mother – an example of what Bennett and Feldman call an inferential tactic – see Bennett and Feldman 1981 supra n.8, p130).

refusing to be admitted to hospital and as a result was later rushed to hospital by ambulance, causing a delay in the delivery and thus potentially threatening the well-being of the child. Although this event was reported as fact and repeated by other professionals there is no hospital or ambulance service record of this ever happening and the consulting physician explicitly challenged the social worker's report regarding this matter. In contrast to the fire incident, this claim on the part of the social worker cannot be seen as the outcome of ineffective investigation. The social worker knew the hospital and doctor concerned and so could have solicited information from them if she suspected that the mother had indeed endangered the child, S, in this way. Given that the social worker made this allegation, only two explanations are tenable. Either, the social worker solicited information from the ambulance service, hospital and consulting physician and chose to deliberately ignore statements contradicting her claim, or she, the social worker, deliberately fabricated the incident.[24]

In a similar vein, the Local Authority made a series of claims about P's behaviour without substantiating evidence, ranging from alleged harassment of doctors in the US, threatening violence, lack of co-operation with the Local Authority, the risk of absconding and her resistance to engagement in therapy (cited in the open hearings of the ECHR). These claims were re-iterated by the UK government in the ECHR proceedings in support of their claim that the actions of the Local Authority and the decisions of the domestic courts were justified. When challenged, however, by the parents' legal team to provide substantiating evidence for these claims, the Government were unable to do so. It is inconceivable that had such evidence existed the Local Authority would have presented it. Their narrative of P as a dangerous mother, was founded upon such claims, and more especially so since Justice Wall had already ruled against their claims that P had actually and actively harmed her daughter, S. The only reasonable interpretation of the failure to produce substantiating evidence for these claims after having had three years to do so, is that the Local Authority did not have such evidence.

As well as making unsubstantiated claims to fact, the Local Authority also sought to mislead the mother and the courts as to the origins

---

[24] It must be remembered here that MSbP mothers supposedly have a keen desire for the dramatic – see especially, HA Schreier and JA Libow, *Hurting for love: Munchausen by proxy syndrome*. (New York: Guilford Press, 1993) and, like the fire incident, the drama of emergency ambulances would fit well with the archetypal MSbP narrative. See also, 23 above.

of the notification to the Local Authority in the UK, attempting to position the parish priest as the person responsible for the notification, rather than the mother's ex-husband. This claim was vehemently denied by the priest concerned and the ECHR later determined that it was in fact the mother's ex-husband who had made the initial notification. The reasons for the Local Authority's misleading claim are unclear, but it seems reasonable to infer that in narrative terms a claim made by a parish priest might hold more weight than a claim by a hostile ex-husband.

3.2.2 A disregard of due process

In addition to a disregard for fact, the case of P, C &S also illustrates a disregard of the process whereby such claims to fact are tested and determined. This disregard for due process is evident in the process of the initial investigations and court proceedings.

With regard to the investigation by the Local Authority, and the Guardian ad Litem, there were several significant failings. Under UK legislation, Local Authorities are required investigate any alleged incident of child abuse or endangerment. This process should involve an investigation into the circumstances of the case and specific risk assessments of those alleged to be a risk to a child. Recommendations and, if necessary, court proceedings are made upon such investigations. In the case of P,C&S, however, although the Local Authority knew of P almost four months before S was born they failed to investigate a number of essential matters. Firstly, prior to the birth of S, the Local Authority failed to conduct full risk assessments of the parents (not even meeting with the father to commence such an assessment). Second, the Local Authority failed to assess the grandparents prior to the birth of child S, to evaluate their potential to care for S during the investigation and court proceedings. Such an evaluation is thought to be good practice in order to keep the child within the natural family if at all possible). Finally, the Local Authority was selective from whom they solicited information, favouring those in the US who were of the opinion that P was dangerous, such as Dr Herbert Schreier, who had never seen the mother or the US child, and the District Attorney who had unsuccessfully prosecuted the felony case against the mother. During the whole investigation the Local Authority did not make contact with other professionals who knew the mother when she was in the US and were of an opposing view.

The lack of due process apparent in the investigation was also apparent in the actions of the Local Authority in keeping documents from the mother, and prior to their withdrawal, her legal team. Throughout the domestic and European proceedings the Local Authority refused to disclose the social work file to the mother or her legal team (referred to in correspondence and inferred from the non-response to requests), and deliberately hid the original psychiatric report by the Local Authority's chosen expert (referred to in the original judgment by Justice Wall) until such time a further (and ultimately more negative) psychiatric expert had been engaged.

In addition to non-disclosure of essential documents, the Local Authority also edited documents, removing, for example, the passages in official documents that referred to their claim that it was the parish priest who had made the initial notification.

Due process was also disregarded in the court proceedings primarily by Justice Wall's ruling that the case would proceed even though the mother was not legally represented. In reviewing the case, the ECHR clearly stated that this lack of legal representation prevented the mother from putting forward her case in a 'proper and effective manner' and was thus a violation of Article 6 of the Human Rights Act. In addition, the mother was denied the opportunity to cross-examine the US doctors upon whose evidence the whole case was centred (particularly after the allegations made about harm to the child S were totally rejected). Furthermore, Justice Wall refused to hear evidence from one of the mother's witnesses about the prevalence of errors in medical records in general (as a counter to the allegations that such errors are a particular feature of cases of MSbP) despite the witness's experience and expertise in regard to these matters. Finally, and a point made by the ECHR, was the apparent rail-roading of the parents by Justice Wall by holding the freeing order hearing only one week after the care proceedings judgement.

In summary, the final court proceedings were characterised by the absence of key players; the absence of legal representation for P; failures of disclosure of evidence; and procedures disadvantageous to the parents. The disregard for fact evident in this particular case, must also be seen in the general context of the Family Courts in which the checks against the dangers of narrative construction available in the criminal courts - the exclusion of hearsay evidence and the threshold of proof being 'clear and convincing' rather than the balance of probabilities – are absent.

3.2.3 A disregard for facticity within the theory of MSbP.

Munchausen syndrome by proxy is a controversial diagnosis. Conceptually confused and confusing, MSbP lacks any empirical base-line research to support some of its primary features and, even after almost 30 years, it is not recognised as a valid diagnostic category in either the Diagnostic and

Statistical Manual of the American Psychiatric Association[25] or the International Classification of Disease of the World Health Organisation.[26]

The identification of MSbP rests upon a combination of observation of the alleged perpetrator, a review of the medical notes and the perpetrator profile developed (in a somewhat ad hoc fashion) over the years. Indicators of the syndrome include discrepancies and errors in the medical records and the personality of the alleged perpetrator. It has been cogently argued, however, that there is no base-line research supporting some of the features of this alleged form of abuse: for example, the frequency, source and significance of discrepancies in medical records[27] or features within the MSbP profile such as marital stress and negative feelings as significant indicators of a potential or actual child abuser.[28]

Furthermore, the reliance upon a 'pattern of presentation' rather than the specifics of any individual presentation allows those constructing a narrative of guilt to avoid having to engage with the facticity and interpretation of specific events. So, for example, in P,C&S the mother submitted a lengthy and detailed critique of the medical records in rebuttal of the MSbP expert's report. The response to this critique was that it was the pattern of presentations that was important (even though the consulting MSbP expert had to admit that he had not had access to all the medical records, and later it being shown that his figures were inaccurate) and, secondly, the recuperation of the mother's statement as 'typical of a Munchausen mother' – that is, itself indicative of MSbP behaviour. In both these ways, the challenge posed by the mother to both the presentation and interpretation of fact was evaded.

In more general terms, MSbP has been criticised by academics, health professionals, lawyers and politicians for being an unproven theory, without scientific basis. Although the proponents of MSbP present it as being a well-developed and proven diagnostic category, it remains the case

---

[25] American Psychiatric Association, Diagnostic and Statistical Manual IV-TR (Arlington, VA, American Psychiatric Association Inc, 2000).

[26] World Health Organisation, International Classification of Disease 10 (WHO, Online, 1994).

[27] CJ Morley, 'Practical concerns about the diagnosis of Munchausen syndrome by proxy', (1995) 72 *Archives of Disease in Childhood* 528.

[28] See especially, E Mart, 'Problems with the diagnosis of factitious disorder by proxy in forensic settings (1999) 17 *American Journal of Forensic Psychology* 69 and EG Mart, *Munchausen's syndrome by proxy reconsidered.* (Manchester, NH: Bally Vaughan Publishing, 2002).

that there is little if any scientifically valid research to support its use.[29] In the US, for example, the use of MSbP evidence has been ruled inadmissible in some courts because it has been successfully argued that it fails to meet the required evidentiary standards (the Daubert standard), including the requirement that a theory be adequately tested and, at least in theory be testable.[30]

These three elements, the lack of an empirical base, the avoidance of the need to engage with factual counter-claims and the failure of the theory to be subjected to empirical testing, lead to the conclusion that within the operationalisation and conceptualisation of MSbP theory there is a significant disregard for facticity.

4. The construction of a persuasive narrative

Even though there was an absence of fact, in the sense described above, Justice Wall still constructed a joint narrative of a dangerous mother and a fair hearing that was persuasive enough to be upheld by the Court of Appeal. The ECHR, however, disagreed and the question thus becomes, what makes a narrative persuasive in the absence of fact? The answer can be found in the way in which the narrative of dangerousness:

> followed a narrative trajectory that limited what could and could not be said;
>
> was presented as embedded within a consensus over the nature and degree of the alleged risk posed by 'Munchausen mothers';
>
> drew upon discourses that favoured the Local Authority's position;
>
> favoured certain narrators over others; and
>
> ignored, glossed over or explained away contradictory evidence or failings on the part of the professionals involved.

4.1 The narrative trajectory

In most legal narratives there is a central action that 'creates the central question that the story must resolve.'[31] In the case of P,C&S the central action, defined by the Local Authority, was MSbP abuse. This definitional tactic, however, is one that needs to be maintained over time, in order to

---

[29] Earl Howe, House of Lords official report (Hansard) (2003) 5 Feb: col 316.

[30] See, C Baldwin, 'Narrative analysis and contested allegations of Munchausen syndrome by proxy', in B Hurwitz, T Greenhalgh and V Skultans (eds), *Narrative research in health and illness* (London: BMJ, 2004) for more detail.

[31] See Bennett and Feldman 1981 supra n.8, p79.

diffuse, deflect or manage challenges made by opposing narratives. One feature of narrative – that of narrative trajectory – builds a substantial degree of self-confirmation into the processes of narrative construction.

Every narrative has a trajectory that holds the story together in its progression towards closure by establishing causality and meaning through the choice of events and the order in which they are related. In cases of MSbP, this trajectory is set by the professionals investigating the case. The trajectory of the chosen narrative determines both the things that it is acceptable to investigate – often set by guidelines, protocols, professional knowledge and good practice but also by the preferences, willingness and abilities of those charged with investigating the complaint – and those things that it is unacceptable to investigate and need to be edited out.

The narrative trajectory set and maintained by the social workers in P,C&S was founded on the joint pillars of a) the opinion of Dr Herbert Schreier in the US, who had never met P or her son before providing a diagnosis; and, b) an archetypal narrative of MSbP abuse: of a deceitful, manipulative and above all dangerous mother, a collusive father, lack of co-operation and denial of the harm done or the risks involved, resistance to therapy and a poor prognosis. This narrative trajectory was operationalised through the (unnecessary and draconian) action of removing the child, S, at birth. The process whereby accounts are brought into conformity with some form of stereotype[32] - narrative smoothing - was then woven into the underlying discourse that presents professionals as benevolent and benign.[33] The presentation of consensus regarding MSbP and thus the trajectory effectively excluded issues surrounding the conduct of the investigation. Indeed, the Local Authority clearly stated that complaints submitted by the parents about the conduct of the investigation would not be investigated until the completion of the investigation thus allowing the trajectory to continue unchallenged.

Even when faced with evidence that contradicted the archetypal MSbP narrative – such as the mother's and father's 'exemplary' parenting skills, the co-operation of the parents in attending innumerable meetings and assessments and providing documents and contacts and the willingness of the parents to address concerns by offering to undertake residential

---

[32] DP Spence, 'Narrative smoothing and clinical wisdom' in TR Sarbin (ed) *Narrative psychology: The storied nature of human conduct.* (New York: Praeger Publishers, 1986).

[33] D Ingleby, 'Professionals as socializers: The "psy complex"' (1985) 7*Research in law, deviance and social control* 79.

assessment and therapy – the social services continued the ratcheting process, that is the tendency for child protection processes to move in a single direction with unwinding, undoing or going back on a decision being very infrequent (if not unknown), even in circumstances where these might seem appropriate.[34]

The judge accepted this trajectory uncritically. Even though he criticised the Local Authority for hiding the first expert report from the parents and the Guardian ad Litem, for pre-judging the case, he failed to make the obvious links between such pre-judgement and its influence on her investigation, report and recommendations. Despite the initial expert's knowledge of the case and her availability, the Local Authority rejected her offer of ongoing involvement and hid her report from the parents and their legal teams until they had acquired the services of another MSbP expert, who subsequently provided an extremely negative report. In making his judgement, Justice Wall claimed that, while unfortunate, the hiding of the report had little if any effect on the outcome of the case. In other words, he failed to see the possibility of an alternative trajectory set by the more sympathetic and open report of the first expert.

In uncritically accepting the trajectory set by the Local Authority and glossing over the possibility of alternative trajectories indicated by direct evidence and expert opinion, the judge was more able to construct a persuasive narrative of professionalism and good practice.

4.2 Presenting consensus

MSbP is a highly contentious and controversial diagnosis and one that has come under increasing scrutiny in recent years. Even at the time of the care proceedings in P,C&S there was mounting criticism by both academics and professionals of which the professionals should have been aware.[35] Indeed

---

[34] See, D Howitt, *Child abuse errors: When good intentions go wrong?* (London, Harvester Wheatsheaf, 1992).

[35] See, DB Allison and MS Roberts, *Disordered mother or disordered diagnosis? : Munchausen by proxy syndrome* (Hillsdale, NJ, Analytic Press, 1998); C Baldwin, 'Munchausen syndrome by proxy: Problems of definition, diagnosis and treatment' (1996) 4 *Health and Social Care in the Community* 159; ML Bergeron, 'Hegemony, law and psychiatry: A perspective on the systematic oppression of "rogue mothers" in *In Aaron S'*, (1996) IV *Feminist Legal Studies* 49; L Blakemore-Brown, 'False illness in children – or simply false accusations?' (1998) 5 *The Therapist* 24; Mart 1999 at 28; Morley 1995 at 27; TM Ryan, 'Munchausen syndrome by proxy: Misogyny or modern medicine?' (1997) Fall *The Association of Trial Lawyers of America's Women Trial Lawyers Caucus Newsletter* 3.

such are the problems with the diagnosis that in the US, courts have ruled testimony regarding MSbP inadmissible because it fails to meet the required standards of evidence.[36]

Even amongst its supporters debates rage about the diagnosis, with some authors questioning whether MSbP is a syndrome at all,[37] whether it is a paediatric diagnosis of the child or a psychiatric diagnosis of the mother[38] and the parameters of its application.[39] Due to its lack of clarity

---

[36] See Baldwin 2004 supra n.30. Since P,C&S, evidence regarding MSbP has also been rejected by the Supreme Court of Queensland in Australia (see, R v LM [2004] QCA 192) because 'it does not relate to an organised or recognised reliable body of knowledge or experience' (para 67). In 2005, Judge Ryder stated that he 'would consign the label MSBP to the history books' and caution against the use of Factitious or Induced Illness (the replacement term for MSbP developed by the Royal College of Paediatricians) 'as a substitute for factual analysis and risk assessment' (see, [2005] EWHC 31 (Fam) para 178). Adding to this controversy, it is also interesting to note that since P,C&S, two of the leading advocates of MSbP have been found guilty of serious professional misconduct by the General Medical Council. In 2004, Prof David Southall was prevented from undertaking any child protection work for three years after identifying, on the basis of a TV documentary and without access to medical records, Stephen Clark as the person responsible for the death of the Clark's son, Harry. In 2005 Sir Roy Meadow, the architect of MSbP, was struck off the medical register for over-stepping the boundaries of his expertise in the case of Sally Clark (Harry's mother who had been charged with the murder of her son). The impact of the GMC's decisions with regard to these two major figures on the status and practice of MSbP is yet to be seen. For example, questions that might flow from these cases might well include, "In how many other cases did Sir Roy Meadow over-step his expertise?" and, "In how many other cases did Prof Southall write reports or give opinions without having access to the facts?"

[37] GC Fisher and I Mitchell, 'Is Munchausen syndrome by proxy really a syndrome?' (1995) 72 *Archives of Disease in Childhood* 530.

[38] See especially, B Bursch, 'Territoriality' (1996) August *National Association of Apnea Professionals Munchausen syndrome by proxy Network Newsletter* 1. See also, R Meadow, 'The history of Munchausen syndrome by proxy' in AV Levin and MS Sheridan (eds), *Munchausen syndrome by proxy: Issues in diagnosis and treatment.* (New York: Lexington Books, 1995).

[39] See, R Meadow, 'What is, and what is not, 'Munchausen syndrome by proxy'?' (1995) 72 *Archives of Disease in Childhood* 534. See also, HA Schreier, 'Repeated false allegations of sexual abuse presenting to sheriffs: When is it Munchausen by proxy?' (1996) 20 *Child Abuse and Neglect* 985 and DPH Jones, 'Commentary: Munchausen syndrome by proxy - is expansion justified?' (1996) 20 *Child Abuse and Neglect* 983.

there are numerous similar but different definitions in current use and even MSbP experts frequently use non-standard definitions in their reports (Pankratz, personal communication). It is notable that MSbP has never been tested under clinical conditions and none of the evidence has ever been approved by a national medical or scientific body.[40]

Despite all the above being known at the time of P,C&S, the professionals involved and the Court acted as if there was general consensus regarding the nature and validity of the concept of MSbP and that MSbP was the appropriate schema to operate within in this case. Schemas are cognitive structures, categories in the mind, that help us assign meaning to incoming information, help to select which information pay attention to and help us to draws inferences about what has happened in the past and about what it likely to happen in the future.[41] Narratives told within a familiar, acceptable and consistent schema appear more persuasive to those who share the schema than those that challenge such schemas or draw on other, less familiar schemas. Judges, as with jurors,

> ... must first recognize the developing contours of a story to accept it, and the perception makes them practical students of preexisting narrative forms. The genre of a story, its familiar form in the telling, is a crucial factor and often the hidden ingredient in courtroom belief.[42]

The primary schema presented by the Local Authority in the case of P,C&S was the orthodox MSbP schema. This schema that would have been familiar to the judge as the judiciary in the UK have received training in MSbP from advocates of the concept such as Sir Roy Meadow. Challenges to that schema (in Bennett and Feldman's terms, attempts to redefine the central action[43]) were either ignored or recuperated into the schema. For example, the use of three differing and non-standard definitions of MSbP by the Local Authority at various times during the case was simply ignored during the whole investigatory and judicial process and the father's questioning of the concept of MSbP was viewed as a reluctance to engage with the Local Authority's concerns regarding the risk posed by P.

---

[40] Howe 2003 supra n.29.

[41] AJ Moore, 'Trial by schema: Cognitive filters in the courtroom' (1989) 37 *UCLA Law Review* 273. See, also, R Sherwin, 'Law frames: Historical truth and narrative necessity in a criminal case' (1994) 47 *Stanford Law Review* 39.

[42] RA Ferguson 1996 supra n.7, p86.

[43] Bennett and Feldman 1981 supra n.8, p102.

The illusion of MSbP as an uncontroversial, generally accepted diagnosis and the use of out-group stereotypes to dismiss conflicting opinions reflect what Janis terms 'groupthink'[44], a mode of thinking engaged in by people in a group situation when the pursuit of unanimity overrides their motivation to realistically appraise alternative courses of action. Features of the conduct of the investigation that favoured the narrative of dangerousness were simply ignored by tacit agreement, thus enhancing its credibility at the expense of proper and realistic appraisal. In the case of P,C&S such groupthink served to advantage the Local Authority in its construction of a narrative of dangerousness and disadvantage the mother's narrative of innocence.

4.3 Supporting discourses

In constructing a persuasive narrative it is commonplace to draw upon discourses that favour that narrative and being able to draw upon common stocks of stories enhances the robustness and persuasiveness of narratives.[45] The uncritical acceptance of such discourses, however, can lead to unreliable evaluations as to the persuasiveness of those narratives that draw up them. This is clearly illustrated in P,C&S where two primary discourses were brought into play: the first being the discourse of professionals as being benevolent and benign[46], the second being that of MSbP itself.

The discourse of professionals as benevolent and benign allowed the judge to ignore, gloss over or explain away contradictory evidence or problems with the investigative and legal processes, for example the problems posed by the expert paediatrician's evidence (see page 8). In accepting the MSbP expert's interpretation of the US medical records Justice Wall seemingly ignored the fact that the doctor was not an expert in the particular area of medicine relevant to that child's illnesses and that he himself had already assessed much of the paediatrician's testimony as erroneous, rejecting as unsubstantiated the allegations made by the paediatrician against P. Drawing from the discourse of professionals being benevolent and benign, the judge rationalised the situation by stating that the paediatrician had expended every effort to find in favour of P but had been unwillingly drawn by the evidence before him to the regrettable

---

[44] I Janis, *Groupthink.* (Boston, Houghton Mifflin, 1982).
[45] BS Jackson, *Law, fact and narrative coherence.* (Lieverpool, Deborah Charles Publications, 1988).
[46] Ingleby 1985 supra n.33.

conclusion that P had harmed her previous child. Such regret, according to MacKinnon,

> ...hides the power that law does have - to intervene or not, to equalize power or not, not to slide down any slope that it doesn't want to[47]

Similarly, the uncritical acceptance of the discourse of MSbP limited the inquisitorial process by avoiding having to address the significant conceptual and empirical problems within that discourse, thus allowing the narrative of dangerousness to be presented as more robust and persuasive than it might otherwise have been (see above under b) Presenting consensus).

4.4 Favoured narrators

Although care proceedings are supposed to be impartial, there is strong evidence that in the case of P,C&S certain narrators were favoured over others. This can be seen in the selective approach by social services to professionals in the US when first investigating the case; the rejection of the first MSbP expert; the failure of the Guardian ad Litem to engage in any significant way with some members of the birth family such as the maternal grandparents or consider other family members as prospective carers for S, despite their obvious ability and qualifications; the Guardian ad Litem's refusal to accept the evidence of the neo-natalist who supported P's account of her ante-natal care; and the silence of the Guardian ad Litem regarding the failings of and deliberate fabrication of evidence by social services whose position she supported throughout. Such actions and subsequent silence on the part of the professionals involved and the Court favoured the construction of the narrative of dangerousness enhancing its persuasiveness by editing out evidence that undermined it.

Even in court certain narrators are favoured with expert witnesses being accorded "courtesy and respect by judges" and protected from "cross examination which is hostile, discourteous, or personal."[48] Such an attitude, coupled with the discourse of professionals being benevolent and benign and the MSbP narrative trajectory, prevented P from questioning expert witnesses as to their credibility, based on their previous records. Such courtesy, respect and protection, however, was not accorded to P whose character was constantly attacked and who had to present her own evidence

---

[47] MacKinnon 1996, p.236 supra n.6.

[48] N Wall 'Judicial attitudes to expert evidence in children's cases'(1997) 76 *Archives of Diseases in Childhood* 185. The author is Justice Wall who heard the domestic proceedings in P,C&S.

without the aid of legal counsel to protect her from cross-examination by two hostile legal teams.

Furthermore, authors such as O'Barr have shown that narrative testimony is deemed more persuasive in the courtroom than fragmented testimony.[49] In P,C&S the favouring of certain narrators and the provision of a more favourable environment for those constructing the narrative of the dangerous mother meant that these narrators were more able to draw upon and present a more cohesive (and thus more persuasive) account.[50] Furthermore, the potential disruption of that narrative through cross-examination[51] of its narrators was forestalled by the absence of the key players, Drs Garcia and Dr Schreier. In this, P can be seen to have been severely disadvantaged from developing her own narrative of innocence.

5. Dealing with contradictory evidence

In order to construct a persuasive narrative some sort of response is required to evidence that threatens to undermine that narrative. In P,C&S we see various attempts to ignore, gloss over or explain away such evidence.

Apart from his remarks over the hiding of a key document (itself glossed over by minimising the seriousness of the event and turning it against the parents), Justice Wall is notably silent on the failings of the social services' investigations and their deliberate attempts to hinder a proper evaluation of the case through fabricating events, altering or censoring documents, their attempted interference with P's independent psychiatric expert and their deception of the parents and other family members. Similarly, although he criticised the Guardian ad Litem for pre-judging the case he ignored the impact this prejudice potentially had on the conduct of her investigation and her subsequent recommendations.

> In acting in this way it can be argued that the judge was displaying elements of groupthink, in particular:
>
> the belief in the inherent morality of the group (i.e. that the social services and expert witnesses were benevolent and benign);
>
> self-censorship (ignoring, glossing over or explaining away contradictory evidence); and

---

[49] WM O'Barr, *Linguistic evidence*. (New York: Academic Press, 1982).

[50] I have explored the issue of a-symmetry in approach to the evidence and testimony of professionals and mothers elsewhere. See, Baldwin 2004 supra n.30.

[51] Jackson 1988 supra n.45.

> self-appointed 'mindguards' (protecting the social services and the expert witnesses from troublesome ideas – either P's cross-examination or the problems of contradictory evidence).

In so doing he also safeguarded the foundations for the narrative of dangerousness, thus enhancing its persuasiveness. Furthermore, by refusing leave to appeal he attempted to silence any further re-telling of the narrative, thus protecting both himself and the Local Authority.

6. Concluding remarks

Care proceedings are predicated on a positivist philosophy that there is a world out there and through careful examination, investigation and testing of claims to factuality it is possible to determine 'what really happened'. While I do not share this positivist world view, even in those terms the narrative of the dangerous mother in P,C&S is seen to be unreliable in that it fails the tests of having due regard to facts, regard for due process and regard for facticity in the conceptualisation and operationalisation of MSbP as a diagnostic category.

In this paper I have therefore sought to indicate other sources of narrative persuasiveness. Some of these sources are those identified by Bennett and Feldman with regard to the US criminal justice system, such as definitional tactics were embodied in both the narrative itself and the process of narrative construction (exemplified by the narrative trajectory of MSbP). Other sources 'centred around relocation, innuendo, manipulation (i.e., addition or deletion) of evidence'[52] – such as the fabrication of events or the interpretation of events within the cognitive schema of MSbP. In addition to these features identified by Bennett and Feldman, the case of P,C&S involved the mobilisation of supporting discourses, the smoothing of the narrative of dangerousness to coincide more closely with the archetypal MSbP narrative and elements of groupthink.

In the case of P,C&S, although the narrators were different, the same arguments were presented to the European Court as had been presented to the domestic courts. One tentative explanation of the ECHR's ruling in favour of P is that, being distanced from the initial proceedings, extraneous sources of narrative persuasiveness played little part, with the focus being on fact, argument and due process. In restoring these to the centre of the case, the ECHR effectively, if not explicitly, undermined both

[52] Bennett and Feldman 1981 p130 supra n.8.

the persuasiveness of the narrative of dangerousness and the reliability of the findings of the domestic courts.

CHAPTER 6

Taking Facts Seriously

Maarten Henket

Utrecht University, The Netherlands

1. Introduction

A primitive definition of 'doing justice' might read: to apply existing law to the facts of the case. From a more sophisticated point of view, this definition is too simple and therefore misleading. What is 'existing law'? What if more than one rule seems applicable? What about the necessary interpretation of rules and precedents? And, on the side of the facts: What is a fact? What is truth? How do we determine which of several different readings of the facts is the true one? Doesn't the theory of narrative coherence argue persuasively that judges and juries do not base their decisions on 'the facts', but on the most convincing narrative of those facts?[1]

And yet, the whole structure of criminal procedure presupposes a belief in the existence of facts. If we give that up, we must give up the search for truth, and declare the search for evidence, including the use of expert witnesses, to be a mere scam, or, to put it in more friendly terms, a part of the ideology that helps in stabilizing society but without having any basis in reality.

In this article, I will defend the view that, even when we take seriously the criticisms of a primitive theory of justice indicated above, we should also keep taking facts seriously. What I mean by that, I hope to explain below. I will do that by making a twofold comparison and juxtaposition. First, I will compare 'fact finding' in common law and in civil law, and secondly, I will compare 'fact finding' in science and in law. As far as law is concerned, I will limit my analysis to criminal law.

---

[1] B.S. Jackson, *Law, Fact and Narrative Coherence* (Liverpool: Deborah Charles Publications, 1988); see also e.g. WL Bennett and M Feldman, *Reconstructing Reality in the Courtroom* (New Brunswick, Rutgers University Press, 1981).

A. Wagner et al. (eds.), Interpretation, Law and the Construction of Meaning, 109–120.

2. Fact Finding in Common Law and in Civil Law

Roughly speaking, criminal procedure in a common law system is adversarial in nature, while in a civil law system it is inquisitorial.[2] Two different philosophies of truth seeking underlie these systems. In civil law there is the idea that the best way to come as close to the truth as possible is to put the investigation in the hands of a judge – a judge who is well versed in the law (including the law of evidence) and who is well equipped to determine for each given case what kind of evidence is needed and what is the evidentiary power of the evidence obtained. In common law, there is the idea that justice is best served if a jury is first confronted with the opposing pieces of evidence presented by the parties in a procedure of direct examination and cross-examination, and then uses its common sense to determine who is right.

In both systems, the official aim of the fact finding part of a criminal trial is to find the truth. To be sure, absolute certainty regarding the facts is not required; in order to find the defendant guilty it suffices that the judge or the jury be convinced 'beyond reasonable doubt'. And on the other hand there are cases where the truth actually *is* found, but cannot lead to a conviction because the evidence is illegitimate. This illustrates that finding the truth is not the *only* aim of a criminal trial.[3] Nevertheless, we can safely say that, within the limits of procedural law, the official aim of collecting and presenting evidence is, to find out 'what really happened'. For the inquisitorial procedure this is generally acknowledged. For the adversarial procedure however, it is controversial. On the one hand there is the view expressed by the Courts. This view can be found in a number of judicial opinions, for instance in *Tehan v. United States*: 'The basic purpose of a trial is the determination of truth.'[4] The same view is also expressed in judge's instructions to the jury: 'It is your duty to decide ... what the facts are.'[5] On the other hand, there is the view that truth is not an end, but only

---

[2] For nuances see e.g. M.R. Damaska, *The Faces of Justice and State Authority* (New Haven and London: Yale University Press, 1986).

[3] See e.g. A.A.S. Zuckerman, *The Principles of Criminal Justice* (Oxford, Oxford University Press, 1989) who mentions three aims: the ascertainment of truth, the protection of the innocent from conviction, and maintenance of adequate standards of propriety in the criminal process.

[4] *Tehan v United States,* 382 U.S. 406, 86 S.Ct. 459, 465 (1966).

[5] Quotation from the *Pattern Jury Instructions for Criminal Cases,* in P. Gaines, 'Ideal and Actual Evidence in the Courtroom: Jurors' and Attorneys' Sense of Facts and Evidence' (2004), paper presented at the 2004 International Round Table for the Semiotics of Law, Lyon (France).

one of several possible means to achieve the end, which is justice. To quote Burnham,

> [T]he idea is not to find 'the truth' of an event, but to find which communicated perception of an event is the most plausible account of that event.[6]

Or, to take a typical attorneys' view, for example the view of Covington: 'The rules of evidence and trial practice are designed primarily to resolve disputes. Truth, if it is found, is a nice-and-desirable-by-product.'[7] So in this view, truth is not the end, but no more than one of the possible means to the end which is dispute resolution and/or justice. And while the judge suggests in his instructions that the evidence will enable the jury to decide what actually happened, in reality what is presented to the jury in an adversarial trial by both the prosecution and the defence, is not evidentiary data from which the truth can be extracted, but rather 'the construction of a possible reality whose presentation is persuasive enough to bring the jury to accept it as the more likely reality.'[8]

These two opposing philosophies as to the nature of evidence and 'truth finding' in an accusatorial procedure result, in the words of Gaines, in an 'inherent schizophrenia in the system.'[9]

In civil law philosophy, this particular schizophrenia does not exist. There is, however, a different kind of schizophrenia that plays a role in any kind of criminal procedure, including the inquisitorial kind, as a result of the various aims of procedural law, which are to a certain extent mutually incompatible. Fact finding is one of them, due process is another one, and so is finality. To warrant due process and finality necessarily means to limit the possibilities to find the truth. I will come back to this in a later section.

3. Convergence of Common Law and Civil Law Fact Finding

In recent times, there have been changes in the law on both sides of the Atlantic that indicate a certain convergence between the two systems of criminal procedure. In continental Europe, a reform is taking place under the influence of the decisions of the European Court of Human Rights in Strasbourg. Notably, the Court's interpretation of the notion of 'fair trial' as

---

[6] W. Burnham, *Introduction to the Law and Legal System of the United States* (St. Paul, MN: West Publishing Company, 1995), at 122. Quoted in Gaines, *supra* n.5, at 6.
[7] J.S. Covington (1993) as quoted in Gaines, *supra* n.5, at 5.
[8] Gaines, *supra* n 5, at 8.
[9] Gaines, *supra* n 5, at 11.

contained in section 6 of the European Convention of Human Rights, forces some member states to revise certain aspects of their traditional procedural practice. For example, in Dutch criminal procedure, witnesses for the prosecution used to be examined by the judge, and not necessarily by the defence. The Kostovski case has put an end to that practice.[10] Some commentators expect that cross-examination will eventually become an integral part of the fact finding process in civil law criminal procedure.

For the United States, we may take as an example the judge-appointed expert witness, made possible in 1975 under FRE (Federal Rules of Evidence) 706 and various state equivalents. While this development has been labelled by critics as 'elitist', 'undemocratic', and even 'totalitarian', both critics and advocates recognize it as a move in the direction of an inquisitorial system.[11]

What the exact consequences of these tendencies will be for the law of evidence both east and west of the Atlantic, remains to be seen. One interesting aspect of this development is a growing interest among European continental scholars in the common law literature on evidence.[12]

4. Natural Science and Law

Objectivity, openness, honesty and a critical attitude; these are said to be the prerequisites of the scientific enterprise. The success of the natural sciences in enabling us to put nature at our service would not be possible without an overall respect for facts. To be sure, not all scientists are objective, honest and open all the time. Every now and then some overly ambitious scientist cannot resist the temptation to falsify research results, but, so it is believed, in the end reality will unmask the fraud.[13]

This picture is actually misleading. Kuhn, Latour and others have shown us that, in science as elsewhere, the notion of 'facts' is not so

---

[10] ECHR 20 November 1989, *NJ* 1990, 245, Slobodan Kostovski/The Netherlands.

[11] See S. Haack, 'Truth and Justice, Inquiry and Advocacy, Science and Law' (2004) *Ratio Juris* 15, at 24.

[12] For the Netherlands, see e.g. J.F. Nijboer, 'Strafrechtelijk bewijs van een andere kant bekeken' (1991) *Delict en Delinquent* 332-44; N. Jörg, 'De exclusionary rule als drijfveer achter de normering van bevoegdheden' (1989) *Delict en Delinquent* 654-670.

[13] For a fascinating account of fraud in science, see W. Broad and N. Wade, *Betrayers of the Truth,* (New York: Simon and Schuster, 1982).

simple.[14] 'Reality' can be 'explained' in different ways, leading paradigms are highly resistant, and which of any two concurring theories prevails depends not only on objective facts, but also on rhetorical talents, economic opportunities and political factors. In other words, 'correspondence to the facts' is a problematic criterion if it comes to choosing between competing *theories* in science. This is true for theories that are proposed in good faith, but also for theories that are put forward by impostors. Therefore, on this level we can not be so sure that 'reality will always unmask the fraud'.

Nevertheless, on the level of *applied* science, we can safely say that denying the facts of nature leads to failure. Our knowledge of the properties of the materials we use for making tools, buildings, vehicles etcetera, is an indispensable ingredient in their design. The consequences of not taking these properties into consideration become clear when poorly designed bridges collapse and space ships explode.

In summary, we might say that in science, fact scepticism on the level of theory building is wise, but fact scepticism on the level of applied science is foolish, and even dangerous. When engineers ignore the laws of nature, Nature is bound to take revenge.

How is the situation in law as compared to science? Is there less objectivity, openness, honesty and critical attitude here? No, I don't think so. But there are two aspects of adjudication that *do* make the situation very different. First of all, there are important differences in method. Legal procedure is in some instances more restrictive, in other instances more permissive than scientific method. On the one hand, fact finding in law is subject to all kinds of limitations, like time limits, the inadmissibility of illegally obtained evidence, and so on. These limits may be there for legitimate reasons, but they clearly undercut the possibilities of fact finding and/or using the facts as a basis for the decision. On the other hand, the law may acknowledge methods and tools of 'fact finding' that are totally unheard of, and would be considered absurd, in science. Like trial by ordeal, torture, and the oath.

The second aspect in which law differs from science with regard to the facts is that judges can ignore the facts without running into Nature's revenge. Badly designed bridges collapse, but a judicial decision that is incongruous with the facts stands as law. It may be overruled by a later

---

[14] T. Kuhn, *The Structure of Scientific Revolutions* (Chicago, Ill., University of Chicago Press, 1962); B Latour, *Science in Action* (Cambridge, Mass., Harvard University Press, 1987).

decision or by the legislator, but those are human interventions, not Nature's revenge. If such interventions don't take place the bad decision remains law. Every uncorrected miscarriage of justice can serve as an example.

5. Convergence of Scientific and Legal Fact Finding

Though lawyers always lag behind in following scientific developments, new scientific insights that are generally accepted eventually find their way into the minds of the legislator or the judge and from there into the law. For example, insights from psychology as to the reliability, or rather unreliability, of the human memory, have led to a re-appreciation of the value of evidence from witnesses and the use thereof in court. Critical analyses of identification-by-confrontation procedures in police stations have resulted in standards that try to enhance the objectivity and reliability of such procedures.

New scientific developments sometimes lead to the introduction of new forms of evidence, the most notorious recent example being that of DNA-based evidence. Countless cases have been reopened and in several instances this has resulted in the rehabilitation of people that had been unjustly convicted, in other instances it has led to finding the hitherto unknown offender. In the Netherlands, the availability of DNA-based evidence has prompted the legislator to lengthen the term of limitation for certain crimes.

These examples show that science influences the collecting of evidence in law in two ways: by influencing the methods and by providing new means.

Interestingly enough, the influence of science is not great enough to completely set aside unscientific methods and tools, not even in the Western world. Trial by ordeal and the weighing of witches have disappeared from Western criminal procedure, but the oath is still there, and so is torture, I'm afraid.

For the sake of balance, let me note that there is also some influence in the other direction. Once it is acknowledged that certain debates in science are undecided, e.g. the debate between adherents and critics of Darwin's theory of the development of species, it becomes interesting to try to formulate rules with regard to the various burdens of proof for the participants in such a debate. And where can be found more expertise on this point than in law?[15] In this context, we should of course not forget to mention Toulmin, who proposes taking jurisprudence as a model for argumentation in other areas. In the introduction of his *The Uses of Argument*, he writes:

> One last preliminary: to break the power of old models and analogies, we can provide ourselves with a new one. Logic is concerned with the soundness of the claims we make – with the solidity of the grounds we produce to support them, the firmness of the backing we provide for them – or, to change the metaphor, with the sort of *case* we present in defence of our claims. The legal analogy implied in this last way of putting the point can for once be a real help. So let us forget about psychology, sociology, technology and mathematics, ignore the echoes of structural engineering and *collage* in the words 'grounds' and 'backing', and take as our model the discipline of jurisprudence. Logic (we may say) is generalized jurisprudence.[16]

The logic Toulmin is talking about here is what Popper has called the logic of discovery, that is, the method of theory building in science. Toulmin's argument is not meant to question or moderate the observance of facts that is indispensable in applied science or engineering.

6. Taking Facts Seriously

In the foregoing sections I have sketched my view on the nature and status of facts and fact finding in law. Starting from there, I can now state more clearly what I mean by taking facts seriously.

Taking into account the rightful criticisms against a naïve positivistic theory of facts, we may grant a number of things. First of all, the sciences sometimes present competing theories of reality, and it is impossible to decide which one is right. Secondly, even if we accept a certain theory of reality as the right one, for example Darwin's theory of the development of species, or Einstein's theory of relativity, and if accordingly we let our perceptions of natural phenomena be coloured by that theory, then still various individuals will differ in their perceptions of the 'reality' around them. And thirdly – and this is especially relevant with regard to fact finding in law – we may agree with Jackson and others that in the appreciation of evidence presented to us by others, what is decisive is

---

[15] See e.g. R.H. Gaskins, *Burdens of Proof in Modern Discourse* (New Haven and London: Yale University Press, 1992).

[16] S. Toulmin, *The Uses of Argument* (Cambridge: Cambridge University Press, 1974), at 7.

not which presentation best matches reality, but which presentation provides the most convincing narrative.

All this being granted, the fact remains that on a rather basic level, some things are real while others are not. For example, that Paris is the capital of France, or that Sunday is followed by Monday, can hardly be denied in any meaningful sense. Also, to take a less trivial example, it is a fact that someone who was not present at the place and time of the murder can not have pulled the trigger.

I shall go one step further in moderating my notion of hard facts. I do acknowledge that the question of which facts are hard facts and which facts are not, is not culturally neutral. For instance, a Medieval Saint who has the enviable gift of *bilocatio* will deny that a person can only be in one place at a time. And an Australian Aboriginal will perhaps deny that a piece of land always is someone's exclusive property, or will perhaps not even understand the notion 'land ownership'. Nevertheless, I maintain that for each given culture there is a set of entities (a collection of phenomena, and objects, and truths, and generalizations) that count as hard facts. And for each of those facts there is a corresponding sentence that counts as unmistakeably true in that culture. It is those facts, I think, that should be taken seriously if we wish to maintain that criminal procedure is about facts.

7. Two Attitudes

I will now for a moment deviate from the direction I have taken in the foregoing section, and return to the two different attitudes towards facts that I sketched in the beginning of this chapter. More specifically, I will point out the implications that each of these attitudes seems to have for criminal procedure.

The first possible attitude is to give up the idea that the aim of a criminal trial is to find the truth. This would imply, I think, a thorough reassessment of what happens in court in terms of evidence. What, against the background of such a philosophy, can be the function of police reports, witness statements and, most of all, expert witnesses? Why call in experts if finding the truth is so relatively unimportant? And what, in this train of thought, can be meant by an expression like 'miscarriage of justice'? As the saying goes, you win some, you loose some, it's all in the game; too bad for the Guildford-Four and the Birmingham-Six.[17] Can an accusatorial criminal trial in its present form be called something other that a stage play? Perhaps this is taking the argument too far. But the existing discrepancy between the 'official' and the 'practical' view of fact finding in an accusatorial procedure should, I think, not be taken lightly. As for the inquisitorial model, this philosophical discrepancy is missing here, and nobody defends the view that finding the truth is unimportant. One would therefore expect that the rules and practices of inquisitorial procedure would optimally warrant due respect for the facts. However, this is not always the case. I will give an example in the next paragraph.

The second possible attitude towards facts is to take facts seriously. This attitude has certain implications for the criminal trial as well. It means that the narratives or stories that are presented in court should be critically evaluated in the light of accepted background knowledge and available evidence.[18] To use a term coined by Crombag *et al*, a narrative should be 'anchored'.[19] It also means that procedural rules and practices should optimally encourage observance of the facts. If we look at the rules of criminal procedure with this idea in mind, we may occasionally find a rule or practice that is clearly counterproductive in this respect, and we then may ask whether that rule or practice is nevertheless sufficiently warranted by the possible arguments in favor of it. As an example I take the rule of Dutch criminal procedure that allows the judge to ignore evidence he doesn't use as a basis for his decision. This means that a suspect in a murder case may be convicted if, say, three out of twenty witnesses recognize him as the shooter, even if all remaining seventeen witnesses say he wasn't the man. Not only that, but the judge does not even have to mention the statements of the seventeen others. I think this rule should be abandoned, and the judge should at least be obliged to state in his decision what evidence has been presented and why he did or did not use it as a basis for his decision. I can't see how the other aims of the criminal trial (due process and finality) could provide sufficient warrant for the rule under discussion.

---

[17] About these cases, see, e.g. C. Mullin, *Error of Judgement* (London, Chatto & Windus, 1986).

[18] For a striking example of disregard for the facts, see C. Baldwin, 'Who Needs Facts When You've Got Narrative? in this volume.

[19] H.F.M. Crombag, P.J. van Koppen, and W.A. Wagenaar, *Anchored Narratives. The Psychology of Criminal Evidence,* (Hempstead, Harvester Weatsheaf and St. Martin's Press, 1993).

For lawyers in an adversarial system, this approach would mean that they should change their philosophy so as to make it coherent with the official view, which is that the adversarial process aims at finding the truth – a view that concurs with the one expressed in jury instructions and official comments. It also means that the judges' instructions to the jury should paint a more realistic picture of what happens in an adversarial trial and should warn jurors against believing that what looks sophisticated and sounds convincing is therefore true.

It will not come as a surprise to the reader that I confess my preference for this second attitude towards facts.

8. Narrativism and Positivism

One serious theoretical question must still be addressed: how can fact-positivism be reconciled with narrativism? How can we, on the one hand, acknowledge that what makes a story convincing is not its truthfulness but its narrative coherence, and at the same time maintain that some basic facts should not be ignored? My answer to this question is as follows. Narrativism is a descriptive theory about how persuasion in the courtroom and elsewhere actually works. The minimal fact-positivism advocated in this paper reflects a normative position regarding how justice should be done in criminal law cases.

As Twining has put it, stories are necessary but dangerous. We must acknowledge that the human mind works the way it does, which implies that telling plausible stories works. This is an analytic and descriptive statement. But at the same time we should, I think, try to minimize the dangers. This means that we should do our best to train our lawyers and arrange our criminal procedure in such a way that plausibility moves in the direction of truthfulness as far as possible. This is a normative statement. Surely, a total convergence of plausibility and truthfulness can never be obtained, but it is an ideal that is worth formulating, and worth striving for.

My view on the relationship between narrativism and positivism implies a 'weak' form of narrativism, where narratives are taken to be representations of a reality that exists separately. There is also a 'strong' form of narrativism, where narratives are taken to constitute reality. This variant seems to me to be irreconcilable with fact-positivism, and therefore to imply that fact-finding cannot be an aim of criminal procedure. The consequences of this attitude as I see them have been sketched briefly in the foregoing paragraph.[20]

9. Conclusion

To take facts seriously is, in my opinion, a necessary condition for criminal justice as long as finding the truth is among the aims of the criminal trial. Finding the truth, however, is not a sufficient condition for criminal justice. This is so because the trial has other ends besides finding the truth, namely finality and due process. On the one hand, the various ends are all part of the greater end, that of justice. On the other hand, these ends require means that sometimes work in opposite directions. For example, the authority to monitor calls between lawyers and their clients is in the interest of crime fighting, but not in the interest of due process. An equilibrium is the best we can hope for. What that equilibrium looks like, and where in that equilibrium the centre of gravity must reside, is a matter of debate. This is only in part a scientific debate. For example, the decision whether the emphasis is on crime fighting or on due process, is a political decision.

According to Merryman, an 'eminent comparative scholar' once stated that if he were innocent, he would prefer to be tried by a civil law court, but that if he were guilty, he would prefer to be tried by a common law court.[21] Be that as it may, I think that both the adversarial and the inquisitorial model have their strong and weak points when it comes to taking facts seriously. Luckily, experts on evidence and criminal investigation from all over the world show a growing interest in each others' work and in each others' models of criminal adjudication, judging by the increasing number of international conferences on these subjects. This development is, of course, not only the fruit of a growing scientific awareness, but also of the growing internationalisation of law. An increasing number of international treaties, the federalization of Europe, the growing number and activities of international tribunals, these are all factors that discourage parochialism. Let me conclude with a statement by Michael Karnavas, an attorney who was trained in the common law, and

---

[20] For these two variants of narrativism, see e.g. P. Brooks and P. Gerwitz (eds.), *Law's Stories: Narrative and Rhetoric in the Law* (New Haven: Yale University, 1996). I was inspired to add this paragraph and reference by reading Baldwin's paper, *supra* n. 18.

[21] J.H. Merryman, *The Civil Law Tradition* (Stanford: Stanford University Press, 1985), at 132.

who is now working as an attorney for the defence at the Yugoslavia Tribunal in The Hague:

> The prosecutors seem to regard the trial as a game that one must try to win. But it should not be that way. These are no ordinary crimes. These are historical trials, where it is important that the truth emerges.[22]

There is no good reason, I think, to regard ordinary trials as different from 'historical trials' when it comes to the question of the importance of truth.

[22] *Trouw*, 16 November 2004 (my translation).

CHAPTER 7

Transforming Ambiguity into Vagueness in Legal Interpretation

Moshe Azar

Haifa University, Israel

1. Introduction

The aim of the paper is to demonstrate courts' inclination to prefer looking at interpretation disputes as if they were cases of vagueness instead of seeing them as what they are: cases of ambiguity. The reason for this preference seems to be the prospect of broadening the spectrum of interpretation offered by vagueness.

My claim is that if one can discern the meaning of the disputed term with the help of the linguistic context, it proves, from a pragmatic interpretation approach, that vagueness is irrelevant to the issue at stake, because we already have reached a non-vague disambiguated meaning. By pragmatic interpretation approach, I mean something not unlike the interpretation approach expressed by Elmer Driedger:

Today there is only one principle or approach, namely, the words of an Act are to be read in their entire context and in their grammatical and ordinary sense harmoniously with the scheme of the Act, the object of the Act, and the intention of Parliament.[1]

The principle by which one has to read an Act, according to Driedger, coincides with pragmatic interpretation approach, which in my view is, basically, trying to understand a text in a way that matches, as far as possible, the writer's intentions as they are communicated *in* the text. According to this view, the meaning of a text is an intentional entity.[2] More than that, meaning and intention are two different words for the same thing.[3] If so, and if 'the object of all reading is always the historical

---

[1] E. Driedger, *Construction of Statutes,* 2nd ed. (Toronto: Butterworths, 1983), at 87.
[2] B.J.F. Lonergan, *Method in Theology,* 2nd ed. (London: Darton, Longman & Todd, 1973), at 159.
[3] The firsts to defend this thesis in its radical form were S. Knapp and W. B. Michaels, 'Against Theory' (1982) 8 *Critical Inquiry* 723. The essay drew much

A. Wagner et al. (eds.), Interpretation, Law and the Construction of Meaning, 121–137.

author's intention, even if the historical author is the universal muse',[4] there can be no difference concerning the search for meaning between a will made by an individual, a contract made by two sides or an Act of Parliament because no meaning exists apart from the author's intended meaning, which is present in the text. The meanings one finds in dictionaries and grammar books cannot be but abstractions of real communication meaning. The real meaning of a text is only what its author intended it to mean. This view of text meaning denies any possibility constructing an interpretation theory to be applied to specific texts, as Knapp and Michaels concluded:

> Meaning is just another name for expressed intention. Knowledge just another name for true belief, but theory is not just another name for practice. It is the name for all the ways people have tried to stand outside practice in order to govern practice from without. Our thesis has been that no one can reach a position outside practice, that theorists should stop trying, and that the theoretical enterprise should therefore come to an end.[5]

The view that intention is not different from meaning means, *inter alia*, that meaning is subjective, a state of mind of an individual or a collective, realized in a text. A collective may have an intention no less clear than an individual, sometimes even clearer, as Sinclair wrote: 'I argue that, to the contrary, there is indeed such a thing as legislative intent, and that it is alive and well and more readily and objectively accessible than the intent of any ordinary person.'[6]

Authorial intention, that is, the meaning of a particular text, cannot be understood by simple observation of the signs; it always needs to be interpreted, which means that no guarantee exists that our understanding of the text is correct. To put it in Henket's words,

---

controversy and many debates, which were collected, together with the original essay, in W. J. T Mitchell, (ed.), *Against Theory: Literary Studies and New pragmatism* (Chicago and London: The University of Chicago Press, 1985).

[4] S. Knapp and W. B. Michaels, 'A Reply to Our Critics' in W. J. T Mitchell, (ed.), *Against Theory: Literary Studies and New Pragmatism* (Chicago and London: The University of Chicago Press, 1985), at 103.

[5] S. Knapp and W. B. Michaels, 'Against Theory', in W. J. T Mitchell (ed.), *Against Theory: Literary Studies and New Pragmatism* (Chicago and London: The University of Chicago Press, 1985), at 30.

[6] M. B. W Sinclair (1997) 46 'Statutory Reasoning', *Drake Law Review* 299, at 303. See also J. R. Searle, 'Collective Intentions and Actions', in P. R. Cohen, J. Morgan and M. A. Pollack (eds.), *Intentions in Communication* (Cambridge: Mass., The MIT Press), 401

> No matter how careful we are and how many particulars we take into consideration, the intentionally we find will always be a conjecture. We can never be sure to have discovered the real subjective intentions of the actor at the time of the act. It is, therefore, at the most a probable intent that serves as a basis for judicial decision-making.[7]

All an interpreter can do, then, is to construct a hypothesis that may best satisfy the entire text. Context, and particularly linguistic context, is the key for the construction of such a hypothesis. There are no rules or directions for creating hypotheses and inferring intentions, because every text is a unique historical event and no theory can predict the nature of that particular event. No interpretation theory can be useful in determining the meaning of a particular text. 'There can be no way of formalizing a set of procedures, or teaching a set of instructions, that would be guaranteed to churn out the right answer each time, any more than there is an algorithm for discovering anything else about the world.'[8]

Uncertainty is always part of text interpretation, certainly when it comes to choosing between two alternatives. But texts sometimes provide linguistic or pragmatic clues that may help to determine which of the alternatives best fits the entire meaning of text. The necessary condition that allows adoption of one of the alternatives on the basis of the pragmatic approach defended in this paper is the recognition that a text cannot mean something different from what the author intended it to mean. Any evidence, be it linguistic or otherwise, which is not aimed at this target is, from a pragmatic viewpoint, irrelevant and must be rejected. For example, the meaning(s) of a word found in dictionaries or in some corpus of texts cannot serve as evidence for the meaning of the same lexical item in the disputed text. A pragmatic linguist does not ask what the meaning of a word is, but what the meaning of a word is in the particular text under consideration.

Some linguists and jurists thought it pertinent to conduct a large-scale linguistic investigation about dictionaries' definitions and people's opinions concerning the meaning of the term *enterprise*.[9] They seem to believe that it is possible to prefer one of the alternatives by investigating

---

[7] M. Henket, 'Contracts, Promises and Meaning: The Question of Intent' (1989) 5 *International Journal for the Semiotics of Law* 129, at 131.

[8] B. Stroud, *Meaning, Understanding, and Practice: Philosophical Essays* (Oxford: Oxford University Press, 2000), at 199.

[9] See J. F. Kaplan, G M. Green, C. D. Cunningham, and J. N. Levi, 'Bringing Linguistics into Judicial Decision-Making: Semantic Analysis Submitted to the US Supreme Court' (1995) 2 *Forensic Linguistics* 81.

the conventional meaning of the disputed word. But if meaning is a particular intention which arises from a particular text, no investigation about others' intentions or potential intentions can solve the interpretation problem. Stanley Fish lucidly described what should be meant by 'linguistic knowledge' in real communication:

> Rather than being distinct from circumstantial (and therefore variable) conditions, linguistic knowledge is unthinkable apart from these circumstances. Linguistic knowledge is contextual rather than abstract, local rather than general, dynamic rather than invariant; every rule is a rule of thumb; every competence grammar is a performance grammar in a disguise.[10]

A pragmatic linguist must exploit any clue and cue in the text itself that can shed light on the author's intentions. One may try, of course, to understand a word in a given text by consulting a dictionary or by looking at other texts to see how people use it and which meanings it can convey. But eventually, the context and circumstances alone determine the particular meaning intended by the author.[11]

The interpretation disputes we deal with in this paper concern disputes over the meaning of lexical units. Two kinds of lexical indeterminacy interest us in this paper: ambiguity and vagueness. Clarifying the difference between these two types of indeterminacy is of utmost importance since, according to pragmatic linguistics as it is understood in this paper, the recognition of a disputed term as a case of vagueness leads to the conclusion that no pragmatic interpretation is possible. On the other hand, recognizing it as a case of ambiguity means usually that one of the two alternatives is pragmatically (or pragma-linguistically) preferable over the other one. And the other way around, the possibility of arriving at a solution based on pragmatic considerations (linguistic context and circumstances) means that the case is an example of ambiguity and not of vagueness, meaning that contemplation about the boundaries of the concept denoted by the disputed term is out of place. Below, two court decisions will be examined, and it will be shown that they reflect the courts' tendency to transform ambiguity cases into vagueness cases in order to make room for judicial discretion.

---

[10] S. Fish, 'Consequences', in W. J. T Mitchell (ed.), *Against Theory: Literary Studies and New Pragmatism* (Chicago and London: The University of Chicago Press, 1985), at 111.

[11] A good example of a pragmatic work that fulfils this principle is J. P. Kaplan, 'Pragmatic Contribution to the Interpretation of a Will' (1998) 5 *Forensic Linguistics* 107.

2. Ambiguity vs. vagueness

The importance of recognizing two major types of indeterminacy is not new. Philosophers, linguists, and jurisprudence scholars paid considerable attention to it. One of the latter puts it very clearly:

> Whereas 'ambiguity' in its classical sense refers to equivocation, 'vagueness' refers to the degree to which, independently of equivocation, language is uncertain in its respective application to a number of particulars.[12]

Let us elaborate on this distinction by looking more closely into those two types of lexical indeterminacy. Four types of semantic indeterminacy or polyvalence exist: homonymy, polysemy, generality, and vagueness.[13]

An expression is homonymous if it has more than one semantically unrelated meaning. The almost canonical example is a *bank* of a river and *bank* as a financial institution. This type of ambiguity is widely recognized by lexicographers, who tend to list a separate dictionary entry for each meaning. The term homonymy refers traditionally to lexical ambiguity, but there is no reason not to apply it as well to morphological and syntactic (or structural) ambiguity. After all, both the latter also have more than one semantically unrelated meaning. Lexical homonymy and morphological homonymy, but not syntactic homonymy, are the types of ambiguity that can be most easily disambiguated by linguistic context. Practically, it is very rare to find in normal communication a misunderstanding or an interpretation dispute caused by lexical or morphological homonymy. Syntactic ambiguity, by contrast, is not rare,[14] and not easily disambiguated by context.

An expression is polysemous if it has two or more meanings having some semantic or rhetorical relationship, or, to put it in another way, if it has two or more senses for one meaning; for example, *table* as a piece of furniture and as a feast. Here too, the term polysemy refers traditionally to lexical ambiguity, but there is no reason not to apply it as well to phrases such as *my book*, which may mean "the book I wrote", "the book I own",

---

[12] R. Dickerson, *The Interpretation and Application of Statutes* (Boston: Little, Brown, 1975), at 49.

[13] See especially Q. Zhang, 'Fuzziness – vagueness – generality – ambiguity' (1998) 29 *Journal of Pragmatics* 13; F. Devos, 'Semantic Vagueness and Lexical Polyvalence' (2003) 57 *Studia Linguistica* 121.

[14] It seems that in English legal text, by far the most prevalent kind of ambiguity is syntactic ambiguity' (Dickerson, *supra* n.12, at 46).

"the book I borrowed from the library", and more.[15] Polysemous words tend to have one dictionary entry with several senses or definitions. Polysemy has a much higher frequency in any language than homonymy. Unlike homonymy, polysemy is not accidental and it may even be predicted. Contrary to homonymy, it is an essential condition for the efficiency of the language as a communication tool. Without polysemy, the language would need an enormous increase of vocabulary.

An expression is general if it denotes something that one can divide more specifically into several things, which may or may not have become lexicalized items. For example, the English word *school* is, in addition to being homonymous and polysemous, general because it stands for any institution in which instruction of any kind is given. This intensional definition comprehends the extensional meaning of *university, high school, school of mines,* etc. Generality becomes actual ambiguity when the general term can be understood in its general (broad) sense as well as in one of its specific (narrow) senses. When hearing the sentence *schools are greenhouses for druggies,* one may understand it as referring only to schools for youngsters, but, linguistically (or semantically), it can refer to all kinds of instructional institutions. Another example is *grandfather,* which stands for both the mother's father and the father's father. In Swedish, instead, the terms are more specific: *morfar* and *farfar* respectively.

Homonymy, polysemy, and generality are potential sources of real communication ambiguity, not so much because the language itself bears some deficiency, but rather because of the user of the language. The user of the language can always avoid linguistic ambiguity if he/she is aware enough. One can always use other terms, other syntactic structures, and periphrases. These three types of ambiguity are indeed pure linguistic ambiguities, and to the extent they can be avoided by the language user, they can be, generally speaking, disambiguated by the addressee thanks to the context and circumstances. The fourth and last type of indeterminacy, vagueness, does not belong, strictly speaking, to linguistic ambiguity[16] and

---

[15] See Zhang, *supra* n.13, at 16. Be aware that Zhang uses the term vagueness instead of polysemy, fuzziness instead of our vagueness, and ambiguity instead of our homonymy.

[16] This is the reason why linguists paid so little attention to this type of indeterminacy. See Devos, *supra* n. 13, at 122.

one cannot expect to be able to de-vaguefy[17] it by context. Williamson provides us a good definition of vagueness:

> An expression or concept is vague if and only if it has borderline cases, that is, actual or potential cases in which it neither clearly applies nor clearly fails to apply. For example, a borderline case for the term 'tall' is someone who is neither clearly tall nor clearly not tall. Even when one can see the person in question without difficulty, one cannot decide whether the term 'tall' applies -or perhaps one decides it one way while other speakers equally familiar with English and with an equally good view of the person decide it the other way.[18]

In other words, vagueness arises when a term that denotes a conceptual category that has a fuzzy zone causes uncertainty as to whether or not an entity in the real world belongs to the category. One may discern two sub-types of vagueness: categorical vagueness and gradual vagueness.[19] The first is due to the uncertainty of the criteria or conditions used in the application of a term. When I say, for example, a *neighbor* of mine, do I mean someone who lives nearby on the same floor, the same building, the same street, or the same quarter? The category itself is not clear. Gradual vagueness is due to the uncertainty of the extent to, or the degree to which, application of certain words is likely. *Tall*, for example, is intrinsically vague concerning the degree to which someone or something has to have greatness of stature in order to be entitled to be qualified as *tall*. Gradual vagueness is more basic in the sense that while categorical vagueness may encompass gradual vagueness, the latter can not be decomposed.

Unlike linguistic ambiguity (or ambiguity *tout court*), which is more or less language-specific (homonymy being entirely and polysemy and generality only partially language-specific), vagueness, it seems, is language-universal, resulting from a language practice of referring to objects, actions, properties, and states of affairs that have a continuous range of values as if they have absolute values. The only way for a user of language to give to a vague term a precise meaning is by providing a stipulative definition. This is exactly what one finds in legal texts such as statutes and contracts. Due to the intrinsic character of vagueness, which has little to do with the text's wording and stylistics, linguistic context provides no clues for the clarification of vague words. Ambiguity, by

---

[17] This neologism, I assume, was coined by Zhang, *supra* n.13, at 27.

[18] T. Williamson, 'Vagueness, Indeterminacy and Social Meaning' (2001) 16 *Critical Studies* 61, at 61.

[19] See Devos, *supra* n.13, at 124.

contrast, in all of its forms, homonymy, polysemy, generality, structural ambiguity, referential ambiguity of indexical terms or demonstratives, is 'extrinsic' in the sense that it is the language packaging that causes the ambiguity and therefore can usually be disambiguated by linguistic context.[20] It is a matter of fact that in real communication, all or almost all potential ambiguities disappear. In other words, 'Although sentences can be ambiguous, utterances cannot. Each particular utterance of an expression is an utterance of it in a certain "way" that removes all ambiguity.'[21] When it comes to real communication, the status of ambiguity is completely different from vagueness. Ambiguity is always in need of disambiguation for the sake of successful communication. Vagueness may, most of the time, remain because it is mutually understood and accepted as such by both parties to the communication event. A simple example may clarify this point. If one says: *David is large*, the hearer must select the intended meaning from at least two of the polysemous meanings which the English language offers ("big", "generous"). Once the term is disambiguated, the speaker and hearer can understand each other even if they do not have the same opinion about the exact amount of the quality needed in order to be worthy of the title *large*.

The fuzzy boundaries of a vague term are frequently the cause of legal disputes.[22] The problem in these cases is not text or communication understanding, but application of terms or conceptual categories to particular cases. In these cases, pragmatic linguistics has nothing to contribute toward solving the problem of vagueness in a particular text. But if it becomes evident that the problem results from ambiguity and the interpreter has to choose the most likely alternative for the author's intended meaning, the pragmatic linguist's input may be of interest, at least for some of the parties concerned.

---

[20] See also Zhang, *supra* n.13, at 27 (who uses fuzziness for our vagueness, and vagueness for what we call polysemy): 'it follows that fuzziness may not be "defuzzified" by a linguistic context alone; whereas disambiguation, 'de-vaguefying', or 'de-generalization' could be done in and by a linguistic context. The reason is that it is difficult for human beings to reach an agreement on the referential applicability of fuzzy expressions."

[21] K. van Deemter, 'Towards a Logic of Ambiguous Expressions,' in K. van Deemter and S. Peters (eds.), *Semantic Ambiguity and Underspecification* (Stanford : CSLI Publication, 1996), at 203 .

[22] See L. M. Solan, 'Law, Language and Lenity' (1998) 40 *William and Mary Law Review* 57, at 78. But Solan, it seems, does not strictly differentiate between vagueness and generality.

If linguists cherish ambiguity because they may have good chance of finding convincing linguistic/pragmatic arguments for the adoption of one of the competitive alternatives, judges cherish vagueness because it opens the door widely for judicial discretion. Decker puts it this way:

> Vagueness analyses seem to me to be devoid of objective tests. Vagueness is a concept that appears heavily dependent on the "I know it when I see it" test, where one begins with a conclusion and thereafter works backward for rational support. Vagueness challenges require a highly subjective mode of analysis that involves an unpredictable assortment of paths a court might take in arriving at a ruling.[23]

We will see, in the two cases discussed below, that courts sometimes treat disputes over the meaning of words as if they were cases of vagueness in spite of the fact that the context clearly enables disambiguation, which proves that vagueness is not the problem.

3. The meaning of *rexev* ("vehicle")

According to an Israeli Act called Act of Compensation for Road-Accident Victims,[24] anyone who has been hurt in a road accident is entitled to receive compensation from a special insurance consortium created by the same law, regardless of insurance coverage for the guilty vehicle or responsibility of the driver. One of its articles defines the Hebrew term *rexev* ("vehicle") and *rexev meno'i* ("motor vehicle") as follows:

> A *rexev meno'i* or a *rexev* [is] a *rexev* propelled by mechanical force, including motorcycle with a side-car, three-wheel motorcycle, bicycle, and three-wheel bicycle with an auxiliary motor, and including vehicle towed or supported by a motor vehicle.[25]

The question that came before the Supreme Court was this: is a train or a locomotive a *rexev* or a *rexev meno'i* (a "vehicle" or a "motor vehicle")? The answer of the court was unanimously (three judges) affirmative: trains and locomotives are included in those terms.

The President of the Israeli Supreme Court, Aharon Barak, wrote, *inter alia*, the following:

> The clear purpose of the law is to cast liability – and parallelly, insurance obligation – due to any body-damage that was caused by the use of a motor

---

[23] J. F. Decker, 'Addressing Vagueness, Ambiguity, and Other Uncertainty in American Criminal Laws' (2002) 80 *Denver University Law Review* 241, at 243.

[24] All the translations from Hebrew to English in this paper are mine.

[25] Supreme Court Verdicts 35(2) 1981, at 64.

> vehicle, be it on a public road or on a private one, or none of them. Thus, for example, a motor vehicle that was built to move only in fields, mountains, seashore, or in courtyards of factories, and was not at all built to move on roadways, is certainly, in my opinion, included in the Act of Compensation. Though we may leave it under further consideration, the Haifa Carmelit (which moves under ground) or a cable-railway (that moves in air between to points on ground) are also within the scope of *'rexev meno'i'* despite the fact that they do not move, and were not built to move, on roadway.[26]

This is a magnificent example of purposivism. Purposivists look beyond the legislative intention in order to find the rationale of the law, and perhaps even how the law should have been conceived. Of course, no judge in the world, and certainly not Aharon Barak, would admit that he or she knows better than the legislature.

Barak goes on to say that the inclusion of trains as part of the notion of motor vehicle has linguistic grounds due to the vagueness of the notion, which permits him to distinguish between a core and penumbra zone.[27] Barak wrote:

> 6. It seems to me that the great majority of interpreters engaged in interpreting the law accept that some situations are undoubtedly included in a certain term, while others may or may not be included. We may call the first situation ... the core of the legal norm. We may call the other ones the 'relative penumbra zone'....
>
> 7. I think that every realistic jurist would assume that a 'private' car, a passenger' car, or a tractor is certainly a *rexev meno'i* as it is meant in the Act of Compensation. This is the core. Now we may ask if there is a difference between a train and the other three. What character does it have that they do not have, and is this difference of character significant in view of the purpose of the law? It seems that the only difference between these three vehicles, which are included in the core of the definition, and the locomotive, which is in the relative penumbra zone', is only that the locomotive runs on a fixed railway while the others do not run on a railway. Is this difference significant? In my opinion, the answer is in the negative ... It seems to me that no legitimate consideration of juridical policy can indicate that the fact that a locomotive runs on a rail way is essential to the extent that it should be excluded from the law.[28]

---

[26] Supreme Court Verdicts 35(2) 1981, at 67.
[27] A distinction that Hart popularized among jurists in his book H. L. A. Hart, *The Concept of Law* (Oxford: Clarendon Press, 1961).
[28] Supreme Court Verdicts 35(2) 1981, at 68-70.

My contention is that the question of whether or not trains can or cannot be included in the 'relative penumbra zone' of the term (or concept) *rexev meno'i* ("motor vehicle") is irrelevant to the interpretation of the given text as seen from a linguistic or pragmatic perspective. It is irrelevant because the text itself defines the term, and the definition, as we will see, inexplicitly excludes trains and locomotives.

The above statutory definition is composed of two parts. The first one is the equation sentence '*rexev meno'i* or a *rexev* [is] a *rexev* propelled by mechanical force'; the second part, the rest of the definition, enumerates some vehicles or means of transport that the lawmakers thought it right, for reasons that we will discuss below, to include as part of the definition. The equation sentence expresses an intensional definition, which is characterized by the formal structure of having a *definiendum* (that which is to be defined) on the left side of the equation, and the *definiens* (that which is defining) on the right side of the equation. What interests us is that the term *rexev* appears on both sides of the equation ('a *rexev* is a *rexev meno'i*'), first as the *definiendum* and then as the *genus* of the *definiens*. However, no circularity arises, since a post-modifier ('propelled by mechanical force') functions as the *differentia specificae*. This *differentia specificae* is necessary for defining the bare noun *rexev*, but adds nothing to the noun phrase *rexev meno'i*: the meaning of *meno'i* ("motorized") is equivalent to the *differentia specificae* 'propelled by mechanical force'. Our conclusion is, therefore, that the first part of the definition is relevant and necessary only for *rexev*, but not for *rexev meno'i*. The first part is necessary because the statute uses the terms *rexev* and *rexev meno'i* interchangeably. The first part tells us, then, that *rexev* and *rexev meno'i* mean the same: *rexev* 'propelled by mechanical force.'

Now, The Hebrew term *rexev* ("vehicle") is ambiguous and vague. It is ambiguous between designating a broad range of means of transport and a much more restricted one. The first meaning conforms to definitions of the kind one may find for the English equivalent term *vehicle*,[29] in this case, trains and locomotives are definitely included. The second, the restricted meaning, definitely excludes trains and locomotives. The terms *rexev* and *kli rexev* ("vehicle") and their two plural form *rexavim* and *kle*

---

[29] In Oxford English Dictionary Online (http://dictionary.oed.com/entrance.dtl) one finds two large definitions: '6. A means of conveyance provided with wheels or runners and used for the carriage of persons or goods; a carriage, cart, wagon, sledge, or similar contrivance. 7.a. Any means of carriage, conveyance, or transport; a receptacle in which anything is placed in order to be moved.'

rexev are the usual and everyday words for designating overland means of transport that run on wheels, especially motorcars and motorcycles.[30] No Modern Hebrew speaker, in everyday speech or writing, would use these words to refer to trains or locomotives.

The terms *rexev*, and consequently, *rexev meno'i*, are, quite naturally, vague in both of their two meanings. It is, therefore, not surprising that the statute gives its own definition for the purpose of the specific law. But we have already seen that the first part of it, the equation sentence, adds nothing to what we already know from *rexev meno'i* ("motor vehicle" = 'vehicle propelled by mechanical force'), except for the determination of the bare term *rexev* as being equal to the phrase *rexev meno'i*. The second part of the statutory definition, which looks like a further or additional part to the main (first) part of the definition, is in fact the key to the overall definition because one can learn from it that the meaning of *rexev* in the text is in accordance only with the narrow, every-day meaning of the word. Trains are not designated by the narrow meaning, nor are they introduced by the second part of the definition.

We repeat here the entire definition:

> A *rexev meno'i* or a *rexev* [is] a *rexev* propelled by mechanical force, including motorcycle with a side-car, three-wheel motorcycle, bicycle, and three-wheel bicycle with an auxiliary motor, and including vehicle towed or supported by a motor vehicle.

If by '*rexev* propelled by mechanical force' the statute means any means of transport propelled by mechanical force (the broad meaning), why was it necessary to include such means of transport as 'motorcycle with a side-car, three-wheel motorcycle'? Are they not already included together with train and other motor vehicles in the broad sense? Only if the meaning of the word is restricted, in accordance with its everyday use, is it reasonable to add as part of the statutory definition a phrase that explicitly includes means of transport that are not part of the core zone of the restricted everyday meaning of the word. Indeed, motorcycle with a side-car and three-wheel motorcycle with an auxiliary motor are not part of the core of *rexev meno'i*, and therefore it makes sense to explicitly include them together with bicycle, which is certainly out of the core zone. Now, if

---

[30] The widely recognized dictionary for Modern Hebrew, the Even-Shoshan Dictionary, gives the following definition for *kli rexev*: 'A general noun for all overland means of transport that runs on wheels, such as wagons, bicycles, motorcars, motorcycles.' (*Even-Shoshan Dictionary* (Israel: Ha-Millon Hexadash, 2003).

the statute's meaning of *rexev* is in accordance with the everyday use of the word and, according to the court, the legislature's purpose was to include trains and locomotives, one cannot understand why the inclusion phrase does not explicitly introduce them since, according to the court itself, they do not belong to the core zone.

It seems, therefore, that if one wishes to understand the statutory definition according to clues provided by the definition itself, the inescapable conclusion is that it inexplicitly excludes trains and locomotives.[31] But the court, it seems, is not bound by such pragmatic considerations. It can decide that the dispute over the meaning of a term can or must be solved by what the court perceives as the purpose of the legal text. The purpose, which is extraneous to the text itself in the sense that it is something that may or may not be inferred from the text itself (intention), determines the outcome of the interpretation dispute; not pragmatic considerations. The court preferred to exercise its judicial discretion, based on the assumption of knowing the purpose of the text, instead of finding a solution by looking closely at the local meaning of the most important part of the text that concerns the interpretation dispute, which is in the case under discussion, the statutory definition. This *tour de force* was possible only because the disputed term *rexev* was indeed vague as a term out of context, but once the term is looked upon in its context, which is the specific statutory definition, vagueness disappears, not because the definition de-vaguefies the term, but because it makes clear that the disputed objects (trains and locomotives) were not in the first place part of the intended meaning of the term. Between the two separate meanings, the broad meaning and the narrow one, one is obliged to opt for the second because. As we have seen, one cannot accommodate a broad meaning, which encompasses all means of transport, with the second part of the statutory definition, the one that starts with the word 'including.' Disregarding linguistic context allows interpreters to ponder core and penumbra zones of terms and concepts as if they were the real problem. This anti-pragmatic way of interpreting terms is even more pronounced when the word is, out of context, ambiguous, because in this case, interpreters can choose a meaning at will and then exercise the contemplation of core and penumbra zones.

---

[31] The Knesset later amended the Act of Compensation in several ways and, *inter alia*, trains and locomotives were explicitly included in the definition of *rexev*. The Knesset, then, accepted the logic of the verdict, but rejected the interpretation of *rexev* and *rexev meno'i* as linguistically including trains and locomotives.

4. The meaning of *use of firearm*

The tendency to examine the meaning of words by contemplating the conceptual categories they denote, which are most of the time without clear-cut boundaries, instead of looking more seriously into the linguistic context, is not unique to the Israeli Supreme Court.

In a well-known case, *Smith v. United States*,[32] the issue was whether the exchange of a machine gun for narcotics constituted a 'use' of a firearm 'during and in relation to ... drug trafficking crime.' The statute imposes a five-year prison term when a gun is so used, and if the weapon is a machine gun, the mandatory sentence is thirty years. The defendant offered to trade a MAC-10 machine gun to an undercover federal agent for two ounces of cocaine. He was convicted of conspiracy to possess and distribute cocaine, and of using the machine gun in relation to the conspiracy, in violation of 924(c)(1). On appeal, Smith argued that trading a gun was not among the 'uses of a firearm' as defined by the statute.

Justice Sandra Day O'Connor, joined by five other Justices, found that giving a gun for acquiring drugs is 'use of a firearm' within the meaning of section 924(c) (1). A three-Justice minority, led by Justice Antonin Scalia, concluded that it is not. In her majority opinion, Justice O'Connor argued that the ordinary meaning of 'use of a firearm' included situations in which a gun was employed to further some end. For authority, she cited definitions from Webster's Second Dictionary and Black's Law Dictionary as well as the meaning Congress gave the word in other parts of section 924, and from dicta in a 109-year-old Supreme Court case, each defining 'use' in terms of employing or deriving service from an instrument. O'Connor concluded that section 924(c)(1) applied to gun-for-drugs trades because such swaps employ firearms as items of barter; Smith had derived service from the weapon 'because it was going to bring him the very drugs he sought.' O'Connor goes on, arguing: 'After all, Congress never said that the statute did not apply to gun-for-drugs swaps. Had Congress intended the narrow construction petitioner urges, it could have so indicated.'[33]

Justice Scalia, on the other hand, argued that by simply reciting dictionary definitions, the majority had determined the possible meanings of use but not its 'ordinary' meaning. In Scalia's view, the ordinary meaning of using an instrument was 'to use it for its intended purpose' – in

---

[32] 113 S. Ct. 2050 (1993).
[33] *Smith v. United States* (91-8674), 508 U.S. 223 (1993).

the case of a machine gun, using it as a weapon. By contrast, the majority's sweeping conception of 'use' would extend section 924(c)(1) to include unlikely employments of firearms that, lacking more specific language, Congress could not have intended to criminalize.

Scalia takes into consideration, at least to some degree, the linguistic context of the phrase *use of firearm*. O'Connor, much like Barak, completely disregards it. O'Connor seems to believe that words' meanings remain the same in any context, but reality tells us that readers and listeners must constantly cope with changes of meanings caused by ever-changing circumstances. It may be of interest to note that a textualist such as O'Connor and a purposivist such as Barak share the same practice of, first, disregarding context, and secondly, adopting some wide intensional definition or conceptual category. Textualists base their arguments on dictionaries and precedents, purposivists on what they conceive as the purpose of the legal text, but eventually, the two approaches finish by contemplating the wide definition or conceptual category and its application to a particular case. Once having a wide definition or concept, the door is open for wide judicial discretion. The only justification interpreters may have for ignoring the linguistic context, which, after all, is universally recognized as crucial for determining the meanings of words, is to claim, explicitly or implicitly, that the indeterminacy at stake is a matter of vagueness, in which local linguistic considerations are of no help.

But is Smith a case of vagueness? In my opinion, it is not, because one can easily find a reasonable solution by closely looking at the linguistic context. Here is the relevant part of the statute:

> Whoever, during and in relation to any crime of violence or drug trafficking crime (including a crime of violence or drug trafficking crime which provides for an enhanced punishment if committed by the use of a deadly or dangerous weapon or device) for which he may be prosecuted in a court of the United States, uses or carries a firearm, shall, in addition to the punishment provided for such crime of violence or drug trafficking crime, be sentenced to imprisonment for five years, and if the firearm is a short-barreled rifle, short-barreled shotgun to imprisonment for ten years, and if the firearm is a machinegun, or a destructive device, or is equipped with a firearm silencer or firearm muffler, to imprisonment for thirty years.[34]

---

[34] J. Polich, 'The Ambiguity of Plain Meaning: Smith v. United States and the New Textualism' (1994) 68 *Southern Californian Law Review* 259, at 259 n.4, quoting from 18 U.S.C. 924(c)(1) (1988 & Supp. III 1991).

For one trying to understand the text using linguistic and pragmatic competence, it is more than likely that the statute was not meant to include cases in which the *use of firearms* is accomplished by providing a firearm as part of a drug-firearm barter.

The use of firearm is, in a similar way as *rexev*, ambiguous in at least two ways: the large meaning as suggested by Justice O'Connor, and the narrow meaning, as suggested by Justice Scalia. One must opt for the narrow meaning, not because of the specific complement ('firearm') of the verb 'use', but because of the larger context. The phrase *use of firearm* is itself ambiguous in the two same ways. The relevant larger linguistic context is the types of firearm the statute considers to be used or carried in relation to the crime and the differentiation of punishment the statute makes for the various types of firearm that may be used during and in relation to a crime. The types of firearm used determine the degree of punishment. The more lethal or of the kind of weapon typically used by criminals it is, the longer the imprisonment. Looking at the relationship between the use of firearm and the punishment, one must conclude that 'use or carries a firearm' in this context does not include giving a firearm as an item of barter. It simply makes no sense to impose an additional punishment of five-year imprisonment if the item of barter is, for example, ten thousand ordinary pistols, but thirty years of imprisonment if the item of barter is one single machinegun or one single pistol 'equipped with a firearm silencer or firearm muffler.'

By acknowledging the rationale of the graduated punishment, one cannot but conclude that the meaning of 'uses or carries a firearm' in the context of 'during and in relation to any crime of violence or drug trafficking crime' falls along the lines of Scalia's narrow meaning: 'to use it for its intended purpose.' It is simply against the rationale of the statute, which clearly targets dangerous criminals who use or carry a variety of firearms as weapons to protect themselves against other criminals or police, rather than using them as items of barter.

Disregard of linguistic context can be found even among linguists. Solan, who comments on Smith, distinguishes between what he calls the 'definition' approach to word meaning and the 'prototype' approach, and opts for the latter. I have no quarrel with him about this issue *per se*. But when he describes the difference of opinions between O'Connor and Scalia as examples of the two approaches, I conclude that Solan too prefers to see the interpretation dispute over *use of firearm* as a case of vagueness. Solan writes:

> O'Connor and Scalia each applied her/his analysis reasonably. That is, swapping a machinegun for drugs really is a 'use' of a machinegun, but it is a very peculiar one, in all likelihood remote from the core concept that motivated Congress to enact the statute and the President to sign it. The issue, then, is not which analysis is performed more competently, but which kind of analysis courts should use ... Typically, but not always, the definitional approach will lead to broad interpretation and the prototypical approach will lead to narrower interpretation.[35]

The problem with this view is that no attempt is made to examine the linguistic context in order to find the meaning that best suits the overall message of the text. Both the definitional approach and the prototypical one are de-vaguefying approaches, which are of no use if the interpretation dispute can be solved by taking seriously the entire available context. Disambiguation, which is choosing between two possible meanings, comes before de-vaguefying because disambiguation, but not de-vaguefying, is crucial for the understanding of the text. De-vaguefying a term by using one approach or another is possible only if the term is understood in a certain, unambiguous way; it cannot replace a process of disambiguation that can be done by paying attention to context.

The conclusion that one can draw from all this is that controversies over the interpretation of words and phrases in legal texts are sometimes treated by courts as if they were cases of vagueness, while they could have been treated and solved by carefully looking at the entire text. Trying to de-vaguefy or to apply a definition on a particular case that can find solution on the basis of linguistic context is an anti-pragmatic move.

---

[35] M. L. Solan, 'Judicial Decisions and Linguistic Analysis: Is There a Linguist in the Court?' (1995) 73 *Washington University Law Quarterly* 1069, at 1076.

PART III

APPLICATION OF LAW IN POLITICAL PRACTICE

CHAPTER 8

The Inclusive/Exclusive Nation: Blacks and Indigenous Peoples in the Construction of the Nation in Colombia

Farid Samir Benavides Vanegas

University of Massachusetts, Amherst, USA

In the second half of the 19th century, Lord Acton identified three ideas that subverted three central principles of modern Europe: Egalitarianism which subverted the principle of aristocracy, communism the principle of property, and nationalism the principle of legitimacy. As Wallerstein has shown, those ideas mirrored the way social sciences were shaped at the end of the 19th century. The principle of aristocracy was related to the social field, property to the economic one, and legitimacy to the political one.[1] Those subversive ideas were developed during modernity and are said to have configured the world in which we now live.[2] They were the result of Revolutions, but just one of them completely changed the face of the world. The French Revolution and its idea of egalitarianism did not go beyond a formal idea without any real application. The communist revolution, which could be understood as a way of correcting the flaws of the French one, did not last more than 70 years and did not bring the elimination of private property, not even in the Soviet camp.[3] The only one that transformed the

---

[1] Immanuel Wallerstein. Open the Social Sciences: Report of the Gulbenkian Foundation on the Restructuring of the Social Sciences (Stanford: California University Press, 1996).

[2] Benedict Anderson. 'Introduction', in Gopal Balakrishnan, *Mapping the Nation.* (London: Verso, 2000).

[3] The life of Marxist legal theorist Eugevny Pashukanis is a good example of this failure, a firm believer that with the elimination of private property the law would disappear, he did not see the danger of sustaining the elimination of the commodity form in a state that had to live within a capitalist world. See Steven Spitzer, 'Marxist Perspectives in the Sociology of Law', *Ann. Rev. Sociol* (1983) 9:103-24 and Piers Beirne and Robert Sharlet (comps), *Pashukanis: Selected Writings on Marxism and Law* (London: Academic Press, 1980).

A. Wagner et al. (eds.), Interpretation, Law and the Construction of Meaning, 141–168.

face of the world was the nationalist Revolution. The world in which we live today is understood along the lines of nation and nationalism.

Despite this agreement on the modern character of nationalism, there has been discussion about the relationship between nationalism and the nation. To some scholars, like Anthony Marx, the nation is the result of the religious struggles in the process of state building in Europe.[4] From this point of view, the nation has a primordialist character and the struggle is about how a nation achieves statehood. This perspective is best summarized in the works of John Stuart Mill, who thought that every nation should live in one state in order to avoid confrontation. One nation, one state, is the idea behind the modern configuration of the state.[5] To others, based on Benedict Anderson's seminal work, the nation cannot be understood without nationalism, that is, there are no primordial communities fighting for statehood. From this perspective, the nation is a community that is imagined in nationalist struggles. As Anderson puts it, the nation is 'an imagined political community – and imagined as both inherently limited and sovereign'.[6]

In his analysis of the nation as an imagined community, Benedict Anderson denounces the conception of nationhood and nationalism as European ideas that were spread around the world. To him, this is Eurocentrism, because in other parts of the world, like in the Latin American case, we find struggles for nation and nationalism that are not related to European nationalism. Anderson is right in considering that these approaches are too centred on European history, because they assume that the modern character of the nation can be explained only from European history without taking into consideration the existence of America and the relationships between Europe and its colonies. From this perspective, the otherness of Europe, which was the base of European nationalism, had to

---

[4] Anthony W. Marx, *Faith in the Nation. Exclusionary Origins of Nationalism.* (Oxford: Oxford University Press, 2003).

[5] John Stuart Mill, *Essays on England, Ireland and the Empire* (Toronto and Buffalo: University of Toronto Press/Routledge and Kegan Paul, 1982); John Stuart Mill. *Considerations on Representative Government.* (Chicago: Regnery, 1962); John Emerich Edward Dalberg-Acton. *Lectures on Modern History* (London/New York: Macmillan and Co. Limited, 1906); John Emerich Edward Dalberg-Acton. *The History of Freedom and other Essays* (London: Macmillan and Co. Limited, 1907).

[6] Benedict Anderson, *Imagined Communities* (London: Verso, 2003), at 6.

be found within Europe and at most in the Orient.[7] Anderson recognizes that there were other political groupings in Latin America that existed before 19th century European nationalism. However, he applies European concepts to the configuration of the nation in Latin America, without taking into account the coloniality of power existing before and after the construction of the nation. To him, the nation that was developed in Latin America is an imagined community which was all-inclusive, serving as a model for the rest of the world. To summarize, Anderson's analysis of the nation is no less Eurocentric than other analysis of nationalism that he labels as such.[8]

What is missing in his analysis of the nation and nationalism is an alternative understanding of modernity that we find in Dussel's and Quijano's work. For the former, modernity cannot be understood without taking into account the fact of the discovery of America. [9] For the latter, the question of the coloniality of power has to be taken into account in order to be able to understand nationalism. To Quijano, 'State formations in Europe and the Americas are linked and distinguished by coloniality of power'.[10]

The history of Colombian struggle for independence supports Dussel's and Quijano's critique of the Eurocentric character of traditional interpretations of the nation and nationalism in Latin America. In this paper I want to show that Colombian struggles for independence are not initially struggles for nationhood but a struggle for equality within the Spanish nation. That is, we cannot understand the Latin American nation-building process without considering the relationships between the Spaniards in

---

[7] I use the word Orient to convey the idea expressed by Edward Said. See Edward Said, *Orientalism* (New York: Pantheon Books, 1978).

[8] I use Carl Schmitt's idea of a political grouping, that is, one based on the dichotomy between friend and enemy, that he sees as the foundation of the political. However, I add the dialectic of inclusion/exclusion that is based on the analysis of capitalism and feudalism in Latin America made by Ruy Mauro Marini and Rodolfo Stavenhagen. See Rodolfo Stavenhagen, Ernesto Laclau & Ruy Mauro Marini. *Tres ensayos sobre America Latina* (Barcelona: Editorial Anagrama, 1980).

[9] Enrique Dussel (1492), El encubrimiento del otro. El origen del mito de la modernidad (Bogota: Anthropos, 1992); Etica de la Liberacion en la edad de la globalizacion y de la exclusion (Madrid: Trotta, 1998), and The Underside of Modernity: Apel, Ricoeur Rorty, Taylor and the Philosophy of Liberation (New Jersey: Humanities Press, 1996).

[10] Anibal Quijano, 'Coloniality of Power, Eurocentrism, and Latin America' *Nepantla Views from the South,* 1.3 (2000), 557.

Spain and the Spaniards in America. This process became, later on, a process for nationhood, but the nation that was proposed is too inclusive on the one hand, because it referred to a mythical *Nuestra America,* and too exclusive on the other hand, because it excluded Indians and blacks from the new nation. I show in this paper that this process of inclusion/exclusion has to be understood along the lines of racial definitions and racial hierarchies.

By showing Colombian fights for independence in 19th century, I want to show that the nation, as an imagined community of equals, formed no part of the discourse of the leaders of these movements. David Bushnell has written that this was a process for Nation Statehood but not for cultural nationhood. However it is more adequate to say that it was a process for the construction of an inclusive/exclusive nation, in which the relations of the colony were replicated in the new Republic. [11]

To understand this process we need to determine the purpose of the fighters for independence. Contrary to Anderson's account of the Latin American case, this paper will show that indigenous peoples and people of African descent were included/excluded from the nation. In order to show this process I want to show the *long duree* of state building in Colombia. Without the exclusion that was at the base of the coloniality of power existing in Colombia, it is impossible to understand the configuration of the Colombian nation.[12]

In the first section I will discuss the question of modernity in Latin America. In the second part I will show the coloniality of power by focusing on the configuration of indigenous peoples and Afro descendants in the juridical discourse of the conquerors, which was part of the discourse of the Republic. In the third part I will show how this discourse was relevant in the configuration of the Republic. The grouping of Afro descendants and Indigenous peoples can be understood from a different point of view, by asking the same question that Chattterjee asks: whose imagined community are we talking about when we say that there is a Colombian imagined community that we call the Colombian nation?[13]

---

[11] David Bushnell, *The Making of Modern Colombia: A Nation in Spite of Itself* (Berkeley/Los Angeles/Oxford: University of California Press, 1993).
[12] Quijano, *supra* n. 10.
[13] Partha Chatterjee, 'Whose Imagined Community', in Balakrishnan, *supra* n.2. See also Partha Chatterjee, *The Politics of the Governed* (New York: Columbia University Press, 2004).

1. Modernity and the management of centrality

Modernity has been defined as the search for the *new* and as the product of European experience. In the Philosophical Discourse of Modernity, Habermas analyzes the philosophical character of modernity and shows how the moderns defined it.[14] According to this account, modernity is the epoch that followed antiquity, and one in which nature was freed from its sacred character and became one that could be used as object of research.[15] Given that modernity is an epoch that desacralizes everything, political power became desacralized too. Traditional forms of legitimation were replaced by legitimation based on popular will. The French Revolution brought about a new way of legitimacy that put into question the principle of aristocracy. Given that the people became the source of legitimacy, a new concept appeared in the discourse of the French revolutionaries. This is the discourse of the Nation as the representative of the people and as the public sphere that mediates between the state and the private sphere of individuals.[16]

However, according to Enrique Dussel, modernity is not the result of internal processes of European medieval cities, but rather the result of the discovery of America, whereby Europe not only became the center of the capitalist world system, but also when Europe had the Other that made possible the process of construction of an identity. To Dussel, the existent interpretation of this process is based on a Eurocentric conception. To Dussel, the experience of the discovery of America is the central element in the constitution of European subjectivity.[17]

Dussel puts it in the following way:

> The first concept is Eurocentric, provincial, and regional. Modernity is an emancipation, a Kantian *Ausgang*, or 'way out,' from immaturity by means of reason, understood as a critical process that affords humanity the possibility of new development. In Europe, this process took place mainly

---

[14] Jurgen Habermas. The Philosophical discourse of modernity. Twelve Lectures. (Cambridge: MIT Press, 1987).

[15] Heidegger shows how European modernity can be seen as a time in which the world became image, that is to say, it was constructed from the subject, who did not contemplate anymore and now intervened in nature. Martin Heideggüer. 'The age of the world picture'. In Martin Heidegger. *The question concerning technology and other essays.* (New York: Harper and Row, 1977).

[16] Habermas. The structural transformation of the public sphere: an inquiry into a category of Bourgeois society. (Cambridge, Mass.: MIT press, 1989).

[17] Dussel. *1492.* Supra n. 9.

> during the eighteenth century. The temporal and spatial dimensions of this phenomenon were described by Hegel and commented on by Jürgen Habermas in his classic work on modernity. Habermas's narrative, unanimously accepted by contemporary European tradition, posits, 'The key historical events for the creation of the principle of [modern] subjectivity are the Reformation, the Enlightenment, and the French Revolution.' As can readily be observed, a spatial-temporal sequence is followed here. Furthermore, other cultural processes are usually added to this sequence as well, from the Italian Renaissance and the German Reformation to the Enlightenment. In a conversation with Paul Ricoeur, Habermas suggested that the English Parliament should also be included. Thus the sequence would run from Italy (fifteenth century) to Germany (sixteenth to eighteenth century) to England (seventeenth century) to France (eighteenth century). I label this perspective 'Eurocentric,' for it indicates intra-European phenomena as the starting point of modernity and explains its later development without making recourse to anything outside of Europe. In a nutshell, this is the provincial, regional view that ranges from Max Weber (I have in mind here his analysis on 'rationalization' and the 'disenchantment of worldviews') to Habermas. For many, Galileo (condemned in 1616), Francis Bacon (*Novum Organum*, 1620), or Descartes (*Discourse on Method*, 1636) could be considered the forebears of the process of modernity in the seventeenth century.[18]

To Dussel, there is an alternative approach to modernity that shows that in the constitution of European identity the central character is the presence of the Other. However, European identity was based not on a presence that is visible, but rather in a presence that is absent. In Spanish Dussel has referred to this not as a process of discovery of the other (*descubrimiento del otro*) but as a process of covering up of the other (*encubrimiento del otro*). This *encubrimiento* will be seen in the debate about the conquest and how indigenous peoples and Africans were constituted as non-presences, that is to say, they were constituted as entities that were covered up and analyzed through European eyes. This same *encubrimiento* would mark the development of the nation in the new Republics. In this way, the nation as a modern concept will be based on a dialectic of *descubrimiento/encubrimiento* that I label as a dialectic of inclusion/exclusion.

---

[18] Enrique Dussel. 'Europe, Modernity and Eurocentrism'. *Nepantla: View from the South 1:3* (2000), aAt 469.

2. Coloniality of Power and Eurocentrism

The modern world system is based on the management of centrality by Europe, that is, the process whereby Europe became the centre of the World System and by which America became its periphery. According to Dussel, the central role of Europe cannot be conceived without America being conceived as its periphery. However, in order for Europe to become central it was necessary to construct it as a colonial power culturally superior to the colonized. As Balibar shows, we cannot understand race without racism.[19] In the same way, the centrality of Europe has been based on the construction of Europeans along racial lines. The conquerors of America thought of themselves as having the right of conquest in the Americas and to the right to subjugate her peoples. The colonization of America was possible, in the juridical discourse, because the conquerors, especially those from the *School of Salamanca*, thought that Spain had a right to conquer and subjugate these peoples, because there was a just cause that made the war of conquest a legitimate one. The dispute about slavery and the rights of the indigenous peoples is read within this framework. However, what is at stake is their westernization, that is, their conversion into western subjects able to be dominated by colonial powers.

Based on this understanding of the colony, Anibal Quijano finds that the identity of Portuguese, Spaniards and Europeans can only be understood by taking into account the racial differentiations between Europe and the rest. 'In other words, race and racial identity were established as instruments of basic social classification'.[20] This racial classification made possible not only the exclusion of slaves from the colonial society as non-subjects but also the exclusion of the indigenous peoples as half way between slaves and subjects with full rights. In the same way, due to territorial belonging there was a classification and hierarchy of those born in the Americas and those who were born in Europe. After independence, as we shall see later, the incorporation of indigenous peoples and Africans was possible only under the category of *worker*, and not under the category of *citizen*. Given the racial classification of subjects in the Americas, whites were seen as privileged, because they were the only ones with the right of access to capital and it was this access to capital that made possible their identification as members of the polity.

---

[19] Etienne Balibar and Immanuel Wallerstein, *Race, Nation, Class: Ambiguous Identities* (London: Verso, 1991).
[20] Quijano. Supra n. 10 at 534.

This centralization of global capitalism around Europe was relevant not only in the European management of centrality, but also in the constitution of identities in the Americas. In fact, the process of state building in Colombia, and this could be extended to the Americas generally, was based on the inclusion/exclusion of Africans and indigenous peoples. The coloniality of power in these countries repressed the indigenous knowledge, practices, and subjectivity and, on the other hand, it imposed European forms of knowledge and political practices. Amongst the elements of the coloniality of power we find the imposition of models of political grouping existent in Europe. The particular political grouping that we call the nation was part of the American experience, but not as an imagined community of equals but rather as a political grouping of unequals, where indigenous peoples and Africans were excluded as non wage earners in the capitalist system.[21]

For Anibal Quijano, one of the elements that show in a better way the tragedy of the coloniality of power is the question of nation and state building and the question of the Nation-State. As Quijano writes, 'a modern nation-state involves the modern institutions of citizenship and political democracy, but only in the way in which citizenship can function as legal, civil, and political equality for socially unequal people'.[22] According to Quijano, it is not enough to imagine a community, because to create a nation the members of the nation need to have something in common that allows them to imagine their political grouping as a nation. As he shows for the Southern Cone, the process of construction of the nation state involved the inclusion/exclusion of indigenous peoples and Africans. The 'nation' in these countries was a political grouping that was based on the inclusion of those peoples as workers but also on their exclusion as citizens. Quijano puts it in the following way: 'Homogenization was achieved not by means of the fundamental democratization of social and political relations, but by the exclusion of a significant part of the population, one that since the

---

[21] Quijano shows how the identity of the different indigenous peoples that lived in the territory of what is today called the Americas was conflated as Indians, and I would add as Native-Americans. For peoples coming from Africa the label was blacks, Negroes, or African Americans. Quijano *supra* n. 10, at 551. See also Devon Carbado for a critique of the dichotomy Black/White in the analysis of racism in the United States. Devon Carbado, 'Critical Race Theory: Race to the Bottom' 49 *UCLA Law Review 1215-1686* (June 2002).

[22] Quijano, *supra* n. 10, at 557.

sixteenth century had been racially classified and marginalized from citizenship and democracy'.[23]

In this way, the process of political grouping in Latin America could not be considered a process of nation building in the sense Anderson understands it, not only due to the lack of democratization but also because of the particular configurations of inclusion/exclusion that the coloniality of power brought about. The loyalty to a political grouping did not achieve the same form that it did in Europe because in the process of nation building in Europe the dialectic of inclusion/exclusion involved two different groups: The inclusion of the people of the nation meant the exclusion of Others, but it was those excluded who were the reference point for the identity of the nation. In the case of Spain, this process involved radical exclusion, and in France and England involved internal exclusion that was not defined in racial terms, therefore it allowed for the group to be included on equal terms as long as it shared the traits of the 'nation'.[24] In the analysis of the construction of the European nation, the fact of the coloniality of power is not taken into account, because what happened in the Americas was perceived as not having anything to do with political processes in Europe. The Colombian case will show that the coloniality of power is an element that has to be analyzed when considering the nation.

3. The Nation as an Imagined Community

As I mentioned at the beginning of this paper, there were three ideas that were putting the status quo in Europe into question. One of them was nationalism. To some authors, nationalism was the awakening of the nation. Even for Ernest Gellner, although nationalism was the product of industrialization, there were some instances in which the nation would wake up and claim its statehood. The nation has been identified as a typical European concept that has spread around the world, in the same way that modernity has done it.

To Miroslav Hroch, the nation is the product of a long and complicated process of historical development in Europe. The process lived through in Europe allows him to identify three elements that are central to understanding the process of nation building. They are:

---

[23] Quijano, *supra* n. 10, at 564.

[24] See Rogers Brubaker, *Citizenship and Nation in France and Germany.* (Cambridge: Harvard University Press, 1992); Marx, *supra* n.4.; and Anibal Quijano, *Reencuentro y Debate. Una Introduccion a Mariategui* (Lima: Mosca Azul Editores, 1981).

1) A memory of some common past, treated as a 'destiny' of the group –or at least of its core constituents;

2) a density of linguistic or cultural ties enabling a higher degree of social communication within the group than beyond it;

3) a conception of the equality of all members of the group organized as civil society.[25]

By analyzing the process in Europe, Hroch determines that different stages in which the process of nation building can be made. All the elements that are identified in Hroch's article about the nation are elements that belong to the historical process of nation building in Europe. In Hroch's defense, we could say that he is not attempting to explain a process in a different part of the world, and therefore to accuse him of being Eurocentric would be to simply state just his field of analysis. Although such a critique could be made, what is relevant for the purposes of this paper is precisely that Hroch assumes the national when he writes that nationalism is a form of national consciousness. However in his analysis he takes into account processes not only internal to Europe but also internal to national formation. In this way, when he explains the process of construction of the nation in the Czech Republic ,he does not take into account the position of this country in the world system and assumes that there is already a national formation wherein national consciousness arises. This is evident when he defines the elements of successful national movements, including a crisis of legitimacy, vertical social mobility, high level of social communication, and nationally relevant conflicts of interest.

Despite the different appreciation of the national movement and nationalism, we find in Gellner a similar Eurocentric conception of the nation. To Gellner, the nation is not a political unit but a cultural unit that is in search of a political form. The combination of sovereignty and culture is the Nation State. To Gellner this combination is a modern product and specifically is the result of industrialization where the culture of the elites becomes the culture of an entire society. What is characteristic of this process is that this kind of society requires a process of homogenization of culture, that is, a process whereby the high culture incorporates all the members of society. However, what Gellner does not mention is that this process needs to be made through the oppression or suppression of at least some people's cultures. This is a process in which, according to Gellner, all

---

[25] Miroslav Hroch, 'From National Movement to the Fully-formed Nation: the Nation-building Process in Europe', in Balakrishnan *supra* n. 2, at 79.

cultures are in competition and at the end one of them wins the allegiance of the masses. Gellner writes,

> The state-cultures live in competition with each other. So this is the end product: a mobile, atomized, egalitarian society with a standard culture, where the culture is a literate, 'high' one, and where its dissemination, maintenance and boundaries are protected by a state. Stated even more briefly: one culture, one state. One state, one culture.[26]

To Gellner the period of nationalism is one in which cultures are striving to obtain the protection of the state, and this process has proven to be a bloody one.

Although Gellner recognizes the constructed character of the nation, the process that he explains is based on the European experience, where some groups were fighting for the protection of the state. However, in the Latin American case what he shows as competition – and this seems not even to be the case in Europe – is just a process of exclusion of groups from the polity, in order not to allow them citizenship and neither, therefore, the protection of the state. But this process also involves a process by which these groups were constituted as subjects and as workers in order to facilitate their capitalist exploitation as living labor. Although Gellner sees nationalism as a bloody process in which some groups are eliminated, the experiences he is showing are European experiences. From this point of view we could say that European nationalism presents these features, or that nationalism, as a European product constituted on the basis of a coloniality of power is necessarily a bloody product because of its configuration of inclusion/exclusion.

Hroch and Gellner explain the nation in different terms. However what they hold in common is that their conception of the nation does not take into account their European character and the different configuration that it had when it was applied in other places of the world.[27] These

---

[26] Ernest Gellner, 'The Coming of Nationalism and its Interpretations: the Myths of Nation and Class', *supra* n. 2, at 111.

[27] Norbu explains the Eurocentric character of the studies on nationalism. He writes that: 'ever since then - that is Renan's work- the term nationalism came to be equated with the modern political doctrine of popular sovereignty, and any nationalism that does not have this pronounced democratic bias is called 'culturalism' or 'traditionalism', as is often described in the case of early Chinese, Indian or Arab nationalism'. Dawa Norbu, *Culture and the politics of Third World Nationalism* (London: Routledege, 1991), at 7. Although I agree that there other forms of political grouping in the so-called Third World, I think that by terming

processes are shown in the analysis of the struggles against colonialism. The bourgeoisie supports the nation state as part of the political grouping after independence, but the fact that the bourgeoisie supports a nation state does not support an idea of a national culture independently from the process of exclusion/inclusion brought about by the coloniality of power. [28]

One question that arises from the discussion about the nation and nationalism is that of the nature of the nation. From a primordialist point of view, the nation would be a pre-existent community of people with similar history and ethnic backgrounds. This ethnic or religious community exists previously and independently of the state and it is fighting for the protection of the state. However, as Benedict Anderson has shown, it is impossible to talk about the nation without talking about nationalism. As an imagined community, the nation is the product of discourses and practices that are created in the process of fighting for it. The nations appear to replace the old communities that constituted the main groupings before the appearance of the nation-state. Pietro Barcellona has shown that this new community is imagined as equal and as a promise. Due to the formal character of this community, its promises remained unfulfilled.[29] The Nation to Anderson appeared to align with the large cultural systems that preceded it, like religious communities and the dynastic realm. It is this 'ancient' character of the nation, a sort of nostalgia of the present, that made it become the main grouping in modernity and the reason why Anderson can say that people would die in modern times for the nation in the same way the had died for their religious communities.[30] The main drive that made it possible for people living in different parts of a territory to identify themselves as part of one nation was print capitalism, that is, the printed word made possible the imposition of high culture onto the masses,

---

them nationalist means to accept the terms of political grouping in European political thought. However, in this paper I want to show that nationalism and the nation as a community of equals was not constructed in terms of equality but rather of exclusion. The fact that we call it nationalism is to show that even European nationalism is based on this exclusion, because as a European concept is based on the coloniality of power.

[28] Franz Fanon, *The Wretched of the Earth* (New York: Grover Weidenfeld, 1991).

[29] Pietro Barcellona, *Il ritorno del legame sociale* (Torino: Bollati Boringhieri, 1990).

[30] Anderson, *supra* n. 6 at 12.

and the possibility of the masses having their own cultural production, due to the existence of a vernacular.[31] Anderson puts it in the following way:

> Why this transformation should be so important for the birth of the imagined community of the nation can best be seen if we consider the basic structure of two forms of imagining which first flowered in Europe in the eighteenth century: the novel and the newspaper. For these forms provided the technical means for re-presenting the kind of imagined community that is the nation.[32]

In these cultural products, Anderson finds authors writing for a community that is being imagined in the novels or the newspapers as a homogenous community, as people who share at least the idea of being imagined.

Benedict Anderson criticizes the Eurocentrism present in most analysis of nationalism. He shows that these analyses consider nationalism as a European invention. According to Anderson, nationalism and its imagination of communities appear for the first time in the new world and is in no way related to the processes existent in Europe at the time. He finds that Creoles in Latin America can be considered pioneers of this new form of imagination. The process that was developed in Latin America, according to Anderson, was different from the one lived in Europe, because there were no different languages that made possible the distinction between communities, and yet, to him, the movement of independence was a national independence movement. According to him, Bolivar and San Martin considered slaves and indigenous peoples as part of the polity that were being imagined in the process of independence. Anderson cites as support of his argument the declaration made by San Martin in 1821, in which he said, 'in the future the aborigines shall not be called Indians or natives; they are children and citizens of Peru and they shall be known as Peruvians'.[33] What is striking to Anderson is the fact that these places did not share any of the features of European nationalism and yet they were national movements. One way to explain this is by appealing to the relations between Spain and the colonies; another, and that preferred by Anderson, is to take into account the administrative separation of the colonies that made possible its future existence and independent political

---

[31] The case of detective novel in England is a good example of how this was made. See Farid Samir Benavides Vanegas, *Derecho y Nacion.* (Bogota: Editorial Juridica Ibanez, 2004).
[32] Anderson, *supra* n. 6 at 25.
[33] Anderson, *supra* n. 6 at 50.

units. The fact that Creoles were Spaniards born in America, who were not truly Spaniard nor truly American, would explain that they identified themselves with the political unit that was created by Spain.

Although Anderson likes to think that Creole nationalism created a community of equals in which slaves and indigenous peoples were included, the history of Latin America proves otherwise. As I shall show with respect to the Colombian case, the process of inclusion/exclusion made it impossible to think of the nation as a homogenous imagined community of equals. Anderson's explanations about the central character of political units are not supported by the facts from the movement of independence, because units did not fight for independence as political units but as America. Anderson does not take into account that Venezuela, Nueva Granada, Ecuador, Peru and Bolivia were the result of the process of independence and the fights against centralization in Caracas – due to it being Bolivar's birth place, and not because of independence. The fact that Bolivar and San Martin met in Peru to discuss the future of the process of independence of the colonies in America is unnoticed by Anderson. Anderson does not take into account that the process of independence was a white process of independence, and it was this whiteness that made it possible for Jorge Luis Borges to say that Americans were Europeans in exile. For Anderson's thesis to be successful there is a need for identification against a group or primordialist identification. Given that Creoles were not communities born in the New World, they could not share a primordial character that made them an ethnic group in search of a nation-state. Anderson is then right in saying that this was not a primordial community. But what kind of imagined community was it? To say that they were Creoles who thought of themselves as non Spaniard and non American is to say that they knew what it meant to be Spaniard and American. That is, they seemed first to be national Spaniards and only after that national Americans. Anderson does not take into account the process of nation building in Spain that served as a model for the Creoles, and he does not take into account that the model constructed in America was based on the process of inclusion/exclusion developed during the life of the colony.

Anderson pays attention only to the experience of Creoles who identified themselves against Spanish policies and who imposed 'national' identity on indigenous peoples and slaves. The fact that Jose de San Martin decided that slaves and indigenous peoples were from that point not *Indios* or *negros* but Peruvians shows the whiteness of the nation, that is, the imposition of an imagined community based on the coloniality of power and a dialectic of inclusion/exclusion.

Anderson's conception of the imagined community does not take into account other forms of political groupings, like those existing in India before the emergence of Nationalism.[34] Chatterje shows that Anderson's conception of nationalism is based on some templates given by Europe and, in the second edition of the book, by the Americas. However, Chatterjee shows that this conception left nothing to be imagined by the colonies. Even imagination remains colonized in Anderson's account. In his book on Third World nationalism, Chatterjee shows how the imposition of western concepts on non-western practices produces illiberal results. Indian nationalism, due to western imposition, instead of liberating people became another way of legitimizing the power of the elite. Based on the analysis of two kinds of nationalism made by Plamenatz, Chatterjee finds that eastern nationalism appeared amongst peoples whose cultures were transformed or repressed by colonial rule. Eastern nationalism tries to appropriate western practices but it cannot imitate them because it cannot completely eliminate the indigenous culture. As a consequence, eastern nationalism presents a dual rejection: of western nationalism for being foreign, and of indigenous practices for not being universal enough. Although Chatterjee does not write in terms of coloniality of power, his critique of the division between European and Eastern nationalism shows that it is the imposition of western models that made eastern nationalism illiberal, that is, it is western nationalism that is illiberal because it is based on the exclusion of peoples defined as inferior and in need of protection by the state but not within the state. In the Colombian case, it is the coloniality of power that was at the base of the illiberal and exclusive nation and that resulted from the wars of independence.

In the following sections I want to show that without a world historical analysis is not possible to understand the relations between the processes of independence in the Americas or the processes of state and nation building in Europe. From a perspective of a *long duree* I want to show that in the conquest and definition of slaves and indigenous peoples in America we find a configuration of the nation as a European concept based on the coloniality of power. The nation and nationalism are European exports that were imposed in the colonies as a new way of normalization and they were based on the dialectic of inclusion/exclusion.

---

[34] Chatterjee, *supra* n. 2 at 216; and Partha Chatterjee, *Nationalist Thought and the Colonial World: A Derivative Discourse.* (London: Zed Books Ltda, 1986).

4. The Constitution of Indigenous peoples and Blacks in the juridical discourse of the Conquest.

The nation in Colombia was based on the dialectic of inclusion and exclusion of the indigenous peoples in Colombia and people from African descent. The fact that the nation in Colombia and in Latin America was constituted based on this exclusion makes it impossible to talk of an imagined community in the way in which Benedict Anderson writes about the nation and nationalism in Latin America. By appealing to an analysis of the situation of the indigenous peoples and peoples of African descent in Latin America, I want to explain the declaration of San Martin with regard to the indigenous peoples of Peru. When he refers to them he, in the same sentence, treats them as children and citizens; that is as subjects of control and normalization, but at the same time as formal members of the polity. Anderson wants to see in this sentence the imagination of the Peruvian nation, my analysis will show that it is part of the constitution of indigenous peoples as western subjects and the constitution of a political grouping based on their exclusion. This is a point that Anderson misses, and this is due to a lack of analysis of the coloniality of power in Latin America.

The construction of nationalism and the nation in Latin America is based on the constitution of the colonial world in the juridical discourse. The fact that America was discovered and that Spain wanted to exploit its treasures had to be justified. The King of Spain wanted to have a justification for the Spanish presence in the new world. This was necessary given that the King believed that Columbus had arrived in the East, which was the center of the World System at the time. Spanish presence in that place needed to be justified. Once the justification was given, the discourse about the indigenous peoples moved from the noble savage, found in Columbus's description of the peoples of the new world, to the Indian described as lazy, dirty, and in need of protection, found in the discourse of *Conquistadores* like Nicolas de Federman. The discourses of justification are related to the perception of America as periphery. Africa did not belong to the World System but America was being incorporated as its periphery. Since Christianity and capitalism were in expansion, this discourse came as both legitimation and explanation of that expansion.

It is in the University of Salamanca that the debates about the conquest of America took place. Francisco de Vitoria, Bartolome de las Casas, Juan Gines de Sepulveda and others intervened to show the legitimacy of the Spanish presence in America. For one of the advisors of the King, the fact that Spain was a Christian power and that they were defending the faith, implied a right of conquest in the new world. This justification was necessary due to the need of possessing the goods of the new world. The king appealed to the doctrine of the just cause, which allowed the enslavement of the defeated and the confiscation of all their possessions. However, the peoples of America were not at war with Spain and for that reason the doctrine of the just war could not be applied to the American conquest. But the constitution of the New World as the periphery of Europe ended up being based on the juridical discourse of the just war. The Pope as representative of Christ on Earth is he who has the right of recovering for the world of Christ what was taken from him.[35] For that reason, and given that the rejection of Christianity was considered a just cause for the subjugation of the infidels, the Crown had a *requerimiento* by which the *conquistadores* read the indigenous peoples a document that explained Christianity, who the Pope was, and the benefits of converting to Catholicism. If they rejected Catholicism they would be considered enemies and for that reason, if captured, they could be considered slaves and subjugated to the total power of the invader. It is the primordial character of Christianity that gave the power and the right to the Spanish crown to exercise war against indigenous peoples and to subjugate them and convert them into slaves and later into serfs.[36] Although Vitoria and de Las Casas agreed in considering Indians as men with a soul, as opposed to Gines de Sepulveda who saw them as lacking a soul and therefore as being by nature subjugated, the three of them were trying to find justifications for the Spanish presence in the Americas. What is coincident in all of them is their consideration of Indians as inferior and Spaniards as superior. Given the superiority of Spain, their cultural products like religion and domination should and had to be accepted by the indigenous peoples. These debates about the nature and dignity of indigenous people would shape the conception of the nation in independent Colombia and currently in the treatment of indigenous peoples under the Constitution of 1991.

As it was the case in the Canary Islands, the Spaniards used the enslavement of Indians in the conquest of America. However this enslavement was not the result of a decision to use them as instruments in a

---

[35] Silvio Zavala, *La filosofia politica en la conquista de America* (Mexico: Fondo de Cultura Economica, 1947), at 27. Also Lewis Hanke, *La lucha por la justicia en la conquista de America* (Madrid: Ediciones Istmo, 1988).

[36] Francisco de Vitoria, *Relecciones sobre los Indios y el Derecho de Guerra* (San Jose: Alma Mater, 1988). About the debates on the New World it can be seen in Antonello Gerbi, *La disputa del Nuevo Mundo: Historia de una Polemica 1750-1900* (Mexico: Fondo de Cultura Economica, 1960).

capitalist enterprise, as it was the case with the African slavery and the Plantation, but the result of the application of the doctrine of the just cause in America. The purpose was not to obtain living labor but rather to obtain money and goods from the indigenous peoples. This is what was called *rescate (ransom)* and it was generally applied during the conquest until the Indians ceased to be enslaved by the Spaniards.[37] It is with the *Real Cedula* of August 2nd 1530 that the Crown prohibited the slavery of indigenous peoples in America. But it is only after 1542 that the Crown prohibited the slavery of Indians in wars or in general in the territory of the colonies. But the liberation of Indians was not the result of the good will of the Crown but rather the result of the beginning of America as a colony and the need to use them as living labor under the dominion of the Spanish colonizer in the *Encomienda.* The liberation of Indians responds, then, to a process of normalization of Indians as Christians and workers without salary, which reflects a process of inclusion/exclusion that would be central in the constitution of the nation in Colombia.[38] In this way the Indians were included as members of that community of Christians, that is to say, as subjects of the Christian message and normalization, and at the same time they were excluded from the colonial polity because only the white colonizer had the right to earn wages for his work. As Gabriel Izquierdo has shown for the Colombian case, the relationship between winner and losers in the wars of conquest in America, in terms of the exploitation of the Indians and the dispossession of their means of production, is seen in the economic institutions of the time. The *Encomienda* is centered on the exploitation of the Indian as labor. After that we will find the *resguardos* based on the constitution of the Indian as individual and therefore in the commodification of their lands.[39] Juan Freire has shown how the entire economy of the colony was based on the exploitation of the indigenous peoples and how at a later stage the conquerors imported African slaves to the new world as labor force to replace the Indians.[40]

---

[37] Silvio Zavala, *Ensayos sobre la colonizacion Espanola en America* (Buenos Aires: Emece Editores, 1944). See also Lewis Hanke, *Uno es todo el genero humano* (Chiapas: Gobierno Constitutcional del Estado de Mexico, 1974).

[38] Zavala, *supra* n.37, at 124.

[39] Gabriel Izquierdo, 'Introduccion', in *Indigenas y Represion en Colombia. Analisis-Denuncia* (Bogota: Cinep, 1978), at 7.

[40] According to Freire this is the reason why there was discussion about the doctrines that denied legitimacy to the conquest. However, I think it can be also viewed as a process of imposition of capitalism in the new world. Juan Freire,

The fate of indigenous peoples in Latin America cannot be understood without the linkage existing in their conversion in serfs and the import of slave labor from Africa. Both practices were part of the constitution of Indians and Africans as living labor, a process by which they contributed to the capitalist world economy without participating in capitalist enterprises.[41] Despite the fact that slavery had been prohibited in the *Leyes de Indias,* the Spanish crown decided to intervene in the slavery of people from Africa. As in the case of the slavery and subjugation of Indians in America, the slavery of Africans was legitimized using the juridical discourse that explained and justified their subjugation by the Spanish power. To Francisco de Vitoria slavery is not based on the Aristotelian doctrine of natural serfdom, because all men are born equal. To Vitoria, the reasons that justify slavery are: being born from a mother who is slave, war made with authority, crime, one's own decision, and contract due to hunger.[42] The doctrine of just war was used to enslave people from Africa, but since they were sent to America, there was no possibility of exploiting them under the system of the *Encomienda.* Although there were some people who opposed slavery, their voices were not heard and slavery remained an economic system of exploitation during the life of the colony.[43]

Bartolome de las Casas was one of the defenders of the Indians who suggested the import of slaves from Africa in order to avoid the elimination of the Indians. Once he saw the results of this import, he rejected the idea of the enslavement of people from Africa. What is interesting about the story of de las Casas is not the mistake he committed, but rather the fact that he considered the slaves from Africa as inferior in dignity to the Indians. But more interesting is the fact that the Crown shared his opinion about the slaves from Africa. This is due to the consideration of the slaves as living labor, and the costs of the exploitation of Africa, then not yet incorporated within the capitalist World System. What the Spaniards and Bartolome de las Casas showed was that the incorporation of the Indians and the Americas within the capitalist World system made their exploitation as slaves more expensive, whereas the

---

Bartolome de las Casas: Precursor del anticolonialismo (Mexico: Siglo XXI editores, 1974).

[41] Stavenhagen, *supra* n. 8.

[42] Jose Luis Cortes Lopez, *La esclavitud negra en la Espana peninsular del siglo XVI* (Salamanca: Universidad de Salamanca, 1989), at 29.

[43] Liliana Obregón, 'Spanish Colonial Critiques of African Slavement', In *Beyond the Law No. 24. Race and Racism in the Global South.* (December 2001).

exploitation of African slaves could not be considered against the owners of the *Plantacion* due to the lack of costs that derived from the non incorporation of Africa to the World system. Once this happened, slavery became non profitable and liberation was incorporated into the political vocabulary of the time.[44]

In the same way as the School of Salamanca developed the juridical justification of the conquest and slavery of indigenous peoples in America, the justification of the slavery of Africans was developed by Spaniard Jesuits in service of the Portuguese Crown.[45] Authors like Domingo de Soto found slavery against the *jus gentium,* which was the law that regulated the relations between peoples in ancient Rome. However, it was the discourse in favor of slavery that was finally imposed. The three pillars that justified slavery, according to Fernao Rebello SJ and Tomas Sanchez SJ were: just war, crime, and a contract in cases of extreme necessity by which the enslaved person or one with the right to do so, sold his/her freedom.[46] Francisco Jose de Jaca and Epifanio de Moirans defended the slaves and for that reason they had to face criminal charges. It is worth mentioning that one of the elements that the two Jesuits took into account was reparation for the fact of the slavery, because slavery is the stealing of the African's freedom. However, the freedom that they granted to the slaves was not due to their status as human beings, but rather to their status as 'humanized beings'. That is, since the Africans came to America they were Christianized and for that reason they became free persons. Christian doctrine prohibited the slavery of Christians. In this case, in order to protect the slaves, Jaca and Moirans wanted the inclusion of Africans in the Christian community, but their inclusion was based on another exclusion, that is, they were included in the Christian community but not as equal persons, only as free-living labor.

One of the questions that the defenders of the Africans asked is why the slavery of Africans was not abolished in the same way as the slavery of Indians. According to Garcia Anoveros, the reasons and the juridical regime of each group were different and that explains why Indians

---

[44] Eulalia Maria Lahmeyer Lobo, 'Bartolome de las Casas e a lenda negra', in Ronaldo Vainfas (org), *America em tempo de conquista* (Rio de Janeiro: Jorge Zaha Editor, 1992).

[45] Jose Tomas Lopez Garcia, *Defensores de los Esclavos Negros en el siglo XVII* (Caracas: Universidad Catolica Andres Bello, 1982).

[46] About the story and doctrines of these two Jesuits, see Obregon, *supra* n. 43 and Lopez Garcia, *supra* n. 45.

were liberated whereas Africans were enslaved after the end of the colony.[47] One of the reasons is that Indians had to be made slaves, that is, they were considered free before the Spaniards came to America and for that reason it was necessary to justify their slavery in stricter terms. On the other hand, according to the juridical discourse of the conquest, Africans were enslaved in Africa, and for that reason they had no right to enjoy freedom in the territory of the Americas. Merchants dealing in Indians had to produce many legal arguments to support their use of Indians as slaves. Those who bought Africans did not have to prove their legal title, because they already had slaves 'made' in Africa. When the Crown could control the merchants, there was no slavery of Indians, but in Brazil, where that control did not exist, merchants subjugated to slavery not only black Africans but also Indians.[48]

The process of the conquest meant for the Indigenous peoples of America and for the Africans a transformation in their identities and their juridical status. For the Indians, the conquest meant their incorporation into the World System as slaves and later on as serfs. They were included in the Christian community as members who were in need of education, protection, and control. They were normalized in order to make them Christians and western. At the same time, their incorporation into the Christian community was not a complete one, because they were considered as children who needed protection and the assistance of the white man. It is the white man who had the privilege of being part of the Christian community as a subject with all his rights and the possibility of earning wages. For the Africans the process was different but led to the same result, that is, the dialectic of inclusion/exclusion. They were brought to America as slaves, that is, there was no need for extensive justification of their status, even if they were Christianized, and they could not be free, because they had never been free. However they were included in the Christian community as objects and as Christians, not as persons. But that inclusion by itself meant the exclusion from the white Christian community; they did not have a right to be part of that community nor to become an active member of it.

---

[47] Jesus Maria Garcia Anoveros, El pensamiento y los argumentos sobre la esclavitud en Europa en el siglo XVI y su aplicacion a los indios americanos y los negros africanos (Madrid: Consejo Superior de Investigaciones Cientificas, 2000), at 215.

[48] For the process of national identity and blackness in the Caribbean, see Nancy Priscilla Naro (ed.), *Blacks, Coloureds and National Identity in Nineteenth-Century Latin America* (London: University of London Press, 2003).

Once we understand this process it is possible to see clearly what Jose de San Martin meant when he said that from now on, Indians were going to be Peruvians. The juridical discourse of the colony shows that Indigenous peoples and Black slaves were not part of the community in which they were living. They did not fully belong to the Christian community, and they did not fully belong to the nation. San Martin's assertion is nothing more than the declaration of a white Creole who decides about the future of quasi subjects and an exercise of the dialectic of inclusion/exclusion. By that gesture, indigenous peoples were included as members of the Peruvian political community, but the same gesture meant that they were not a real part of that community, because they were children and citizens, that is, members of the community that needed to be protected and controlled by those who had all full rights and ability to do so: the white Creole. In the following section I want to show the process of inclusion and exclusion in the Colombian case.

5. Up with the king and down with the bad government: the constitution of the 'Nation' in 19th century Colombia.

The history of indigenous peoples in Colombia and their relationship with the white man was marked by violence and by the appropriation of the means of production of the indigenous peoples in Colombia. The coloniality of power defined them as inferior and power relations in the new world were based on that definition. With independence, the situation of Indigenous peoples did not change in a substantial way, although they did formally become part of the Colombian polity. With respect to black communities, their situation of slavery remained the same until the second half of the century, when they were incorporated into the Colombian polity in the same way as Indians. From the beginning of the Republic (1819), the interests of the State are identified with the interests of the rural aristocracy, who were dispossessing them of their lands. After the *Encomienda,* that was, under the control of the *conquistadores,* Indian lands were regulated under the regime of the *resguardo,* a way in which the colony guaranteed free Indian labor without depriving them of their freedom and without subjecting them to the control of the *conquistador,* whose behaviour could lead to disastrous economic results.[49]

The process of Independence did not begin with the purpose of creating a Colombian nation. In fact, the process began due to the influence of the Revolution of slaves in Haiti, the French Revolution and the

[49] Izquierdo Supra n. 39 at 13.

American Revolution. The translation of the document entitled 'Rights of Men' by Antonio Narino was a central element in the independence of Colombia. However, in the discourse of the *libertadores* there was no mention of total independence of Colombia from Spain. In Cartagena, on November 11 1809, and in Bogotá on July 20 1810, the purpose of the movements of Creoles was aimed at changing the bad government and maintaining loyalty to the King. If we define the nation as the place to which a person has loyalty, it seems clear that the Creoles who wanted the transformation of the *status quo* in 1810 were not thinking of a new imagined community to which they could give allegiance. As Campa has written, the movement for independence in Latin America did not bring about radical transformations in the region. If we want to talk about nationalism in Latin America this was not the case for the movement of independence in Colombia, because the leaders of the movement wanted to be part of Spain. To Campa, the beginning of the struggle for independence was a struggle only to follow the caudillo, not one to imagine a community of equals.[50] Soler has shown that the construction of the nation in America was the result of processes of construction of the nation in Spain. In the Constitution of Cadiz 1812, after the revolts in Latin America, the Spanish government declared the equality of all Spanish people born in Spain or born in the Americas.[51] In a newspaper published in Lima, that did not necessarily mirror the opinion of the Spaniards in Spain but did mirror the opinion of white Creoles, we find that the nation is defined as 'the reunion of all Spaniards from both hemispheres and for that reason this is or common *patria*'. In the discourse of the Creoles there was no attempt, at the beginning of the movement, for independence of a new nation. This is clearly found in one of the first documents in which the Creoles expressed their intention of making the promises of the French Revolution a reality. Camilo Torres in his *Memorial de Agravios (1809)* says that 'the Americas are not made up from foreigners to the Spanish Nation.' and 'Americans are as Spanish as the heirs of don Pelayo'.[52] One of the claims of the Creoles was for representation in the *Junta Central* for the Spanish from the Americas. What is evident from these discourses for independence is

---

[50] Ricardo Campa. *Il potere politico nell'America Latina.* (Milano: Edizione di Comunita, 1968). at 120.

[51] This process was favoured by the French occupation in Spain. See Juan Freire. *La otra verdad. La independencia americana vista por los espanoles.* (Bogota: Tercer Mundo Ediciones, 1972).

[52] Guillermo Hernandez de Alba (comp), *Como nacio la Republica de Colombia.* (Bogota: Banco de la Republica, 1965).

that the movement did not begin as part of a movement for the construction of a new nation, but rather as part of the construction of the Spanish nation. It is important to notice that the Creoles were talking about members of the Spanish nation, that is, Spaniards born in both sides of the Ocean. This means that those who were born in Africa or were in America before the Spanish presence could not be part of the Hispanic American nation, those people were not Spaniards and therefore those could not be part of the new Spanish nation.[53]

Indigenous peoples, such as born in America, became part of the rhetoric of independence, but this did not mean that they were part of the nation or that their situation improved. Spanish Creoles in America used the history of oppression of Indians as part of their rhetoric against the Spanish Crown; in this case, Creoles took for themselves the condition of indigenous peoples as victims of Spanish colonial power.[54] In one pamphlet of the independency movement, we see that the Creoles transformed their domination and exploitation of Indians in domination and exploitation of the Spanish Crown against Spaniards in America:

> With horror we take out of our sight the 300 years of oppression, miseries, suffering of all kinds, that our country accumulated over the ferocity of its conquerors and Spanish governors, whose history posterity could not read without being admired of their sufferings.[55]

As a result of the unequal commercial relations between the colonies and Spain, the movement for autonomy became a movement for independence from Spain. Given the lack of government in Spain, the Spaniards in America assumed the discourse of popular sovereignty as part of the control of these territories not only against France but also because the sovereign was unable to govern in America.[56] It is in this moment that the bourgeoisie and the high aristocrats decide to declare their independence from Spain. But this movement is not one of independence of the particular units as such, as Anderson wants to think, but a movement of

---

[53] Ricaurte Soler, Idea y Cuestion Nacional Latinoamericanas. De la Independencia a la emergencia del imperialismo (Mexico: Siglo XXI, 1980).

[54] Hans Joachim Konig, En el camino hacia la nacion. Nacionalismo en el proceso de formacion del Estado y de la Nacion de la Nueva Granada, 1750-1856 (Bogota: Banco de la Republica, 1994), at 236.

[55] Act of the Independency of Cartagena, in Konig, *supra* n. 54, at 242

[56] This factor explains why in Brazil the independence was peaceful. See Javier Ocampo Lopez, 'El proceso politico, militar y social de la Independencia', *Manual de Historia de Colombia Tomo II* (Bogota: Instituto Colombiano de Cultura, 1979), at 91.

the Americas as a whole. The movement for independence was in that way assembled under the motto of *Our America.* From Anderson's point of view, *Nuestra America* could be understood as the seed of the nation in the American republics. However, when we see in more detail what people were part of *Nuestra America* – in Bolivar's and San Martin's understanding – we can easily see that only white Creoles were seen as part of this community. It is in this moment that Spanish Americans, who used to see themselves as Spanish born in the Americas, saw themselves as Hispanic Americans, that is, Americans with roots in Spain. The *patria* is in that way conceived within the broader confines of America, and not within the limits of the administrative units. To be sure, the movement of independence is a movement for the independence of *Nuestra America* and that consciousness is reflected in the attempts of Bolivar and San Martin to liberate the entire continent from Argentina to Mexico. Due to the coloniality of power, established by Spain from the beginning of colonial power in America, indigenous peoples and blacks were excluded from *Nuestra America.* With regard to blacks the claim was based on their identity as foreigners, as Africans. And with regard to Indigenous peoples they were excluded as children, as uncivilized. Alba defines the fate of indigenous peoples in the following way: 'the conquest was the work of the Indians; independence was the work of the Spaniards'.[57] It is worth mentioning that some indigenous groups did not see the process of independence as an improvement in their situation, and rather they saw it as something even worse than Spanish dominion. For that reason, in the South of Colombia, in the region of Narino, some indigenous peoples supported the Spanish Crown and fought against Bolivar troops.[58]

In the discourse of the revolutionaries the word *citizen* is found as part of the rhetoric to get the support of the masses.[59] But this evocation of the word citizen appeals to the consciousness of Spaniards in America as Spanish citizens. As I have mentioned, in the movement for total independence, the question was transformed into a question of citizenship

---

[57] This process has been labelled as one of independence without nationalism. Victor Alba, *Nationalists without Nations: The Oligarchy versus the People in Latin America* (New York: Frederick A. Praeger Publishers, 1968), at 19. See also Antonio Garcia, *La estrctura del atraso en America Latina* (Buenos Aires: Editorial Pleamar, 1969).

[58] Fernan E. Gonzalez Gonzalez, Para leer la politica: ensayos de Historia Politica Colombiana (Bogota: Cinep, 1997).

[59] Guillermo Hernandez de Alba (comp), *Como nacio la Republica de Colombia segunda serie (1812-1817)* (Bogota: Banco de la Republica, 1981).

of Spaniards in *Nuestra America.* In 1830, Simon Bolivar showed this identity of citizenship to be part of the discourse of the nation in Colombia, but the audience of this message was only white Creoles, who extended colonial power over blacks and Indians and who were part of the incorporation of the new Republics in the capitalist World System.

The revolutionary movement did not bring about real independence from Spain and instead opened Colombia to English penetration. To Bushnell this fact explains the end of slavery in regions like Antioquia, in the north part of Colombia, because the incorporation of this region into the World System required new capitalist forms of labour and not the colonial ones, and also due to the fact that Antioquia did not have an extensive plantation system like Brazil or Cuba. Bushnell has described it in the following terms:

> When they adopted the free birth principle, therefore *Antioquenos* could assume that –along with the growing free black and *pardo* (brown) population –enough of the free born offspring of slaves would be willing to work for pay in the mining industry to meet its labour requirements.[60]

6. Conclusion

The dialectic of inclusion/exclusion of indigenous peoples led to an incomplete incorporation into the nation building process. Mariategui has noticed that in Peru the tolerance of communities was part of the feudal regime of the colony. In times of the Republic this practice led to a collective incorporation of indigenous peoples into the nation, which Mariategui explains as exploiting in a collective way the work of indigenous peoples. Indians are not part of the capitalist system as individuals, a process yet to be completed, but as a collectivity. It is this that explains why during the Republic and the colony the collective and communal practices of indigenous peoples were accepted at the same time as the practices of western capitalism.[61] But the process of consolidation of the Republic and the Colombian Nation can not be understood without examining the process of transformation of indigenous peoples as individuals. One of the first acts of the patriots after the first movement for independence in Colombia was the elimination of the *Resguardos* because they violated the individual rights of Indians. This process was followed after the independence of Colombia with the intention of liberalizing

---

[60] Bushnel, *supra* n. 11 at 42.

[61] Jose Carlos Mariategui, *Siete Ensayos de Interpretacion de la Realidad Peruana.* (Lima: Serie Popular, 1979), at 77.

indigenous peoples in Colombia, that is, in order to make them liberal subjects and commodify their lands. As a result of the laws of 22 June 1848 and that of June 3 1848, indigenous peoples became, as individuals, owners of their lands. Given their situation as poor peasants they were forced to sell their lands to *latifundistas* who became exploiters of indigenous labour. One of the leaders of liberalism in 1850s Colombia, Salvador Roldan, wrote about the situation in Colombia in the following terms:

> They sold their land immediately to their bosses for prices ridiculously low. Indians became wage earners with wages of 10 cents a day, food became scarce, lands for agriculture became lands for cattle and the rests of the Indian race, owners of these lands before, had to go to warm lands in search for better salaries, where their situation has not improved.[62]

This situation remained the same until the Constitution of 1991, when the rights of indigenous peoples were recognized by the Constitution, but a new attempt to make them liberal subjects under the discourse of human rights began under the umbrella of the discourse of universal human rights.[63]

The current process in Colombia is one of liberalization of indigenous peoples as part of their inclusion/exclusion in the Colombian nation. This process has taken new forms. As shown in an investigation of the Tukanoans in the Vaupes, this group have become Indians as a result of pressures from outside their community. According to the Colombian constitutions they are citizens and ethnic groups. Whites surrounding the area where they live have exercised pressure to make them Indians, telling them what is to be Indians and how to be Indian. This process is just another way of the dialectical incorporation in the Colombian nation.[64]

---

[62] Salvador Camacho Roldan in Dario Fajardo, 'Los sectores indigenas en el desarrollo del capitalismo en Colombia', in Juan Friede et al. *Indigenismo y Aniquilamiento de Indigenas en Colombia* (Bogota, Universidad Nacional de Colmbia, 1975), at 43. About the role of intellectuals in the imagination of the Latin American nation, see Nicola Miller, *In the Shadow of the State: Intellectuals and the Quest for National Identity in Twentieth Century Spanish America* (London: Verso, 1999).

[63] As in the colony, indigenous peoples have a right to their culture as long as it is respectful of universal human rights. See Antonio Garcia, *Legislacion Indigenista de Colombia* (Mexico: Instituto Indigenista Interamericano, 1952).

[64] Jean E. Jackson, 'Being and becoming an Indian in the Vaupes', in Greg Urban and Joel Sherzer, *Nation-States and Indians in Latin America* (Austin: University of Texas Press, 1991).

In the current discussion about globalization and the end of the nation, ideas about cultural nationalism and the separation between the political and the cultural are emerging.[65] From this discussion, the question of nationalism and the nation are no longer associated with Mill's ideas about the Nation and the State, ideas that permeated how the debate on multiculturalism was understood in the 1980s.[66] However in the new form of nationhood and nationalism we need to take into account the coloniality of power that has shaped modern nations.

---

[65] Arjun Appadurai, *Modernity at Large: Cultural Dimensions of Globalization.* (Minneapolis: University of Minnesota Press, 1996).
[66] Will Kymlicka, Multicultural Citizenship: A Liberal Theory of Minority Rights (Oxford: Oxford University Press, 1995).

CHAPTER 9

Global Values and Floating Borders in the Brazilian Amazon

Pekka Virtanen

University of Tampere, Finland

1. Introduction

In recent years, critical researchers have expressed serious doubts about the ability of even popular and democratic governments in developing countries to resist the globalising pressure of international capital and local elite interests, which are dominating development policies in the global South. In this context, globalisation refers to a process whereby a specific local entity expands its influence over the whole world, developing in this process a capacity to constitute pre-existing entities elsewhere as local, and eventually to re-construct them according to its own needs. At the same time, however, some of the same elements of globalisation are used by local actors to defend their rights and cultural identities from the homogenising forces of globalisation. This multi-faced process is quite clearly discernible in the changing character of normative systems, where the role of the state has undergone profound alterations. One prominent example, which is discussed in this chapter, is the case of Brazilian Amazon.

Globalisation has been analysed in the framework of such new intellectual trends as post-colonialism and subaltern studies, which are used in the following section as a basis that I develop further with support from semiotic theory following Yuri Loman. In the third section I use this framework to discuss the process of globalisation and the changing character of borders in the context of the Brazilian Amazon. I start by analysing how international merchant capitalism penetrated the area in the second half of the 19th century, how the region was subsequently integrated into the national economy in a subordinate position in the late 20th century, and how the homogenising national project was finally contested by minority groups from the national periphery, who had constructed independent linkages to the global level. In the fourth section I address the process of democratisation and penetration of international standards in

A. Wagner et al. (eds.), Interpretation, Law and the Construction of Meaning, 169–193.

such areas as environmental and cultural rights, which are reflected in the legislative process at the federal level, but are frequently challenged at state level. In the fourth section the focus is on independent certification, an international market-based system of standards which provides an alternative to traditional state-based normative systems for regulating the use of natural resources and related social processes. Independent certification, which has gained a strong foothold in Brazil, provides an example of the new kind of borderland spaces arising from the contradictions that emerge at the interface of different cultural formations.

2. Globalisation, interculturality and borders

In Brazil the coming to power of a new government headed by the Workers' Party in 2003 created strong expectations of more equitable and environmentally sound government policy that would also respect the rights of indigenous peoples and other minority groups. The expected changes in government policy have, however, failed to materialise and representatives of environmental and indigenist NGOs – many of them previous supporters of the government – are criticising more and more openly the government's deplorable performance with regard to such global issues as deforestation in the Amazon and protection of indigenous peoples' rights.[1] The disappointing record of Brazil and other recently democratised developing countries such as South Africa, has cast serious doubts on the ability of democratically elected governments in developing countries to guarantee the rights of indigenous and other minority populations or to protect the environment in the face of increasing pressure from international markets and local elite interests.[2]

According to Boaventura de Sousa Santos, globalisation is a process whereby a specific local condition or entity expands its influence over the whole world, developing in this process a capacity to constitute other existing social conditions or entities as local. This definition has two major implications. On the one hand, what we in the West presently call globalisation is merely a successful internationalisation of a certain type of

---

1 See eg M Santilli, *A retalhação da floresta amazônica* (http://www.socioambiental.org.br, 09/12/2004); O Braga de Souza, *Fórum lança manifesto cotra política indigenista do governo Lula* (http://www.socioambiental.org/website/ index.cfm, 01/04/2005).

2 R Peet, Ideology, discourse, and the geography of hegemony: from socialist to neoliberal development in postapartheid South Africa (2002), *Antipode*: 54-84; J Petras and H Veltmeyer, Whither Lula's Brazil? Neo-liberalism and 'third way' ideology (2003), *The Journal of Peasant Studies* 31: 1-44.

local culture. Secondly, localisation is an obligatory counterpart of globalisation, for something can be defined as global only in relation to other entities which, in the same context, are defined or re-defined as local. *Globalised localism* refers, therefore, to a situation where a local phenomenon is successfully transformed to an internationally accepted standard, while *localised globalism* refers to the specific impact of transnational practices and norms on local conditions, which are thereby de-constructed and re-constructed according to the demands of the former.[3]

Transformation of the European legal system into an internationally dominant standard provides a prime example of globalised localism. Historically, the normative European system was based on Roman law and the canon law of the Catholic Church, which were mixed with local traditions of customary law and feudalism. Under the influence of the Enlightenment, this essentially European tradition developed into a universalist doctrine of law and subsequently to the hypothesis of legal positivism.[4] With the conversion of the positivist legal hypothesis to a hegemonic thesis of law, the exclusive position of the state in the normative sphere was converted into a given, and law came to mean state-law.[5] Subsequently, Western colonial powers succeeded in transplanting this European model of a constitutional-liberal state with a unified legal system all over the world.

The current international system is, however, characterised by increasing complexity of the normative framework. Along with local and national normative systems, new kinds of supra-national orders are emerging in such areas as economy, environment and human rights. One typical feature of the new orders is their bifurcated basis on local and global levels, thus surpassing the dominant idea of state sovereignty in the sphere of law. At the same time, the boundaries between different systems have become softer while their systemic identities have turned fuzzy. Instead of autonomous normative frameworks based on nation-states, the present international system is, therefore, characterised by a constellation of

---

[3] B de Sousa Santos, 'Por uma concepção multicultural de direitos humanos' in B de Sousa Santos (ed) *Reconhecer para libertar: os caminhos do cosmopolitismo multicultural* (Rio de Janeiro, Civilização Brasileira, 2003).

[4] See, eg O Robinson, T Fergus and W Gordon, *An introduction to European legal history* (Oxon: Professional Books, 1987).

[5] B de Sousa Santos, 'O estado heterogéneo e o pluralismo jurídico' in B de Sousa Santos and JC Trindade (eds), *Conflito e transformação social: uma paisagem das justiças em Moçambique, vol. 1* (Porto: Edições Afrontamento, 2003), at 53.

interdependent issue-based frameworks.[6] This change is reflected also in the semantic content of such concepts as *multiculturalism*, which used to signify coexistence of cultural forms or groups within the territorial borders of one nation-state, but is now increasingly used to depict cultures that interact and influence each other irrespective of national borders.[7]

In the following, the thesis of Santos will be further elaborated on the basis of Yuri Lotman's ideas about borders and identity. According to Lotman the continued existence of a semiotic system – of which states are one example – depends on two interlinked processes. First, one part of the system, which emerges as the 'centre', must succeed in expanding its own normative system over the whole semiotic space, thus making an entire synchronic section of the system appear as something unified. The second condition underlined by Lotman is that each semiotic system must establish a boundary between Self and Other, which helps the system to assert its identity in sameness and to stabilise it. It must, however, be noted that both systemic identities and the borders that delimit them are contemporary representations created by one part of the system and are thus open to contestation.[8]

Despite the increasing complexity of the international system, the constitutional-liberal state form persists as the primary set of institutions for regulating resources, investments and populations, and constitutes, therefore, a privileged site of contestation for political projects.[9] The changing character of international relations has, however, irrevocably changed the function of inter-systemic borders, which can no longer be conceived primarily as a means to maintain states as socio-culturally homogeneous and geographically discrete entities. While the basic function of a semiotic boundary is to control, filter and adapt the external into the internal, the concept is by nature ambivalent. It is always a border with something and thus belongs to both contiguous spheres. Contemporary borders must, therefore, be understood as ongoing, dialectical processes that generate multiple borderland spaces which are not necessarily

---

[6] B Santos 2003 at 49.
[7] B de Sousa Santos and J Arriscado Nunes, 'Introdução: para ampliar o cânone do reconhecimento, da diferença e da igualdade' in B de Sousa Santos (ed) *Reconhecer para libertar: os caminhos do cosmopolitismo multicultural* (Rio de Janeiro, Civilização Brasileira, 2003).
[8] Y Lotman, Universe of the mind: a semiotic theory of culture (London, I.B. Tauris, 1990), 130-35.
[9] L Lowe and D Lloyd, 'Introduction' in L Lowe and D Lloyd (eds) *The politics of culture in the shadow of capital* (Durham, Duke University Press, 1997), at 7.

contiguous. They can be discontinuous, fragmented, or refracted in terms of space and scale. Aside from challenging the exclusive position of national borders in the normative sphere, this means that new counter-forces to the homogenising currents of Eurocentric globalisation must be sought from the increasingly dynamic interface where the 'global' is translated into the 'local'.[10]

3. Localised globalism in the Brazilian Amazon

3.1 The penetration of international merchant capital

The Amazon basin, which constitutes the largest continuous area of tropical forest in the world, was colonised by the Portuguese at the beginning of the 17th century. The conquest took place despite an international treaty signed in Tordesillas in 1494, which placed the area within the Spanish sphere of interest. Portuguese rule over the area was formalised in the Treaty of Madrid in 1750, which defined the international boundary in the Amazon basin much as it is today, recognising thus the principle of *uti possidetis de facto*, or actual possession, as a legitimate basis for territorial claims and subsequent exclusive dominion.[11]

The policy of closed territorial borders continued during the early post-colonial decades until the 1850s, whereupon Imperial Brazil ceded to international pressure and gradually opened the Amazon basin for international navigation. Thereafter such technical innovations as steam ships and an increasing demand for key raw materials such as rubber in industrial markets turned Amazonia into a major new frontier-region of international capitalism. Latex of the rubber tree (*Hevea brasiliensis*) had traditionally been used by the indigenous population for waterproofing, and small-scale production was started in Brazil at the end of the 18th century. Invention of vulcanisation in Britain in 1839 led, however, to rapid growth of industrial demand, and during the peak years of 1886-1915 more than 70 per cent of Brazilian rubber was exported, making it the main export commodity along with coffee.[12]

---

[10] P Price, 'Inscribing the border: schizoprenia and the aesthetics of Aztlán' (2000), *Social and Cultural Geography* 1: 101-116; Y Lotman 1990 at 136-42.
[11] C de Meira Mattos, *Uma geopolítica pan-amazônica* (Rio de Janeiro, Biblioteca do Exército, 1980), at 32-48.
[12] W Dean, A luta pela borracha no Brasil: Um estudo de história ecológica (São Paulo, Nobel, 1989).

In nature, rubber tree grow dispersed over large areas and extracting wild rubber is, therefore, heavily labour-intensive. The extremely low population density in Amazonia, consisting mainly of dispersed indigenous groups and a small *'caboclo'* population of mixed European and indigenous stock, did not provide sufficient labour to meet growing international demand during the 'rubber boom', and hundreds of thousands of migrants were enticed to the region to work in rubber extraction. The majority came from the north-east of Brazil where peasants were driven off by droughts, but workers were also recruited from abroad, notably from Peru and Bolivia.[13] Rapid expansion of rubber production posed, however, a threat to the survival of indigenous peoples and cultures as new lands were brought within the system of rubber extraction which expanded rapidly across the Amazon basin. In the process, which was in many ways a continuation of the assimilation/extermination policy pursued in the south and north-east of Brazil during previous decades, rubber tappers and their patrons invariably either decimated or drove away indigenous groups or, in some cases, incorporated their members as cheap labour.[14]

Traditionally rubber had been extracted by independent collectors using very rudimentary technology, but in response to increasing demand a new system to control access to rubber trees was developed while the extraction technology remained virtually unchanged. In this system the basic management unit was a large-scale land concession or 'rubber estate', which usually controlled a small tributary of the river system. A depot at the mouth served as headquarters, while rubber tappers worked their rubber trails individually further up the tributary. The latter were tied to the patron of the estate through a system of debt bondage known as '*aviamento*', whereby the patron provided on credit the necessary tools and other basic equipment, and placed the worker in one of the holdings of his estate. Even though the price paid for rubber by the patron was extremely low, the tappers were not allowed to sell their product to others, while they were expected to buy everything they needed from the patron's depot for highly inflated prices. In many cases, the annual income from rubber accumulated by the worker during the year was not sufficient to cover the bill accrued at the depot, and he remained in permanent debt to the patron. The patron, on the other hand, was tied to commercial houses in Manaus and Belém,

---

[13] E Pontes Pinto, *Rondônia: evolução histórica* (Rio de Janeiro, Expressão e Cultura, 1993), at 101; W Dean 1989 at 68-74.

[14] O Ianni, *A luta pela terra* (Petrópolis, Vozes, 1978), at 28-41; F Pinto 1993 at 101-105.

which operated with European and North-American capital exporting raw rubber to industrial markets.[15]

The 'rubber boom' in the north had its parallel in the centre-south, where the expansion of coffee production was dominated by a wealthy elite that acquired large landholdings on a moving frontier expanding south and westward from Rio de Janeiro and São Paulo. While this process was linked to expansion of the agricultural export economy, the increase in production was not based on technical intensification but on more extensive use of land and labour. In Brazil, land continued to be cheap whereas capital was expensive, thus reinforcing a pattern of production based on extensive landholdings and intensive control over labour in order to depress wages, which characterised both the Amazon region and the centre-south. With increasing specialisation in one commodity (rubber and coffee) destined for external markets, the regional economies became, however, dependent on world prices for primary commodities. The weakness of this system became apparent with the world-wide economic depression of the 1930s.[16]

3.2 National integration and localised globalism

The world price for rubber fell drastically after the second decade of the 20th century, as natural rubber from south-east Asian plantations and – after World War II – synthetic rubber flooded the market. While the coffee-based export economy of the centre-south was saved from collapse during the world depression by strong state intervention, equally strong support for rubber was not forthcoming. Thus foreign investors dismantled their export networks in the Amazon basin and most of the middlemen and merchants moved out of the region along with a large number of rubber tappers, leading to a major decline in the region's population. Even so, many of the rubber tappers remained while diversifying their bases of livelihood, thus following the example of indigenous and long-established *caboclo* populations. Their livelihood strategies also became more subsistence-oriented, based on relatively autonomous households scattered in the forest

---

[15] S Schwartzman, 'Extractive reserves: the rubber tappers' strategy for sustainable use of the Amazon rainforest' in J Browder (ed), *Fragile lands of Latin America: strategies for sustainable development* (Boulder, Westview Press, 1989), at 153-54; O Ianni 1978 at 42-56; see also W Dean 1989 at 71-74 and F Pinto 1993 at 98-110.

[16] M Grindle, *State and countryside: development policy and agrarian politics in Latin America* (Baltimore, The Johns Hopkins University Press, 1986), 38-44; W Dean 1989 at 51-87.

and subsisting mainly on swidden cultivation (slash and burn), fishing, hunting and collecting various wild forest products.[17]

This relative isolation was broken in the 1950s, when the federal government started to construct a highway linking the city of Belém to Brasília, the new capital built in the central region. This project had a major effect on the population dynamics of Amazonia, which soon replaced southern Brazil as the frontier region absorbing impoverished peasants expelled by drought in the north-east and by mechanisation of agriculture in the centre-south.[18] After a military coup in 1964, the new government adopted a more determined approach, seeking actively to integrate the northern hinterlands into the national administrative and economic network controlled by the agro-industrial and commercial elite of the industrialised centre-south. A military-style 'Operation Amazonia' was geared towards concentrating investments in specific growth poles, providing fiscal incentives such as tax exemptions and access to cheap credit to private investors, and promoting infrastructure development. The generous terms granted to private investors led to a dramatic expansion of large-scale cattle ranching, which was also supported by multilateral organisations such as the World Bank and the Inter-American Development Bank, reflecting expanding demand for beef in international markets.[19]

In the early 1970s there was a change of emphasis in government policy, as construction of two major highways crossing Amazonia were used as spinal columns for settling small farmers in the region. The settlers were mainly migrants coming from the north-east, but also from the centre and south where mechanisation of agriculture led to expulsion of surplus labour. The results were, however, chaotic as the government failed to create the essential infrastructure and social services. At the same time, the agro-industrial and commercial elite from the centre-south continued to

---

[17] O Ianni 1978 at 57-66; S Schwartzman 1989 at 155-57

[18] See, eg B Becker, 'Síntese do processo de ocupação da Amazônia - lições do passado e desafios do presente' in *Causas e dinâmica do desmatamento na Amazônia* (Brasília, MMA, 2001); A Hall, *Developing Amazonia: deforestation and social conflict in Brazil's Carajás programme* (Manchester, Manchester University Press, 1989).

[19] S Hecht, 'Environment, development and politics: capital accumulation and the livestock sector in Eastern Amazonia' (1985), *World Development* 13: 663-684; A Hall 1989 at 6-9.

exert considerable influence on government policy, and succeeded in moving the emphasis back to large-scale ranching.[20]

The negative environmental and social effects of large-scale livestock ranches and large hydroelectric dams, as well as inadequately planned colonisation, road building and mining projects in the Amazon basin, have been extensively documented.[21] Displacement of indigenous peoples and long-established extractivist and agricultural populations from their lands, invasion of indigenous reserves and conservation areas, a chaotic surge of immigrants, use of ecologically and socially inadequate production methods leading to large-scale deforestation and depletion of soil, and consequent loss of biodiversity, were directly linked to the military government's attempt to impose its externally conceived and centrally manipulated model of economic development and socio-political integration over a culturally and geographically diverse peripheral region. Imported agricultural methods which replaced local practices deemed 'stagnant and unproductive' proved, however, to be unsustainable in the tropical environment, leading to creation of wastelands and a nomadic rural population constantly on the move to a new frontier.[22]

The demographic and cultural consequences of the integration policy were shattering for the region's traditional and indigenous populations. In 1960 the Amazon region had only 2.6 million inhabitants, but in twenty years the population more than doubled, and during the 1980s another 1.4 million immigrants arrived.[23] Some Amazonian states suffered

---

[20] M Coy, 'Desenvolvimento regional na periferia Amazônica. Organização do espaço, conflitos de interesses e programas de planejamento dentro de uma região de 'fronteira': o caso de Rondônia' in C Aubertin (ed) *Fronteiras* (Brasília, Editora Universidade de Brasília, 1988); A Hall 1989 at 6-25.

[21] Eg L Mougeot, 'Planejamento hidroelétrico e reinstalação de populações na Amazônia: primeiras lições de Tucurui, Pará' in C Aubertin (ed) *Fronteiras* (Brasília, Editora Universidade de Brasília, 1988); P Fearnside, 'Environmental impacts of Brazil's Tucurui Dam: unlearned lessons for hydroelectric development in Amazonia' (2001), *Environmental Management* 27: 377-96; A Hall 1989; O Ianni 1978; M Coy 1988.

[22] E Botelho de Andrade, 'Desmatamento, solos e agricultura na Amazônia Legal' in *Causas e dinâmica do desmatamento na Amazônia* (Brasília, MMA, 2001); S Hecht, A Anderson and P May, 'The subsidy from nature: shifting cultivation, successional palm forests, and rural development' (1988), *Human Organization* 47: 25-35; S Hecht 1985 at 673-678

[23] P Léna, 'Diversidade da fronteira agrícola na Amazônia' in C Aubertin (ed) *Fronteiras* (Brasília, Editora Universidade de Brasília, 1988), at 94.

even more drastic changes, and, for example, in Rondônia the population increased from 70,000 in 1960 to 500,000 in 1980.[24] This demographic growth was linked to a major structural change from a relatively self-sufficient rural society organised along the river network to a largely urban society settled primarily along the road network and dependent on external markets.[25] In this process, ecologically well adapted local production systems, including indigenous cultures but also long-established subsistence-oriented *caboclo* and extractivist cultures, were profoundly altered.[26]

The integration policy pursued by the military government was, however, essentially a repetition of an earlier scenario played out in the centre-south. There the politically powerful landed elite, which had emerged in the late 19th century during the 'coffee boom' and had survived the depression of the 1930s with state support, succeeded in discouraging state initiatives to tax landholdings or to intrude in the regulation of rural labour relations. At the same time it demanded and received public investment in infrastructure, subvented credit and directed official subsidies for agricultural inputs and services. After World War II, the centre-south rapidly became the most dynamic centre of industrial growth in the country, feeding the development of mechanised agriculture which was heavily subsidised by the central state. By the 1970s, modern capitalist agriculture had become dominant in the region, while its expansion to the northern hinterlands by the same elite group served as a means to convert

---

[24] K Brown and S Rosendo, 'Environmentalists, rubber-tappers and empowerment: the politics and economics of extractive reserves' (2000), *Development and Change* 31: 201-227.

[25] While about 70 per cent of the population was rural in 1960, by 1980 over 60 per cent of the population had become urban. See D Sawyer, 'Evolução demográfica, qualidade de vida e desmatamento na Amazônia' in *Causas e dinâmica do desmatamento na Amazônia* (Brasília, MMA, 2001), at 75-79; P Léna 1988 at 94-95.

[26] See, eg S Hecht, 'Indigenous soil management in the Amazon basin: some implications for development' in J Browder (ed) *Fragile lands of Latin America: strategies for sustainable development* (Boulder, Westview Press, 1989); D Lima and J Pozzobon, 'Amazônia socioambiental – sustentabilidade ecológica e diversidade social' in IC Guimarães Vieira, JM Cardoso da Silva, DC Oren and MA D'Incao (eds), *Biological and cultural diversity of Amazônia* (Belém, Museu Paraense Emílio Goeldi, 2001); S Gram, L Kvist and A Cáseres, 'The importance of products extracted from Amazonian flood plain forests' (2001), *Ambio* 30: 365-368.

the peripheral populations and their cultural forms into conformity with the government's project of universal modernisation.[27]

3.3 Development, environment and multiculturalism

The military government's policy which sought to expand a unitary socio-economic model of development over the whole national territory did not, however, go unopposed. Already in the 1970s Brazil's indigenous population started to organise nation-wide, and despite continuing repression by the government, this movement developed into new forms of collaboration in the 1980s. Common concerns of the indigenous population included resistance to the government's resuscitated assimilation policy, demands for the right of indigenous groups to represent themselves instead of being represented by the respective state organ (*Fundação Nacional do Índio*, FUNAI) and calls for the immediate demarcation of lands claimed by the country's 215 indigenous groups, as well as their protection against invasions.[28] At the same time, the remaining rubber tappers started to organise resistance to prevent ranchers and loggers from cutting down rubber trees which provided their major source of income. This led to the formation of a national organisation (*Conselho Nacional de Seringueiros*, CNS) in 1985. The rubber tappers' example was followed by other extractivist groups such as fishermen and brazil-nut collectors, who organised themselves in order to protect local natural resources which provided the mainstay of their livelihoods.[29]

By the late 1980s these groups from the national periphery, which had in common ecologically sustainable livelihood strategies that had been condemned as anachronistic by the centre, formed a coalition for the conservation of the Amazonian rain forest based on sustainable use and guardianship by long-established indigenous and traditional populations.[30] Credit for raising awareness of environmental issues in the Brazilian

---

[27] M Grindle 1986 at 41-44, 72-73; A Hall 1989 at 6-40.

[28] L de Oliveira Neves, 'Olhos mágicos do sul (do sul): lutas contra-hegemônicas dos povos indígenas no Brasil' in B de Sousa Santos (ed) *Reconhecer para libertar: os caminhos do cosmopolitismo multicultural* (Rio de Janeiro, Civilização Brasileira, 2003), at 115-121.

[29] H Hadsell, 'Profits, parrots, peons: ethical perplexities in the Amazon' in BR Taylor (ed) *Ecological resistance movements: the global emergence of radical and popular environmentalism* (Albany, State University of New York Press, 1995); A Hall 1989 at 207-208.

[30] M da Cunha and M de Almeida, 'Indigenous people, traditional people, and conservation in the Amazon' (2000), *Daedalus* 129: 315-38.

Amazon, and subsequent changes in government policy, has often been given to Western environmental NGOs and international media.[31] As Brazilian researchers have pointed out, however, the visible international media coverage given to large-scale deforestation taking place in the region in the 1980s was a reflection of the environment-related struggles already taking place at the national level. The role of external actors was rather to translate environmental concerns already expressed by indigenous and traditional populations to fit with Western ecopolitical discourse, and thus to provide additional and indirect – albeit crucial – leverage for the principal Brazilian actors in negotiations with their own government.[32]

In Brazil, the dualist government policy that favours agrarian capitalism and yet seeks increasingly to promote social equity is rooted in contradictory political expectations placed on the government. While the land-owning elite of capitalist entrepreneurs from the centre-south has formed a strong political lobby to guarantee continuing privileged treatment from the government, with the return to democratic rule in the 1980s and simultaneous economic decline, the concern voiced by the opposition over the failure of agricultural modernisation to alleviate mass poverty has gained increasing political weight. Direct government interventions such as the Amazonian settlement schemes of the early 1970s, land reform proposals of the mid 1980s, and finally the change of government in 2003 are some results of this concern.[33]

What was new in the approach of the Brazilian opposition during the 1980s was the project of constructing an alternative model of development based on images of 'forest people' living in harmony with nature, which was used to challenge the homogenising rhetoric of the centre.[34] Like all identities, however, this new identity was not simply a residue of the 'pre-modern' society, but represented a compound of social formations which were rooted in a long history of antagonism and adaptation.[35] As described above, the key elements of 'forest people' were

---

[31] Eg A Hurrell, 'Brazil and the international politics of Amazonian deforestation' in A Hurrell and A Kingsbury (eds), *The international politics of environment: actors, interests and institutions* (Oxford, Clarendon Press, 1992).
[32] See, eg L Barbosa, 'Save the rainforest! NGOs and grassroots organisations in the dialectics of Brazilian Amazonia' (2003), *International Social Science Journal* 55: 583-591; P Pinheiro, 'Democratic governance, violence, and the (un)rule of law' (2000), Daedalus 129: 119-143; M da Cunha and M de Almeida 2000.
[33] Generally, see M Grindle 1986 and A Hall 1989.
[34] L Barbosa 2003 at 586; M da Cunha and M de Almeida 2000 at 335.
[35] L Lowe and D Lloyd 1997 at 15.

put together from various local and global elements operating in the Amazon region. Indigenous societies and traditional populations in their present form were constructed in border-like processes set in motion by the penetration of globalising institutions – early colonialism and merchant capitalism – into the Amazon basin, where existing populations suffered profound changes and new identities emerged. The new image of authentic local grassroots groups was constructed on this rather unstable basis with support from foreign researchers,[36] and used tactically with the help of international environmental NGOs to question multilateral financing for the continuation of a socially, culturally and environmentally destructive programme of national integration in Brazil's northern periphery.[37]

4. Law, Power and Political community

4.1 Landed property and its social function

As described above, in Brazil the indigenous and traditional peoples' movement is struggling against a long history of authoritarian rule benefiting a small economic and political elite from the centre-south. Despite more or less regular elections carried out since the early 19th century, both electoral politics and legislation in Brazil have historically been geared to control the patrimonial state and to use public power for the advancement of private interests.[38] One critical researcher has even argued that in Brazil land law is 'an instrument of calculated disorder by means of which illegal practices produce law and extralegal solutions are smuggled into the judicial process'.[39]

While in many ways the above quotation seems to represent an accurate view of land tenure and development policies pursued in the Amazon region, it provides too narrow a picture of state and politics in Brazil. I would argue rather that the Brazilian legal system reflects, like legal systems in general albeit in a more extreme way, a contradiction

---

[36] Eg S Schwartzman 1989.

[37] B Bramble and G Porter, 'Non-governmental organizations and the making of US international environmental policy' in A Hurrell and A Kingsbury (eds), *The international politics of environment: actors, interests and institutions* (Oxford, Clarendon Press, 1992), 327-333; K Brown and S Rosendo 2000 at 206-216; A Hall 1989 at 200-205.

[38] L Bethell, 'Politics in Brazil: from elections without democracy to democracy without citizenship' (2000), *Daedalus* 129: 1-27.

[39] J Holston, 'The misrule of law: land and usurpation in Brazil' (1991), *Comparative Studies in Society and History* 33: 695-725, at 695.

between the private economic interest of a dominant group and the broader social interests of the political community. In Brazil the 'civilist' legal discourse based on Roman law, which provides strong protection for private property and individual rights, has been dominant ever since the Imperial Constitution of 1824. On the other hand, the social function of property, meaning that it must be used adequately and rationally to produce economic goods in a manner that is socially beneficial, has gained an increasingly strong foothold at the federal level since the Constitution of 1946, gaining prominence in the present (1988) Constitution.[40]

During the last few decades the notion of social function has acquired an increasingly broad meaning in the Brazilian normative system, encompassing both cultural rights and environmental values in addition to economic and social rights. For example, in forestry legislation trees were initially considered solely as an economic good, but already in the 1965 Forest Code specific protected areas were envisaged. While in most cases protection was justified by utilitarian reasoning such as preventing erosion, the statute also acknowledged a linkage between environmental quality and human welfare, referring to aesthetic and cultural values of nature. Under the influence of both international environmental discourse and concern expressed by domestic civil society, new statutes have been enacted and environmental administration has been gradually unified from the 1970s onwards. As a result, Brazil had a relatively comprehensive framework of environmental legislation at the federal level by the 1990s, and for example, the principles of environmental sustainability and public obligation to defend nature are inscribed in the 1988 Constitution.[41]

Contradictory pressures are also evident in public discourse about the status of the indigenous population, where respect for cultural difference has gradually replaced cultural homogenisation and economic integration as dominant trends. Historically, Brazil's official policy towards the indigenous population has been based on temporary state guardianship, which was considered necessary before members of indigenous groups could be fully assimilated into the dominant national culture on an individual basis. While this approach was formally in conformity with the

---

[40] O Mello Alvarenga, Política e direito agroambiental: Comentários à nova Lei de reforma agrária (Lei no 8.629, de 2 de Fevereiro de 1993) (Rio de Janeiro, Forense, 1995), at 2-41.

[41] M do Socorro Flores, O meio ambiente e a proteção dos recursos florestais no Pará: uma abordagem jurídica (Belém, Universidade Federal do Pará, 1999).

then dominant international view,[42] the pretext of Christianising and instilling a Western work ethic was, in many cases, used to legitimise forced labour or expropriation of indigenous lands for the benefit of European settlers.[43]

The indigenous land issue was also a major point of contestation during a public debate on constitutional reform in the 1980s. By then legal shortcomings impairing indigenous rights had become quite clear, especially regarding the rights of outsiders to harness hydroelectric power and access mineral riches in indigenous lands. Restrictions to access by non-indigenous Brazilians were debated vociferously, but eventually the line supporting indigenous peoples' special status prevailed. In the final text of the 1988 Constitution, indigenous land rights are declared 'originary', that is, justified by their historical foundations and limiting, therefore, the state's role to recognise them.[44] In general the present federal legislation recognises cultural difference and indigenous peoples' communal rights to land, and is thus in line with recent international agreements such as the ILO Convention on indigenous and tribal peoples in independent countries of 1989 and the UN Convention on biological diversity of 1992, both of which Brazil has ratified.[45]

The model of collectively managed indigenous lands, where nature conservation had been pursued along with sustainable use ever since the Xingu Indigenous Park was created in 1960, has subsequently been taken up by traditional *caboclo* populations gathered under the CNS. By building upon their role as guardians of the rainforest against externally imposed destructive modes of land-use, such as cattle-ranching, rubber tappers and other extractivists have managed to create a powerful counter-image of socially and ecologically correct 'traditional populations'. As a result of this struggle a new type of settlement destined for extractive production under communal tenure (*Projeto de Assentamento Extrativista*, PAE) was officially established in 1987, and another collective modality called

---

[42] Eg ILO Convention no. 107 of 1957 concerning the protection and integration of indigenous and other tribal and semi-tribal populations in independent countries (http://www.ilo.org/public, 2005).

[43] See, eg E Cordeiro, Política indigenista Brasileira e promoção internacional dos direitos das populações indígenas (Brasília, CEE, 1999).

[44] M da Cunha and M de Almeida 2000 at 317-321.

[45] E Cordeiro 1999 at 124-138

extractive reserve, which is intended for sustainable use by traditional populations, was institutionalised in 1990.[46]

4.2 Federal legislation, state judiciary and defensive borders

Even though Brazil's present federal legislation is in harmony with current international principles of environmental sustainability and socio-cultural pluralism, its impact on jurisdiction in member states remains indecisive. To some extent this situation arises from the 1988 Constitution, which – aside from being environmentally and socially progressive – changed the distribution of competence between the federal state and lower level authorities. The centralised power of the federal state practically disappeared in a decentralisation process which allocated competence to different authorities in a complex system that is open to conflicting interpretations.[47]

While in principle federal legislation is superior to state laws and municipal by-laws, in the Brazilian system the constitutionality of laws passed by the federal legislature can be challenged relatively easily. This is because decisions about constitutionality taken by the Supreme Court fail to carry the force of *erga omnes* and *stare decisis* principles, that is they do not constitute binding precedents in all analogous cases for all judges in the federation. The judiciary has, therefore, become a roundabout way for vetoing and even changing majority decisions made in the political sphere against the interests of local elite groups.[48] For example the constitutionality of creating indigenous reserves without allowing claims by third parties to be heard was contested in the 1990s. Despite widespread resistance a new statute was enacted, allowing private interests as well as state and local governments to contest the size of indigenous reserves – challenging thus the originary character of indigenous land rights guaranteed by the very constitution.[49]

---

[46] Instituto Brasileiro do Meio Ambiente e dos Recursos Naturais Renováveis, *Amazônia: reservas extrativistas, estrategias 2010* (Brasília, Edições IBAMA, 2002).

[47] F Craveiro de Araújo, 'A repartição de competências em matéria ambiental' in *Causas e dinâmica do desmatamento na Amazônia* (Brasília, MMA, 2001); O Alvarenga 1995 at 128-129.

[48] A Stepan, 'Brazil's decentralized federalism: bringing government closer to the citizens?' (2000), *Daedalus* 129: 145-169.

[49] M da Cunha and M de Almeida 2000 at 318.

Another problem is that while progressive federal statutes have been passed during the last decade, environmental legislation, for example, it is poorly enforced at state level.[50] The laws have various loopholes which make fraudulent practices viable, and it has been estimated that up to 80 per cent of timber coming from the Amazon region is harvested illegally.[51] The prevalence of fraudulent practices traces back to the Imperial period, when there was no serious effort to enforce imperial law against the interests of local political elites who were the local supports of the political system.[52] Especially in the north and north-east, local politics was controlled until the 1970s by *coroneis*, local political bosses representing powerful landed oligarchies.[53] During the subsequent national integration process the *coroneis* were replaced by a new political-commercial elite from the centre-south, but organised violence continues to be frequently used by the dominant groups.[54]

Yet another colonial legacy in the Brazilian Amazon concerns land tenure. The majority of land is formally owned by the federal or state governments, and since the 1934 Constitution, constant and unopposed occupation (*usucapião*) of public land for ten years has been acknowledged as a valid basis for gaining usage rights in the case of small farmers.[55] However, even though practically no public land has passed to private ownership through regular sale since 1987, public control over indigenous lands, conservation areas and other lands in the public domain is extremely weak. Large areas of land are constantly lost through illegal invasions, which are frequently regularised by state or municipal level authorities in arrear. Without formal title, small farmers, extractivist communities and indigenous groups whose lands have not been regularised are vulnerable in the face of land speculators (*grileiros*) who use forged deeds, often in

---

[50] See, eg E Eve, F Arguelles and P Fearnside, 'How well does Brazil's environmental law work in practice? Environmental impact assessment and the case of the Itapiranga private sustainable logging plan' (2000), *Environmental Management* 26: 251-67; M Murrieta, *Direito ambiental e exploração de recursos naturais: um estudo do setor madeireiro em Portel/Marajó* (Belém, Editora Paka-tatu, 2003); M Flores 1999.

[51] P Amaral and MA Neto, Manejo florestal comunitário na Amazônia Brasileira: situação atual, desafios e perspectivas (Brasília, IIEB, 2000), at 13.

[52] M Flores 1999 at 53-54.

[53] L Bethell 2000 at 4; for the concept see F Itami Campos, *Coronelismo em Goiás* (Goiânia, Editora Vieira, 2003).

[54] Eg P Pinheiro 2000; A Hall 1989, O Ianni 1978.

[55] O Alvarenga 1995 at 23.

combination with bribery, threats and violence, to obtain large areas illegally. In this context the federal authorities have estimated that in Brazil about three quarters of large properties (over 10,000 ha) have invalid titles.[56]

While the increasing penetration of international normative discourse has strengthened the position of previously marginalised groups of civil society in Brazil, the political struggle has been transposed to lower levels, where small elite groups remain powerful in most northern states. At this level, the colonial principle of *uti possidetis de facto* continues to serve as the main basis for access to land, while progressive federal statutes remain a dead letter. In Brazil the normative system established at the federal level does not, therefore, provide a unifying national code which would guarantee enforcement of the internationally agreed principles protecting cultural difference and environmentally sound use of land throughout the political community. Instead, the state judiciary and the mechanisms of political power are being used to build a new defensive boundary to protect the narrow economic interests of dominant elite groups, displacing thus the increasingly porous national level.

5. Forest communities and certification in the Amazon

5.1 Certification as a boundary

In international development discourse the concept of sustainable development, understood broadly as environmentally sound and socially equitable economic growth, displaced the narrow economic models of development in the 1980s. The new international standards of development were endorsed in international fora such as the UN Conference on sustainable development held in Rio de Janeiro in 1992, and formally ratified in the form of international conventions by most governments.[57] As the case of Brazil shows, however, the commitment and ability of public authorities in developing countries to enforce the various objectives implied by sustainable development are often relatively weak. Increasing porosity

---

[56] P Fearnside, 'Land tenure issues as factors in environmental destruction in Brazilian Amazonia: the case of Southern Pará' (2001), *World Development* 29: 1361-72.

[57] D Burger, 'Making Rio work: the vision of sustainable development and its implication through forest certification' in K von Gadow, T Pukkala and M Tomé (eds), *Sustainable forest management* (Dordrecht, Kluwer Academic Publishers, 2000); P Virtanen and E Palmujoki, *Sustainable forest management through multilateral agreements and market-based mechanisms* (Helsinki, MFA, 2002).

of the boundaries between normative systems at different levels has, on the other hand, created new spaces for alternative practices and normative systems in such spheres as culture and economy.

International networks of independent certification such as the Fairtrade Labelling Organizations International (FLO), the International Federation of Organic Agriculture Movements (IFOAM) and the Forest Stewardship Council (FSC) provide one such alternative. While the certification criteria of these networks focus on different aspects such as social and ecological production conditions and fair trade, all of them seek to establish a normative framework which is based on global standards developed through an open and participatory process by independent civil society actors.[58] Due to their bifurcated basis on local and global normative systems their actual operation can, however, be understood only in the broader context of international market conventions, national legislation and local production systems.[59]

The Forest Stewardship Council, which is the leading international forest certification network, was founded in 1993 by representatives of environmental, economic and social organisations from all over the world. It has three main roles: to endorse regional forest stewardship standards based on international principles and criteria, to accredit and monitor organisations providing certification services under the FSC framework, and to provide information and training. It is an open membership association with a general assembly as its highest organ. In the assembly membership, voting is structured into three chambers to provide a balance between environmental, social and economic interests from the North and the South. FSC promotes the formation of regional and national working groups which draw up criteria and indicators that correspond to the specific ecological, social and economic conditions of each region or country. Along with thematic international working groups and annual meetings, these regional groups provide spaces for local involvement in the development of a global normative system. The product of the consultative elements in the certification process is an agreed definition of how forests should be managed, which forms a binding contractual basis between the certifier and the certified operation.[60]

---

[58] L Raynolds, D. Murray and P Taylor, 'Fair trade coffee: building producer capacity via global networks' (2004), *Journal of International Development* 16: 1109-1121; D Burger 2000 at 177-191.

[59] Cf B Santos 2003 at 49.

[60] D Burger 2000 at 177-187; P Virtanen and E Palmujoki 2002 at 28-30

By January 2005 more than 50 million hectares had been certified by the FSC, which had forest management and chain of custody certificates in 75 countries. Among the 12 countries with more than one million hectares certified, there were five former socialist countries from Europe, three developing countries (South Africa, Bolivia and Brazil), two West-European countries, and two North-American countries.[61] Especially in countries such as Brazil, where the state has only a limited capacity to regulate forest use, the checks and balances provided by an independent certification can offer more solid performance guarantees than state-centred systems. Under the transparent model of standards development and monitoring promoted by certification, a great deal of the control function traditionally held by governments can be transferred to civil society and market constituencies. For example, in areas where indigenous peoples are well organised, FSC certification has provided local communities with leverage for the recognition of their customary rights by companies who seek to certify their forestry operations in areas with pre-existing indigenous claims.[62]

Like the modern concept of border, certification denotes an ongoing, dialectical process that generates multiple borderland spaces which are refracted in terms of space and scale.[63] While standards forged in international institutions become codified in certification modalities, they are subsequently adapted to regional and local socio-economic and ecological conditions, and finally made intelligible to local producers by accredited certifiers. Therefore, even though the standards-based certification paradigm is based on such Western cultural traits as professionalisation, documentation and commensurability, certification is essentially a process of transposing standards into local practice and vice versa.[64] As local communities learn about certification, their representatives

---

[61] Forest Stewardship Council, Currently certified forests and chain of custody operations (http://www.fsc.org, 2005).

[62] D Irvine, *Certification and community forestry: current trends, challenges and potential* (A background paper for the World Bank/WWF Alliance workshop on independent certification, Washington, DC, November 9-10, 1999); K Thornber and M Markopoulos, *Certification: its impacts and prospects for community forests, stakeholders and markets* (London, IIED, 2000).

[63] P Price 2000; Y Lotman 1990 at 136-42.

[64] T Mutersbaugh, 'Serve and certify: paradoxes of service work in organic-coffee certification' (2004), *Environment and Planning D: Society and Space* 22: 533-552; I Iorgulescu, J Bowling and R Schlaepfler, 'Field testing criteria and indicators for forest and wood workers in Ghana' in A Franc, O Laroussinie and T

become integrated into the ongoing process, which provides the communities with an opportunity to shape the evolution of certification, transforming it to a border-like process of mutual translation. Examples of this adaptive process include the FSC guidelines for group certification from 1998 and the ongoing development of guidelines for non-timber forest products (NTFPs), among others.[65]

5.2 Independent forest certification in the Brazilian Amazon

Forest certification began to take root in Brazil in the late 1990s, in response to both local and international developments. Societal demands for sustainable development had by then become an international market convention, affecting the parameters for competition. The Brazilian wood industry had, therefore, to deal with the negative image deriving from the controversial social and environmental impacts of deforestation, monoculture plantations and use of child labour which were prevalent in the country. In this context a few leading enterprises resolved to pursue new technological directions and seek mutually beneficial relations with neighbouring communities in order to rebuild their image as environmentally and socially responsible.[66]

The FSC was introduced to Brazil in 1994, and national standards for different types of forest have since been prepared. The process was not, however, driven solely by international markets. Brazil is itself a significant consumer as well as producer of tropical timber, and certification of domestic chains of custody has become an important area of activity. A Brazilian Certified Wood Buyers' Group was established in 1997, and by the year 2000 it accounted for ten per cent of national wood demand. At the same time, several FSC-accredited forest certifiers launched their activities in Brazil, including national associates of three major certification organisations based in the USA and Europe.[67] By the end of 2004 the

---

Karjalainen (eds), *Criteria and indicators for sustainable forest management at the forest management unit level* (Joensuu, European Forest Institute, 2001); Thornber and Markopoulos 2000 at 15-19.

[65] D Irvine 1999 at 6-7.

[66] P May, *Forest certification in Brazil: trade and environmental enhancement* (A paper prepared for the Consumer Choice Council, 2002), at 3.

[67] P May 2002 at 4-5.

country had more than 2.6 million hectares of certified forests, out of which about one half were native forests situated in the Amazon region.[68]

Brazil has rapidly become a leading country in the certification of communally managed forests, and independent certification is seen as an important means for strengthening the economic and socio-political position of traditional populations.[69] By the end of 2004 there were five FSC certifications for communal management in Brazil, all of them natural forests in the Amazon region.[70] Four of them are in government agro-extractivist settlement schemes (PAE) in the state of Acre. These lands are former rubber-estates which were turned into unproductive ranches, and subsequently expropriated by the federal authority for land reform. The fifth is a state-managed conservation area in the State of Amapá, where traditional and indigenous communities have legally guaranteed use-rights. Concentration of communally managed projects in two states reflects the close interlinkage needed between national/sub-national and international normative systems: both Acre and Amapá are presently ruled by state governments that are favourable for traditional and indigenous populations, and have actively supported their endeavours.[71]

FSC certified community management projects in the Amazon region have had an important role in the adaptation of international standards to local conditions. The traditional populations involved are using forest resources in a highly diversified manner, and logging is only one activity among others even in those cases where management for certified timber production is included. Along with timber, most associations produce certified NTFPs such as oil, resin, nuts, palm fruits and seeds and wild rubber under FSC or other international schemes. In the global context, certification of NTFPs has been rather problematic due to lack of scientific knowledge for planning and monitoring sustainable production, and one of the Brazilian FSC accredited certifiers (Imaflora) has had a pioneering role in the development of regional NTFP certification guidelines. Copaiba oil produced in Amapá was actually the first NTFP to

---

[68] Forest Stewardship Council, *Currently certified forests and chain of custody operations* (http://www.fsc.org.br, 2004).

[69] See eg Ministério do Meio Ambiente, Avaliação de ações prioritárias para a conservação, utilização sustentável e repartição dos benefícios da biodiversidade na Amazônia Brasileira (Brasília, MMA/SBF, 2001).

[70] Forest Stewardship Council 2004.

[71] Cf I Iorgulescu, J Bowling and R Schlaepfler 2001.

obtain FSC certification under community management.[72] Another example of the mutual adaptation process is the PAE Pedro Peixoto in Acre, which operates as a test case for the development of Small and Low Intensity Managed Forest (SLIMF) streamlined certification procedures for the FSC.[73] These are, however, slow and laborious processes and the economic viability of small-scale forest certification is yet to be proved.

While in terms of land area and volume of production the certified community management forests in Brazil are still rather insignificant, they are likely to provide an interesting alternative normative framework for encouraging ecologically sound and socially just forest management that respects the cultural rights of indigenous and traditional peoples. The crucial difference between state-centred normative systems and voluntary international systems such as independent certification lies in the radically different way the latter conceive systemic borders. Instead of serving as geographically fixed limits for internally homogeneous nation-states with unified standards, the borderland spaces are fragmented over nation-states and serve to identify those enterprises and communities who share certain social, environmental and economic principles. But instead of trying to homogenise these producers according to a preconceived model, the international certification networks seek to engage them in a dialectical process whereby the constantly evolving national and regional standards and practices are reflected in the international standards and vice versa. Independent certification provides, therefore, an alternative to dominant forms of globalisation which seek to control the global periphery through the normative apparatuses of formally sovereign nation-states.

6. Conclusion

The history of the Brazilian Amazon provides an interesting example of the changes that globalisation has suffered during the last two hundred years. The entry of the region to the global world system through the penetration of merchant capital in the second half of the 19th century, and the subsequent process of national integration under an authoritarian central

---

[72] L Brown, D Robinson and M Karmann, The Forest Stewardship Council and non-timber forest certification: a discussion paper (Bonn, FSC, 2002); Instituto de Manejo e Certificação Florestal e Agrícola (Imaflora), Resumo público de certificação de COMARU - Cooperativa Mista dos Produtores Extrativistas dos Rio Iratapuru (http://www.smartwood.org, 2004).

[73] Instituto de Manejo e Certificação Florestal e Agrícola (Imaflora), Resumo público de certificação de APRUMA - Associação dos produtores rurais em Manejo Florestal e Agricultura (http://www.smartwood.org, 2003).

state in the late 20th century after an intermission of 50 years, implied a massive conversion of populations and their cultural forms into conformity with the project of universal modernisation. In this process, traditional Amazonian societies and their cultural diversity were reshaped to produce subjects who would function in terms of externally defined patterns as political subjects of the state, economic subjects of the international market economy, and cultural subjects of the nation. In line with contemporary international conventions, the border was constituted to mean a geographical line separating the sovereign state of Brazil from other states and their normative systems.[74]

An important finding that emerges from the case of the Brazilian Amazon is, however, that globalisation does not necessarily lead to socio-cultural homogenisation. Various apparently backward cultural forms such as traditional rubber extractivism, which seem incompatible with international market economy, have actually both permitted market integration and provided elements for the emergence of alternative modes. Globalisation does not, therefore, simply transform or destroy local social forms even though unification is a central element in the operational logic of semiotic systems. Rather, current international relations are characterised by interpenetration of different normative systems, which in Brazil can be observed at the level of federal legislation which is becoming increasingly compatible with international normative frameworks. As both antagonism and adaptation are part of the globalisation process, alternative forms emerge from the contradictions of the transformation process which takes place at the border zone between local and global cultural forms. But while openness to international influence during the last two decades has encouraged the institutionalisation of alternative socio-cultural modalities emerging from the local level, in Brazil, exclusive elite groups remain powerful at state level, which has replaced the nation as the main locus for the protection of elite interests.

The weakness of the central government when confronted with powerful elite interests has encouraged the development of independent normative frameworks which can offer an alternative basis for the development and monitoring of performance standards that fulfil internationally agreed social, economic and ecological criteria. This process has been reinforced by an increasing globalisation of markets, which has changed the parameters for competition affecting individual companies. In the case of independent certification, a great deal of the control functions

---

[74] Cf L Lowe and D Lloyd 1997 at 7.

traditionally held by governments have been transferred to civil society and market constituencies. The crucial difference between state-centred normative systems and voluntary international systems lies, however, in the radically new concept of systemic borders embraced by the latter. In the system of independent certification borderland spaces are fragmented across nation-states and serve to identify those enterprises and communities who share certain social, environmental and economic principles. Instead of trying to impose one externally conceived model on these producers, international certification is essentially a process of transposing standards into local practice and vice versa. While it is still an emerging system with limited geographical coverage, it provides an interesting alternative to the prevalent forms of unidirectional and homogenising globalisation.

CHAPTER 10

Landmarks for Aboriginal Law in Australia[1]

Agnes T.M. Schreiner[2]

University of Amsterdam, the Netherlands

It is not the new building of the AIATSIS (Australian Institute of Aboriginal and Torres Strait Islander Studies) inaugurated in 2001 in Canberra that I want to discuss here, nor the Aboriginal Embassy, nor the Corroboree 2000[3], not even the Mabo, Native Title, the Wik decision, the Indigenous Land Use Agreements with governments, miners, and farmers[4] – to sum up some landmarks in the struggle for Aboriginal rights in the last few years.[5]

The landmarks I will focus on are the marks carried by the land itself, because the land the Australian indigenous people claim as their land, can be read by its features.[6] One has to be initiated, of course, to be able to read the country. Every registration under the state's or territory's

---

[1] An earlier draft of this paper was presented at the 2001 LSA/RCSL Conference Budapest July 4-7, 2001, *Law: Its Material Manifestations,* Session 1305

[2] All comments on this paper are very welcome. Please email the author: a.t.m.schreiner@uva.nl.

[3]http://www.cultureandrecreation.gov.au/articles/reconciliation/
http://www.austlii.edu.au/au/orgs/car/towards/index.htm

[4] See for instance the ILUA between Australia's largest beef producer, Australian Agricultural Company (AACo) and the Waluwarra/Georgina River people in October 2004 http://savanna.ntu.edu.au/publications/savanna_links30/indigenous_l_use.html

[5] See for a recent overview of native title Greame Neate (2004) *An overview of native title in Australia - some recent milestones and the way ahead.* Paper delivered at 11th Annual Cultural Heritage & Native Title Conference 'Building Partnerships and Finding Solutions for Better Outcomes', Brisbane Queensland http://www.nntt.gov.au/metacard/files/Overview/An%20overview%20of%20native%20title%20in%20Australia%20%20some%20recent%20milestones%20and%20the%20way%20ahead.pdf.

[6] See Krim Benterrak, Stephen Mueke & Paddy Roe (1984) *Reading the Country. Introduction to Nomadology.* Fremantle WA: Fremantle Arts Centre Press; Ian Hughes (1996) Yolgnu 'rom': indigenous knowledge in north Australia. Pp. 184-190 Blunt, Peter and Warren, D. Michael (1996) *Indigenous organisations and development*. London: Intermediate technology publications, at 185.

A. Wagner et al. (eds.), Interpretation, Law and the Construction of Meaning, 195–206.

Aboriginal land rights legislation, as well as under the Native Title Act (1993), or the amended Native Title Act (1998), bears witness to Australian indigenous people being able to read their country. Although many affidavits are blanked out due to the confidentiality, or the secrecy, of the knowledge therein, we understand that they have testified and in several cases complied with the conditions for application.[7]

Reading the land is like mapping the country. Imagine: here are some sand dunes, there a forest, and over there another one. In the middle, we have a salt lake, a dry lakebed, a sandy beach. We see gullies and a sandbank with a settlement at the far end. It is the map of Djarrakpi being described, a map Howard Morphy (1983) provided in his article commenting, *'Now you understand': an analysis of the way Yolgnu have used sacred knowledge to retain their autonomy* (fig.1).

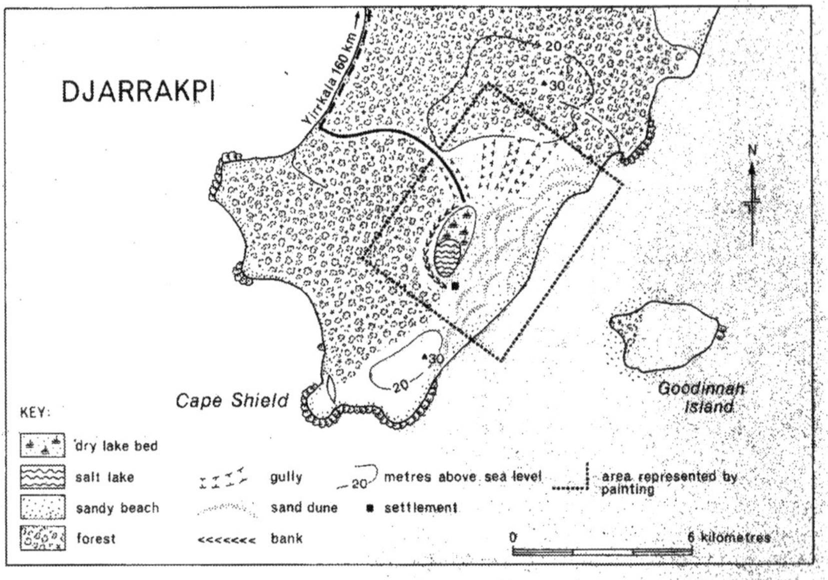

If we go to the Land Register and see the map with the general scheme or outline of the Djarrakpi country and seashore, we would be able

[7] See for the difficulties to give evidence Jane Simpson (1994) Confidentiality of linguistic material: the case of Aboriginal land claims. Pp. 428-439 Gibbons, John (1994) *Language and the law.* London/New York: Longman; Neate, *supra* n. 5, at 13-15

to find out who the owner is. Law manifests itself in a certificated piece of paper that marks the boundaries of an estate. Moreover, when we go back to a registered piece of land, we would find, in most cases, something like a fence, a pole, or a prohibition plate, which the law uses to manifest itself. Pieces of paper, fences, and poles serve as tokens of the law.

Remarkably, without ever being in Djarrakpi, we are able to think of it as a piece of landed property. How so? We as jurists have learned to analyse a given situation through the perspective of an abstract legal system that provides definitions and regulations, which in turn build up to that abstract system. It is the way we, Europeans lawyers and legal scholars, think most of the time; and not only when we think of law. We are able to read the map (fig. 1) that represents Djarrakpi as such, because we have learned to analyse a landscape with the perspective of geography, and we have learned to read its keys. In that manner, we are able to recognise an abstract map as a particular landscape.

But what has become of the actual sand dunes, the forest, the salt lake, and the sandy beach of Djarrakpi? During this explication, we have forgotten all about it. The analytical way of thinking steers us away from the specific into the general.[8] The general is studied profoundly by specialists. Those specialists have to justify the analytical – in our case legal – system by proving its adequacy.[9] They almost tautologically justify their operations by using the analytical – and again in our case legal – terms.[10] Of course, this requires sophisticated argument which is hard for a lay person to follow, but it is public and without secrecy. What will be left, when the result is given, are the specialists who remain specialists working within the legal system, and of course the laity, the public, who will knock on their doors the moment they are convinced that their rights are being neglected.

Still, we are not yet close enough to the land just described. How can we stay in the country and turn our minds to it? After thrice trying it becomes clear that we have to switch to another type of thinking about things. Let us try to think in the manner of *analogical* thinking, a mode that can be considered as the very opposite of the *analytical*.[11] Analogy is used,

---

[8] From the actual estate into the concept 'real estate', for example.

[9] 'Real estate' well balanced between all other property issues.

[10] See *supra* n. 8.

[11] See Bernard S. Jackson (2001) A semiotic perspective on the comparison of analogical reasoning in secular and religious legal systems. Pp. 295-325 Soeteman,

and is useful, when it comes to remembering things, i.e. not to forget something, to keep knowledge and experience alive. It is a mental instrument that needs to be exercised and learns by heart. Analogy truly is an art of memory as said by Francis Yates.[12]

> Analogy works both ways. Let us say we focus on the land and construct along its features - from left to right: the trees, the lake, the sand hills - a narrative about important things of life, like eating and breading. We now know about this eating and breading just by reading the country from left to right. At the same time, however, we can listen to that story and construct along its features (from the beginning to the end) the sight on a landscape, and become aware of where we are and what is behind and in front of us. One should not think that one understands this analogy by putting one and two together to conclude that this is all about the necessities of life. That would be analytical once again, with this consequence that one has missed the gullies and the sandbank from the Djarrakpi land. Or, the consequence that one will miss the possums climbing up the tree in the following story.
>
> 'Two Guwak [Cuckoo birds] sitting on top of a native cashew tree, feeding off the nuts. Each night on their journey across Arnhem Land from Donydji in the centre to Djarrakpi in the south-east they rested at the top of the trees and instructed their workers, the Possum Ancestors, to climb up the tree spinning their fur into lengths of string. They gave lengths of the string to members of Aboriginal groups living in the area where they camp that night so that they could be used in manufacturing sacred object to commemorate them. They were accompanied by the Emu Ancestors who scratched the ground looking for water, creating waterholes at the places they visit.'[13]

This narrative brings the ancestors, the food, the land, the journey, the work, the ritual, the water, the day and the night into our minds. It is told alongside its central figures: the Guwak, the Possum, and the Emu. If one knows these figures one is able memorise the Ancestor story.

Arend (ed.) *Pluralism and Law.* Dordrecht: Kluwer Academic Press. If Jackson's distinction between propositional and non-propositional analogy is used (*Ibid.* at 297), I would think the non-propositional analogy is most adequate to describe Australian indigenous reasoning.

[12] Francis A. Yates (1974) *The art of memory.* Chicago: The University of Chicago Press

[13] Howard Morphy (1983) 'Now you understand': an analysis of the way Yolgnu have used sacred knowledge to retain their autonomy. Pp. 110-145 Peterson, Nicolas & Langton, Marcia (eds.) *Aborigines, land and landrights.* Canberra: Australian Institute of Aboriginals Studies at 112-113

The analogy does not stop here. Alongside these figures the people of Djarrakpi, the Manggalili clan, can construct and reconstruct a great deal more. Everything they know, have experienced, and have found to be important can be stored in this alphabet of the Guwak, the Possum, the Emu. They can store the skills to make strings, to collect ochre, to manufacture sacred objects, and to paint clan designs. The analogy can be read vertically, horizontally, and diagonally, when a Manggalili bark painting is presented (fig. 2). And, thanks to the analogy, we are able to place ourselves back in the Djarrakpi country again while reading this painting: from the gullies in the sand hills (formed by the lengths of string laid out by the Guwak to gather several clans), along the edge of the lake, up to plum/cashew trees, down along the lake to the sand bank and the settlement – if we are reading Morphy's description of the bark painting correctly. Of course, to do it perfectly one has to be initiated. We can understand, however, how the mental instrument of analogy works.[14]

We understand that the Manggalili are able to reconstruct the Ancestor story by following the Guwak, the Possum, and the Emu. They are able to start again and reconstruct the land along the alphabetical series of the sand hills, the gullies, the trees, the lake and sandbank. They are able to pick up another starting point and reconstruct the ceremonies step by step through the sacred objects. Or, to begin at another end and reconstruct the law, that what is known and what has to be known, along these series of landmarks.[15]

---

[14] We are able to understand the working of the mental instrument of analogy *in general*, of course. After all this is an analytical analysis. I like to recall the title of Howard Morphy's article *'Now you understand': an analysis of the way Yolgnu have used sacred knowledge to retain their autonomy.* The analogies that Morphy's informant did reveal in order to help him understand, are being analysed to explain the retained autonomy of the Yolgnu clan Manggalili. The formula 'now you understand', however, might be read as a closing phrase of the exchange of some layers of sacred knowledge, the initiation in some sort of a stage. Or one can say with Jackson the teaching instead of the explanation (Jackson, *supra* n. 11, at 322 and his n. 94)

[15] One must realize that not every Manggalili clan member is equally trained to make these reconstructions, or to say it in other words equally initiated in these stories and qualified to tell them. See for instance Michael Walsh (1994) Interactional styles in the courtroom: an example from northern Australia. Pp. 217-233 Gibbons, John (1994) *Language and the law.* London/New York: Longman;

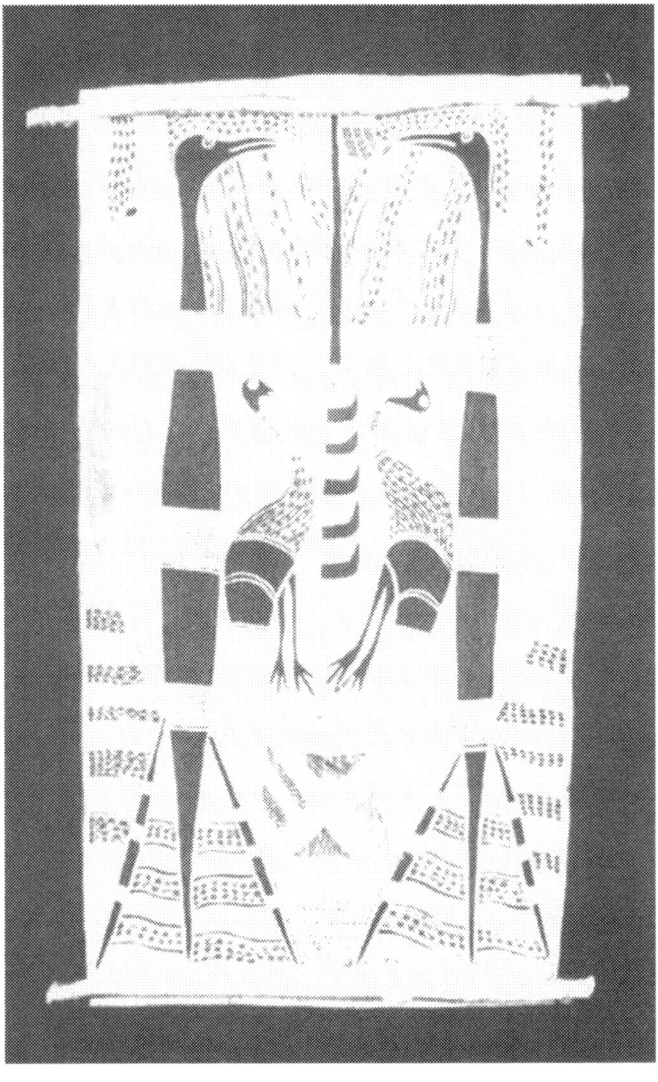

Agnes T.M. Schreiner (2003) The Ritual Manifesto. eEdition. Amsterdam/Internet: 1001Publishers http://www.1001publishers.com/index_uk.html.

It might even be some member of an affiliated clan is trained as a 'ritual manager' to make a particular reconstruction. See Bruce Chatwin (1988) *The Songlines* Penguin Books at 27, 97-98, 151, 258; Maddock, Kenneth (1981) Warlpiri Land Tenure: a Test Case in Legal Anthropology. 52/2 *Oceania* 85-102 at 94; Schreiner, Agnes T.M. (2004) Observing the differences. Pp. 87-94 Arend Soeteman (ed.) *Pluralism and Law. Proceedings of the 20th IVR World Congress.* Volume 3: Global Problems (ARSP-Beiheft 90). Stuttgart: Franz Steiner Verlag at 88.

The summing up of the reconstructions that can be made, might, however, lead to an analytical interpretation, which would recognise four concepts: the Ancestor dreaming, the land, the ceremony, and the law. Each concept would contain at a deeper and more abstract level a general idea. For instance, the Ancestor dreaming symbolises or refers to their cultural and historical heritage; the land to their social and economical conditions; the ceremony to their artistic, cultural, and spiritual activities; the law to their social, moral, and legal rules. *Separation* is crucial for analytical reasoning, whereas *combination* is the core of analogical reasoning. The outcomes of these types of thinking are truly opposed and non-communicative in relation to each other, although both are intelligible. It is the same opposition which holds between the symbolic interpretation versus the emblematic or allegorical one. The first one sees the general in the particular. The general in that case is, or has become something that is, underlying and is expected to be discovered. The second one, the emblematic reasoning, however, sees the particular in the general. The general then is superficial, recognisable by its features and memorizable by the art of combinations between the particularities. Those combinations can be observed, read, reconstructed, or else produced.[16] Moreover, the combination of sand dunes, forest, salt lake, dry lake bed, sandy beach, gullies, bank, and settlement (the land) is a particular itself which can be taken as a part of a new set of combinations, which corresponds with another set. The art of memory is actually one big play of combinatorial exchanges.

To demonstrate a combinatorial exchange I will rely on a representative of the Borroloola community who clarifies the Aboriginal law:

> A lot of law is very strong, the Aborigines have. Which is called, that is ceremony, which is called 'guaniwirri'. It is coming from Australia, maybe North Australia. (...) That ceremony is a very long story and is connected with land. A lot of Aborigines go by that law, we all go by that ceremony, every one of us, a lot of, every Aborigine goes by that ceremony. There is only one law, Aborigines people have, which is in the ceremony and the ceremony is connected with the land, and the land itself will go by that law.

---

[16] This distinction between symbol and emblem goes back via Walter Benjamin to Goethe, see Agnes T.M. Schreiner (1997) So, this is how it is done ... Pp. 123-144 Lindgren, J. Ralph & Jay Knaack (eds.) *Ritual and Semiotics*. Critic of Institutions Vol. 14: Law. New York etc: Peter Lang at 125 and 140

He speaks here in front of a camera operated by his own people. It is the film *Two Laws* made by Indigenous Australians from Borroloola.[17] From start to finish it represents their own indigenous view. Accordingly, the speaker is explaining Aboriginal law in a manner that is most familiar and comprehensible to him.

The 'law' the Aborigines have is 'cere–mony', is a 'long story', is connected with the 'land', while the 'land' in turn is connected with the 'law'. By way of threading a string of beads, Aboriginal law, ritual, and land are linked by a common line. Yes, a common 'songline'. Singing is an excellent way to memorise. Even more so when it is moulded into a ritual form, like the ritual form of poetry which the Australian Aborigines chant, using boomerangs or digging sticks for percussion. Their art of memory reaches the highest level of perfection when they combine the musical bars of that songline with the score the landscape offers. Indeed, it is that series of landmarks they travel across that is intended.[18] It is thus, as the Aboriginal said, literally a 'long story'. He does not say that he needs a very roundabout story to explain what Aboriginal law is, and that he has only just begun to reveal the first ingredients. That would be the case if symbolic reading and, thus, analytical reasoning were at work. What our Aboriginal informant demonstrates, however, is better understood as allegoric reading with the use of analogical reasoning. It is exactly as he

---

[17] The film *Two Laws* has been made in 1980 and consists of four separate reels with four distinct storylines - like independent chapters. Each part has its own title. The first part, *Police Times,* shows the Borroloola Aboriginals during the 1930s by means of a dramatized reconstruction of an event in 1933. The second part, *Welfare Times,* gives a sketch of life in Borroloola during the period of the welfare provisions of the 1950s. The ties the Aboriginals have with their land, their struggle for the land and for their sacred places, and the official claim that the Borroloola Aboriginals lodged under the *Land Rights Act* (Northern Territory) of 1976, are the subject of the third part, *Struggle for our Land.* The final part, *Living with Two Laws,* deals with the movement among Aboriginals to return to their original territories and to set up cattle farms in remote homelands. The filmmakers Carolyn Strachan and Alessandro Cavadini we find on the payroll were hired by the Borroloola community to train them in the technique of film.

[18] See *The Songlines*, Bruce Chatwin's Australian travel book that has been categorized as a myth and pigeonholed as 'fiction', with the author's consent by the way (Bruce Chatwin (1989) *What am I doing here.* London: Picador at 64). And yet it is one out of books that really hold ground and give a remarkable account of the 'songlines'. Like Howard Morphy, I would make it compulsory reading for anthropologists (Morphy, *supra* n. 13, at 20).

puts it: the land goes by that law, that is ceremony, that is, a long story connected with the land; the land itself is therefore also the law or the 'strong' line, the rule that every Aboriginal follows.[19] He knows, he goes, every Aborigine goes by that line, that law, that reading of the particular landmarks. The Manggalili go by the reading of those of the Djarrakpi. Along this line of reasoning it is perfectly right to say that these landmarks, as memorised, are the true appearances of native title.[20]

In concluding I want to mention three consequences that affect the Anglo Australian legal system among all the consequences of this analogical type of reasoning.

The first consequence of analogical reasoning is that one is able (and has to be able) to fabricate analogies, correspondences and combinations, or else there is no longer an art of memory, and with that, no memory, no knowledge. On the other hand, because it is memorized in accordance with the actual landmarks, these fabrications do not stem from fantasy. That is why the Yolgnu, Manggalili, and many other indigenous Australians tell 'true stories'.[21]

---

[19] Even in the manner of clarifying Aboriginal law, this indigenous infor–mant is showing us how a 'songline' is completed step by step.

[20] Native title claimants have found Anglo Australian Judges on their site. See *Daniel v Western Australia* [2003] FCA 666 at [421] in which it was decided that the claimants may still have connection - as found in s 223(1)(b) of the Native Title Act - to the claimed area, being no residents of the area (anymore), when they are able to memorise the landmarks, or to 'conduct and maintain cultural, spiritual and religious practices and institutions through ceremonies and proper and appropriate maintenance and use of the Determination Area' as has been decided in *Kaurareg People v Queensland*, consent determination of native title, 23 May 2001, Order 6(d)(iii). See also for more cases Neate *supra* n 5.

[21] Understandably, the lawyers of the parties who oppose the Australian Indigenous claimants confront these true stories with the allegation of fabrication. This came up in the Hindmarsh case, where women of the Ngarrindjeri clan claimed - under Aboriginal and Torres Strait Islander Heritage Protection Act 1984 - 'woman's business' on Hindmarsh Island. It came even to an installation of a State investigation commission, the Hindmarsh Bridge Royal Commission, 16 June 1995. See James F. Weiner (1995) Anthropologists, historians and the secret of social klowledge. 11/5 *Anthropology Today* 3-7 at 3. In this case the fact even that not every Ngarrindjeri woman had knowledge of this woman's business was hold against the claimants, although this not being informed can be inline with the 'knowledge economy' among Aboriginal people as Walsh calls it, see Walsh,

The second consequence of this type of reasoning is that one is able (and has to be able) to incorporate new landmarks in the established series of existing features; otherwise the combinatorial exchange would stop, and with this the art of memory. That is why the Yolgnu, Manggalili, and many other indigenous Australians struggle with the condition of a 'traditional connection' to the land.[22]

The third consequence of analogical thinking is that it respects the general, which consists of all the features in its own terms, and is not explained, revealed or discovered by the correspondences, the analogies or combinations made up for memorization. The general holds its mystery. That is why the Yolgnu, Manggalili, and many other indigenous Australians keep their secrets.

---

supra n. 15, at 225. The Commissioner concluded that secret Ngarrindjeri 'women's business' was a fabrication. So the Federal Court decided in favour of the developers of the marine on Hindmarsh island who wanted the bridge to be built (*Chapman v. Tickner* (1995) 55 FCR 316). Many litigations followed but without changing this outcome: http://www.marina-hi.com.au/index.html.

[22] In the Mabo case (*Mabo v Queensland (No 2)* (1992) 175 CLR 1 at 57, 58, it is determined that there exists a native title according common law, which relies on the analytical concept of traditional. Judge Brennan: "The term 'native title' conveniently describes the interests and rights of indigenous inhabitants in land, whether communal, group or individual, possessed under the *traditional laws* acknowledged by and the *traditional customs* observed by the indigenous inhabitants. ... Native title has its origin in and is given its content by the *traditional laws* acknowledged by and the *traditional customs* observed by the indigenous inhabitants of a territory. The nature and incidents of native title must be ascertained as a matter of fact by reference to *those laws and customs.*' (emphasis added by Greame Neate (2004) *The 'tidal wave of justice' and the 'tide of history': ebbs and flows in Indigenous land rights in Australia.* Paper delivered at the 5th world Summit of Nobel Peace Laureates, Rome. http://www.nntt.gov.au/metacard/files/Justice/Ebbs%20and%20flows%20in%20Indigenous%20land%20rights%20in%20Australia.pdf at 15). Judge Brennan also said that 'when the tide of history has washed away any real acknowledgment of traditional law and any real observance of traditional customs, the foundation of native title has disappeared.' From then on it is hard to establish the traditional link or connection to the country. In the Yorta Yorta case (*Members of the Yorta Yorta Aboriginal Community v Victoria* [1998] FCA 1606; (2001) 110 FCR 244, 180 ALR 655; (2002) 214 CLR 422; 194 ALR 538) it was decided that the native title was therefore extinguished (Kenneth Maddock (2001) Native Title and the tide of History in Australia: reflection on *Yorta Yorta.* 34 *International Union of Anthropology and Ethnological Sciences, Commission on Folk Law and Legal Pluralism Newsletter* 35-43; Neate, *ibid.* at 17).

REFERENCES

Aarnio, Aulis and Maccormic, D.Neil (ed), *Legal Reasoning*, vol. II (Aldershot: Darthmouth Publishing Company).

Allison, DB., and Roberts, M.S., *Disordered mother or disordered diagnosis? : Munchausen by proxy syndrome* (Hillsdale, NJ, Analytic Press, 1998).

Amin Razavi, Mehdi and Ambuel, David (eds.) (Albany: State University of New York Press, 1997).

Anderson, Benedict, *Imagined Communities.* (London: Verso, 2003).

Appadurai, Arjun, *Modernity at large: cultural dimensions of globalization.* (Minneapolis: University of Minnesota Press, 1996).

Artingstall, K., *Practical aspects of Munchausen by proxy and Munchausen syndrome investigation* (London: CRC Press, 1999).

Astedt-Kurki, P and Heikkinen, RL 'Two approaches to the study of experiences of health and old age: The thematic interview and the narrative method', (1994) 20 *Journal of Advanced Nursing* 418.

Aubertin, C. (ed) *Fronteiras* (Brasília, Editora Universidade de Brasília, 1988).

Austin, J.L., *How to do Things With Words* (Cambridge, Harvard University Press, 1962).

Bach, Kent and Harnish, Robert M. *Linguistic Communication and Speech Acts* (Cambridge, The MIT Press, 1979).

Balakrishnan, Gopal, *Mapping the Nation.* (London: Verso, 2000).

Baldwin, C., 'Letter to the editor. Removal of a baby for adoption' (2002) 10 *British Journal of Midwifery* 668.

Baldwin, C., 'Munchausen syndrome by proxy: Problems of definition, diagnosis and treatment' (1996) 4 *Health and Social Care in the Community* 159.

Baldwin, C., *Munchausen syndrome by proxy: Telling tales of illness* (Unpublished PhD thesis, University of Sheffield, 2000).

Balibar, Etienne and Wallerstein, Immanuel, *Race, nation, class: ambiguous identities.* (London: Verso, 1991).

Barbosa, L., 'Save the rainforest! NGOs and grassroots organisations in the dialectics of Brazilian Amazonia' (2003), *International Social Science Journal* 55: 583-591.

Barcellona, Pietro, *Il ritorno del legame sociale.* (Torino: Bollati Boringhieri, 1990).

Beirne, Piers and Sharlet, Robert (comps). *Pashukanis: selected writings on Marxism and law.* (London: Academic Press, 1980).

Beitz, Charles, *Political Theory and International Relations* (Princeton: Princeton University Press, 1979).

Bennett, WL, and Feldman, MS, *Reconstructing reality in the courtroom: Justice and judgment in American culture* (New Brunswick: Rutgers University Press, 1981).

Benterrak, Krim, Stephen Mueke & Paddy Roe *Reading the Country. Introduction to Nomadology. (*Fremantle WA: Fremantle Arts Centre Press, 1984)

Bergeron, M.L., 'Hegemony, law and psychiatry: A perspective on the systematic oppression of "rogue mothers" in *In Aaron S',* (1996) IV *Feminist Legal Studies* 49.

Bethell, L., 'Politics in Brazil: from elections without democracy to democracy without citizenship' (2000), *Daedalus* 129: 1-27.

Blakemore-Brown, L., 'False illness in children – or simply false accusations?' (1998) 5 *The Therapist* 24; Mart 1999.

Botelho de Andrade, E., 'Desmatamento, solos e agricultura na Amazônia Legal' in *Causas e dinâmica do desmatamento na Amazônia* (Brasília, MMA, 2001).

Bowers, Frederick, *The Linguistic Aspects of Legislative Expression* (Vancouver, University of British Columbia, 1989).

Broad, W. and Wade, N., *Betrayers of the Truth,* (Simon and Schuster, New York, 1982).

Brooks, P. and Gerwitz, P. (eds), *Law's stories: Narrative and rhetoric in the law* (New Haven: Yale University, 1996).

Browder, J. (ed) *Fragile lands of Latin America: strategies for sustainable development* (Boulder, Westview Press, 1989).

Brown, K., and Rosendo, S., 'Environmentalists, rubber-tappers and empowerment: the politics and economics of extractive reserves' (2000), *Development and Change* 31: 201-227.

Brubaker, Rogers, *Citizenship and nation in France and Germany.* (Cambridge: Harvard University Press, 1992).

Burnham, W., Introduction to the Law and Legal System of the United States (West Publishing Company, St. Paul, MN, 1995).

Bursch, B., 'Territoriality' *August National Association of Apnea Professionals Munchausen syndrome by proxy Network Newsletter* 1 (1996).

Bushnell, David, *The Making of Modern Colombia. A nation in spite of itself.* (Berkeley/Los Angeles/Oxford: University of California Press, 1993).

Chandler, David (ed.) *Rethinking Human Rights : Critical Approaches to International Politics* (New York: Palgrave Macmillan 2003).

Chatterjee, Partha, *The Politics of the Governed.* (New York: Columbia University Press, 2004).

Cohen, P.R., at al. (eds.), *Intentions in Communication* (Cambridge, Mass., The MIT Press).

Cooke, Maeve, (ed.) *On the Pragmatics of Communication* (Cambridge, The MIT Press, 1998).

Cortazzi, M., *Narrative analysis* (London: The Falmer Press 1993).

Cunningham, Clark D. and C. J. Fillmore, 'Using Common Sense: A Linguistic Perspective on Judicial Interpretation of "Use a Firearm'', 73 *Wash. U. L.Q.* 1159 (1995)

Dahbour, Omar, 'Three Models of Global Community', *The Journal of Ethics* 9, no. 1-2 (2005): 201-24.

Damaska, M.R., *The Faces of Justice and State Authority* (Yale University Press, New Haven and London, 1986).

Danet, Brenda, 'Language in the Legal Process', (1980) *Law and Society,* 14(3): 447-63.

De Gregorio E. Borensztein, J. and J-W. Lee, "How Does Foreign Direct Investment Affect Economic Growth?" *Journal of International Economics* 45 (1998), 115-135.

De la Potterie B. Van Pottellsberghe, "Does Foreign Direct Investment Transfer Technology Across Borders?" *Review of Economics and Statistics* 83 (2001), 490-497.

Dean, W., A luta pela borracha no Brasil: Um estudo de história ecológica (São Paulo, Nobel, 1989).

Decker, F., 'Addressing Vagueness, Ambiguity, and Other Uncertainty in American Criminal Laws' (2002) 80 *Denver University Law Review* 241.

Deemter, K van, and Peters, S (eds.), *Semantic Ambiguity and Underspecification* (CSLI Publication, Stanford, 1996).

Devos, F., 'Semantic Vagueness and Lexical Polyvalence' (2003) 57 *Studia Linguistica* 121.

Dickerson, R., *The Interpretation and Application of Statutes* (Boston, Little, Brown, 1975).

Driedger, E., *Construction of Statutes* (2d ed. Toronto, Butterworths, 1983).

Dussel, Enrique, "Europe, Modernity and Eurocentrism". *Nepantla: view from the South 1:3* (2000).

Dussel, Enrique, *El encubrimiento del otro. El origen del mito de la modernidad.* (Bogota, Anthropos, 1992).

Dussel, Enrique, *Etica de la Liberacion en la edad de la globalizacion y de la exclusion.* (Madrid: Trotta, 1998).

Dussel, Enrique, The *Underside of Modernity. Apel, Ricoeur Rorty, Taylor and the Philosophy of Liberation.* (New Jersey: Humanities Press, 1996).

Emerich Edward Dalberg-Acton, John. First Baron Acton. *The history of freedom and other essays.* (London: Macmillan and co. Limited, 1907).

Emerich, John Edward, First Baron Acton. *Lectures on Modern History.* (London/New York: Macmillan and Co., Limited, 1906).

Endicott, T.A.O. *Vagueness in Law* (Oxford, OUP, 2000).

Fanon, Franz, *The wretched of the Earth.* (New York: Grover Weidenfeld, 1991).

Fearnside, P., 'Environmental impacts of Brazil's Tucurui Dam: unlearned lessons for hydroelectric development in Amazonia' (2001), *Environmental Management* 27: 377-96.

Fisher, G.C., and Mitchell, I., 'Is Munchausen syndrome by proxy really a syndrome?' (1995) 72 *Archives of Disease in Childhood* 530.

Flew, A. (ed.), *Logic and Language (*1st series). Cambridge, Blackwell, 1951).

Freeman, Richard B., 'Are your Wages Set in Beijing?', *Journal of Economic Perspectives*, vol. 9 (Summer 1995), No.3, pp. 15-32.

Gadow, K von, Pukkala, T. and Tomé, M. (eds), *Sustainable forest management* (Dordrecht, Kluwer Academic Publishers, 2000).

Gaines, P., 'Ideal and Actual Evidence in the Courtroom: Jurors' and Attorneys' Sense of Facts and Evidence' (2004), paper presented at the 2004 International Round Table for the Semiotics of Law, Lyon (France).

Garcia Anoveros, Jesus Maria, El pensamiento y los argumentos sobre la esclavitud en Europa en el siglo XVI y su aplicacion a los indios americanos y los negros africanos. (Madrid: Consejo Superior de Investigaciones Cientificas, 2000).

Garcia, Antonio, *Legislacion Indigenista de Colombia.* (Mexico: Instituto Indigenista Interamericano, 1952).

Gaskins, R.H., *Burdens of Proof in Modern Discourse* (Yale University Press, New Haven and London, 1992).

Gerbi, Antonello, La disputa del Nuevo Mundo. Historia de una Polemica 1750-1900. (Mexico: Fondo de Cultura Economica, 1960).

Gonzalez, Fernan E., Para leer la politica: ensayos de Historia Politica Colombiana. (Bogota: Cinep, 1997).

Gram, S., Kvist, L. and Cáseres, A., 'The importance of products extracted from Amazonian flood plain forests' (2001), *Ambio* 30: 365-368.

Grice, H.P., *Studies in the way of words* (collected papers) (Harvard University Press: Cambridge, Mass. 1989).

Grindle, M., *State and countryside: development policy and agrarian politics in Latin America* (Baltimore, The Johns Hopkins University Press, 1986).

Guillermo Hernandez de Alba (comp). *Como nacio la Republica de Colombia.* (Bogota: Banco de la Republica, 1965).

Guimarães Vieira, IC., Cardoso da Silva, J.M., Oren, D.C. and D'Incao, M.A. (eds), *Biological and cultural diversity of Amazônia* (Belém, Museu Paraense Emílio Goeldi, 2001).

Haack, S., 'Truth and Justice, Inquiry and Advocacy, Science and Law' (2004) *Ratio Juris*, 15.

Haack, Susan, 'Truth, truths, "truth", and "truths" in the law', *The Journal of Philosophy, Science and Law,* Volume 3, 2003.

Habermas, Jürgen, *Between Facts and Norms: Contributions to a Discourse Theory of Law and Democracy*, translated by William Rehg (Cambridge, the MIT Press, 1996).

Habermas, Jürgen, *On the Pragmatics of Communication* (Cambridge, the MIT Press, 1989).

Habermas, Jürgen, The Philosophical discourse of modernity. Twelve Lectures. (Cambridge: MIT Press, 1987).

Habermas, Jürgen, *The structural transformation of the public sphere: an inquiry into a category of Bourgeois society.* (Cambridge, Mass.: MIT press, 1989).

Hale, Sir Matthew, *History of the Pleas of the Crown* (1736). (London: Professional Books, I971.

Hall, A., *Developing Amazonia: deforestation and social conflict in Brazil's Carajás programme* (Manchester, Manchester University Press, 1989).

Hanke, Lewis, La lucha por la justicia en la conquista de America. (Madrid: Ediciones Istmo, 1988).

Hanke, Lewis, *Uno es todo el genero humano.* (Chiapas: Gobierno Constitutcional del Estado de Mexico, 1974).

Hart, H.L.A., *Essays in Jurisprudence and Philosophy* (Oxford: Clarendon Press, 1983).

Hart, H.L.A., *The concept of law* (Oxford, Clarendon, 1961-1994).

Hatch, J.A., and Wisniewski, R., (eds), *Life history and narrative* (London: The Falmer Press, 1995).

Hecht, S., Anderson, A. and May, P., 'The subsidy from nature: shifting cultivation, successional palm forests, and rural development' (1988), *Human Organization* 47: 25-35.

Heidegger, Martin, *The question concerning technology and other essays.* (New York: Harper and Row, 1977).

Henket, M., 'Contracts, Promises and Meaning: The question of Intent' (1989) 5 *International Journal for the Semiotics of Law* 129.

Hewson, B. et al , 'The appearance of fairness' (2002) 152 *New Law Journal* 1245.

Holmes, Oliver Wendell, 'The Path of the Law', in *Harvard Law Review* 457 (1897).

Holston, J., 'The misrule of law: land and usurpation in Brazil' (1991), *Comparative Studies in Society and History* 33: 695-725.

Howitt, D., *Child abuse errors: When good intentions go wrong?* (London, Harvester Wheatsheaf, 1992).

Hughes, Ian 'Yolgnu 'rom': indigenous knowledge in north Australia': 184-190. In Blunt, Peter and Warren, D. Michael (1996) *Indigenous organisations and development.* (London: Intermediate technology publications, 1996)

Hurrell, A. and Kingsbury, A., (eds), *The international politics of environment: actors, interests and institutions* (Oxford, Clarendon Press, 1992).

Hurwitz, B., et al (eds), *Narrative research in health and illness* (London: BMJ, 2004).

Hyman, D., 'Lies, damned lies, and narrative (1997) 73 *Indiana Law Journal* 797.

Ingleby, D., 'Professionals as socializers: The "psy complex"' (1985) 7*Research in law, deviance and social control* 79.

Jackson, Bernard S. 'A semiotic perspective on the comparison of analogical reasoning in secular and religious legal systems' : 295-325. In Soeteman, Arend (ed.) *Pluralism and Law.* (Dordrecht: Kluwer Academic Press, 2001)

Jackson, BS., *Law, fact and narrative coherence.* (Roby, Deborah Charles Publications, 1988).

Janis, I., *Groupthink.* (Boston, Houghton Mifflin, 1982).

Johnstone, Diana, *Fool's Crusade: Yugoslavia, NATO and Western Delusions* (New York: Monthly Review Press, 2002).

Jokic, Aleksandar (ed.) *Lessons of Kosovo: The Dangers of Humanitarian Intervention* (Calgary: Broadview Press, 2003).

Jokic, Aleksandar, 'Activism, Language, and International Law', *International Journal for the Semiotic of Law* 15 (2002): 107-120.

Jokic, Aleksandar, 'Genocidalism', *The Journal of Ethics* 8, No. 3 (2004): 251-297.

Jones, DPH, 'Commentary: Munchausen syndrome by proxy - is expansion justified?' (1996) 20 *Child Abuse and Neglect* 983.

Jori, M., 'Legal Performative', *The Encyclopedia of Language and Linguistics*, Volume 4, (Oxford, Pergamon Press, 1994).

Kaplan, J.F. et al., 'Bringing Linguistics into Judicial Decision-Making: Semantic Analysis Submitted to the US Supreme Court' (1995) 2 *Forensic Linguistics* 81.

Kelsen, Hans, *Reine Rechtslehre* (Wien: Österreichische Staatsdruckerei, 1992).

Koops, B.J, Schooten, H. van and Prins, M., *Recht naar binnen kijken. Een toekomstverkenning van huisrecht, lichamelijke integriteit en nieuwe opsporingstechnieken* [Looking Right In: A Prospective Study of the Sanctity of the Home, Bodily Integrity and New Investigation Techniques] (Den Haag: Sdu Uitgevers, 2004)

Kripke, S.A., *Wittgenstein on rules and private language* (Blackwell, Oxford, 1982).

Kuhn, T., *The Structure of Scientific Revolutions* (University of Chicago Press, 1962).

Kurzon, Dennis, *It is Hereby Performed ... Explorations in Legal Speech Acts* (Amsterdam, John Benjamins Publishing Company, 1986).

Kymlicka, Will, *Multicultural citizenship. A liberal theory of minority rights*. (Oxford: Oxford University Press, 1995).

Lagerspetz, Eerik, *The Opposite Mirrors: An Essay on the Conventionalist Theory of Institutions* (Dordrecht: Kluwer Academic Publishers, 1995).

Latour, B., *Science in Action* (Harvard University Press, 1987).

Lewy, Guenter, *America in Vietnam* (New York: Oxford University Press, 1978).

Lieber, Francis, *Legal and Political Hermeneutics or Principles of Interpretation and Construction in Law and Politics with Remarks on Precedents and Authorities,* 3rd ed. (St.Lous: F.H.Thomas, 1880).

Lonergan, B.J.F., *Method in theology, Second edition.* (London, Darton, Longman & Todd 1973).

Lopez Garcia, Jose Tomas, *Defensores de los Esclavos Negros en el siglo XVII.* (Caracas: Universidad Catolica Andres Bello, 1982).

Lotman, Y., *Universe of the mind: a semiotic theory of culture* (London, I.B. Tauris, 1990).

Lowe, L., and Lloyd, D. (eds) *The politics of culture in the shadow of capital* (Durham, Duke University Press, 1997).

MacCormick, Neil and Weinberger, Ota, *An Institutional Theory of Law: New Approaches to Legal Positivism* (Dordrecht: Kluwer Academic Publishers, 1986).

Maddock, Kenneth 'Native Title and the tide of History in Australia: reflection on Yorta Yorta' (2001) 34 *International Union of Anthropology and Ethnological Sciences, Commission on Folk Law and Legal Pluralism Newsletter* 35-43

Maddock, Kenneth 'Warlpiri Land Tenure: a Test Case in Legal Anthropology', (1981) 52/2 *Oceania* 85-102

Mariategui, Jose Carlos, Siete Ensayos de Interpretacion de la Realidad Peruana. (Lima: Serie Popular,, 1979).

Mart, E., 'Problems with the diagnosis of factitious disorder by proxy in forensic settings (1999) 17 *American Journal of Forensic Psychology* 69.

Mart, E.G., *Munchausen's syndrome by proxy reconsidered.* (Manchester, NH: Bally Vaughan Publishing, 2002).

Marx, Anthony W., *Faith in the Nation. Exclusionary origins of nationalism.* (Oxford: Oxford University Press, 2003).

Meadow, R., 'The history of Munchausen syndrome by proxy' in Levin, A.V., and Sheridan, M.S. (eds), *Munchausen syndrome by proxy: Issues in diagnosis and treatment.* (New York: Lexington Books, 1995).

Meira Mattos, C. de, *Uma geopolítica pan-amazônica* (Rio de Janeiro, Biblioteca do Exército, 1980).

Mello Alvarenga, O., Política e direito agroambiental: Comentários à nova Lei de reforma agrária (Lei no 8.629, de 2 de Fevereiro de 1993) (Rio de Janeiro, Forense, 1995).

Merryman, J.H., *The Civil Law Tradition* (Stanford University Press, Stanford, CA, 1985).

Mill, John Stuart. *Essays on England, Ireland and the Empire.* (Toronto and Buffalo: University of Toronto Press/Routledge and Kegan Paul, 1982).

Mill, John Stuart. *Del Gobierno Representativo.* (Madrid: Tecnos, 1985).

Mitchell, W.J.T., (ed.), *Against Theory: Literary Studies and New pragmatism* (Chicago and London, The University of Chicago Press, 1985).

Moore, AJ., 'Trial by schema: Cognitive filters in the courtroom' (1989) 37 *UCLA Law Review* 273.

Moore, T. (ed.), *New trends in cognitive representation* (Hillsdale NJ, Erlbaum, 1983).

Morley, C.J., 'Practical concerns about the diagnosis of Munchausen syndrome by proxy', (1995) 72 *Archives of Disease in Childhood* 528.

Morphy, Howard, ''Now you understand': an analysis of the way Yolgnu have used sacred knowledge to retain their autonomy': 110-145. In Peterson, Nicolas & Langton, Marcia (eds.) *Aborigines, land and landrights* (Canberra: Australian Institute of Aboriginals Studies, 1983)

Naro, Nancy Priscilla (ed). *Blacks, coloureds and national identity in Nineteenth-Century Latin America.* (London: University of London Press, 2003).

Neate, Greame '*The 'tidal wave of justice' and the 'tide of history': ebbs and flows in Indigenous land rights in Australia'*, Paper delivered at the 5th world Summit of Nobel Peace Laureates, (2004b) Rome. http://www.nntt.gov.au/metacard/files/Justice/Ebbs%20and%20flows%20in%20Indigenous%20land%20rights%20in%20Australia.pdf

Neate, Greame, '*An overview of native title in Australia — some recent milestones and the way ahead'*, Paper delivered at 11th Annual Cultural Heritage & Native Title Conference 'Building Partnerships and Finding Solutions for Better Outcomes', (2004a) Brisbane Queensland http://www.nntt.gov.au/metacard/files/Overview/An%20overview%20of%20native%20title%20in%20Australia%20-%20some%20recent%20milestones%20and%20the%20way%20ahead.pdf

Norbu, Dawa, *Culture and the politics of Third World Nationalism.* (London: Routledege, 1991).

O'Barr, WM, *Linguistic evidence.* (New York: Academic Press, 1982).

Ogden, C.K., *Bentham's Theory of Fictions* (New York: Harcourt, Brace and Company, 1942).

Patterson, D.M., (ed) *Wittgenstein and legal theory* (Boulder CO, Westview., 1992).

Peet, R., Ideology, discourse, and the geography of hegemony: from socialist to neoliberal development in postapartheid South África (2002), *Antipode*: 54-84.

Perelman, Chaim and Olbrechts-Tyteca, Luac, *The New Rhetoric. A Treatise on Argumentation*, (Notre-Dame – London, 1969).

Perkins, Dwight, *Economics of Development* (New York: W.W. Norton & Company, 2001).

Petras, J. and Veltmeyer, H., 'Whither Lula's Brazil? Neo-liberalism and 'third way' ideology', *The Journal of Peasant Studies* 31 (2003): 1-44.

Pinheiro, P., 'Democratic governance, violence, and the (un)rule of law' (2000), *Daedalus* 129: 119-143.

Pogge, Thomas, *Realizing Rawls* (Ithaca: Cornell University Press, 1989).

Pogge, Thomas, *World Poverty and Human rights* (Cambridge: Polity Press, 2002).

Polich, J., 'The Ambiguity of plain meaning: Smith v. United States and the new Textualism' (1994) 68 *Southern Californian Law review* 259.

Pontes Pinto, E., *Rondônia: evolução histórica* (Rio de Janeiro, Expressão e Cultura, 1993).

Power, Samantha, *A Problem from Hell: America and the Age of Genocide* (New York: Basic Books, 2002).

Putnam, H., 'The meaning of "meaning"' in *Mind, language and reality* (vol. 2) (Cambridge, CUP, 1975).

Quijano, Anibal, "Coloniality of Power, Eurocentrism, and Latin America". *Nepantla. Views from the South.* 1.3 (2000).

Quijano, Anibal, *Reencuentro y Debate. Una Introduccion a Mariategui.* (Lima: Mosca Azul Editores, 1981).

Quintilianus, Marcus Fabius, *The Institutio Oratoria of Quintilian*, (London, 1951).

Rawls, John, *Political Liberalism* (New York: Columbia University Press 1993).

Raynolds, L., Murray, D. and Taylor, P., 'Fair trade coffee: building producer capacity via global networks' (2004), *Journal of International Development* 16: 1109-1121.

Recanati, F., *Literal meaning* (Cambridge, CUP, 2004).

Riessman, C.K., *Narrative analysis* (London: Sage, 1993).

Robinson, O., Fergus, T. and Gordon, W., *An introduction to European legal history* (Oxon: Professional Books, 1987).

Ruiter, Dick W.P., *Legal Institutions* (Dordrecht: Kluwer Academic Publishers, 2001).

Ryan, T.M., 'Munchausen syndrome by proxy: Misogyny or modern medicine?' (1997) Fall *The Association of Trial Lawyers of America's Women Trial Lawyers Caucus Newsletter* 3.

Schauer, F., *Playing by the rules* (Oxford, Clarendon, 1991).

Schooten, Hanneke van (ed.), *Semiotics and Legislation: Jurisprudential, Institutional and Sociological Perspectives* (Liverpool: Deborah Charles Publications, 1999).

Schooten, Hanneke van, 'A New Conceptual Framework for Analysing a Case Study on ICT and the Sanctity of the Home', *International Journal for the Semiotics of Law* (forthcoming, 2005)

Schreier, H.A., 'Repeated false allegations of sexual abuse presenting to sheriffs: When is it Munchausen by proxy?' (1996) 20 *Child Abuse and Neglect* 985.

Schreier, H.A., and Libow, J.A., *Hurting for love: Munchausen by proxy syndrome*. (New York: Guilford Press, 1993).

Schreiner, Agnes T.M. 'Observing the differences': 87-94. In Arend Soeteman (ed.) *Pluralism and Law. Proceedings of the 20th IVR World Congress.* Volume 3: Global Problems (ARSP-Beiheft 90) (Stuttgart: Franz Steiner Verlag, 2004).

Schreiner, Agnes T.M. 'So, this is how it is done ...': 123-144. In Lindgren, J. Ralph & Jay Knaack (eds.) *Ritual and Semiotics.* Critic of Institutions Vol. 14: Law (New York etc: Peter Lang, 1997)

Schreiner, Agnes T.M. 'The Ritual Manifesto'. (2003) eEdition. Amsterdam/Internet: 1001Publishers http://www.1001publishers.com/index_uk.html

Searle, John R., *Expression and Meaning: Essays in the Theory of Speech Acts* (Cambridge, Cambridge University Press, 1979).

Searle, John R., 'Literal meaning' in *Expression and meaning*. (Cambridge, CUP, 1979).

Searle, John R., *Mind, Language and Society: Philosophy in the Real World* (New York, Basic Books, 1988).

Searle, John R., *Speech Acts*: *An Essay in the Philosophy of Language* (Cambridge: Cambridge University Press, 1969-1970).

Shapiro, Ian and Brilmayer, Lea (eds.), *Global Justice* (New York: New York University Press, 1999).

Sherwin, R., 'Law frames: Historical truth and narrative necessity in a criminal case' (1994) 47 *Stanford Law Review* 39.

Sherwin, R., 'The narrative construction of legal reality' (1994), 18 *Vermont Law Review* 681.

Simpson, Jane, 'Confidentiality of linguistic material: the case of Aboriginal land claims': 428-439. In Gibbons, John (1994) *Language and the law* (London/New York: Longman, 1994).

Sinclair, M.B.W., 'Statutory Reasoning',(1997) 46 *Drake Law Review* 299.

Singer, Peter, *One World: The Ethics of Globalization* (New Haven: Yale University Pres, 2002).

Socorro Flores, M do, *O meio ambiente e a proteção dos recursos florestais no Pará: uma abordagem jurídica* (Belém, Universidade Federal do Pará, 1999).

Solan, L. M., 'Judicial Decisions and linguistic analysis: is there a linguist in the court?' (1995) 73 *Washington University Law Quarterly* 1069.

Solan, L.M., 'Law, language and lenity' (1998) 40 *William and Mary Law Review* 57.

Sousa Santos, B de (ed) *Reconhecer para libertar: os caminhos do cosmopolitismo multicultural* (Rio de Janeiro, Civilização Brasileira, 2003).

Sousa Santos, B de and Trindade, J.C. (eds), *Conflito e transformação social: uma paisagem das justiças em Moçambique, vol. 1* (Porto: Edições Afrontamento, 2003).

Spence, D.P., 'Narrative smoothing and clinical wisdom' in Sarbin, T.R., (ed) *Narrative psychology: The storied nature of human conduct.* (New York: Praeger Publishers, 1986).

Spitzer, Steven, "Marxist Perspectives in the Sociology of Law". *Ann. Rev. Sociol.* 1983. 9:103-24.

Stavenhagen, Rodolfo et al. *Tres ensayos sobre America Latina.* (Barcelona: Editorial Anagrama, 1980).

Stone, Julius, Legal System and Lawyers' Reasoning (London, 1964).

Stroud, B., *Meaning, understanding, and Practice: Philosophical Essays* (Oxford, Oxford University press, 2000)

Taylor, BR., (ed) *Ecological resistance movements: the global emergence of radical and popular environmentalism* (Albany, State University of New York Press, 1995).

Toulmin, S., *The Uses of Argument* (Cambridge University Press, 1974).

Travis, C., *The uses of sense: Wittgenstein's philosophy of language.* (Oxford, Clarendon:1989).

Urban, Greg and Sherzer. Joel, *Nation-States and Indians in Latin America.* (Austin: University of Texas Press, 1991).

Viehweg, Theodor, *Topics and Law*, (Frankfurt am Mein: Peter Lang, 1993).

Virtanen, P. and Palmujoki, E., *Sustainable forest management through multilateral agreements and market-based mechanisms* (Helsinki, MFA, 2002).

Wagenaar, WA, *Anchored Narratives. The Psychology of Criminal Evidence,* (Harvester Weatsheaf and St. Martin's Press, 1993).

Wall, N., 'Judicial attitudes to expert evidence in children's cases'(1997) 76 *Archives of Diseases in Childhood* 185.

Wallerstein, Immanuel, *Open the Social Sciences. Report of the Gulbenkian Foundation on the Restructuring of the Social Science.* (Stanford: California University Press, 1996).

Walsh, Michael (1994) 'Interactional styles in the courtroom: an example from northern Australia': 217-233. In Gibbons, John (1994) *Language and the law* (London/New York: Longman).

Weiner, James F. (1995) 'Anthropologists, historians and the secret of social knowledge' 11/5 *Anthropology Today*, 3-7

Williamson, T., 'Vagueness, Indeterminacy and Social Meaning' (2001) 16 *Critical Studies* 61.

Wittgenstein, L., *Philosophical Investigations* (Oxford, Blackwell, 1953).

Wood, Adrian, 'How trade Hurt Unskilled Workers', in *Journal of Economic Perspectives*, vol. 9 (Summer 1995).

Wood, Adrian, *North-South Trade, Employment and Inequality: Changing Fortunes in a Skill-Driven World* (Oxford: Clarendon Press 1994).

Yates, Francis A. (1974) *The art of memory* (Chicago: The University of Chicago Press).

Zavala, Silvio, *Ensayos sobre la colonizacion Espanola en America.* (Buenos Aires: Emece Editores, 1944).

Zavala, Silvio, *La filosofia politica en la conquista de America.* (Mexico: Fondo de Cultura Economica, 1947). Benavides Vanegas, Farid Samir, *Derecho y Nacion.* (Bogota: Editorial Juridica Ibanez, 2004).

Zhang, Q., 'Fuzziness – vagueness – generality – ambiguity' (1998) 29 *Journal of Pragmatics* 13.

Zuckerman, A.S.S, *The principles of Criminal Justice* (Oxford, 1989).

9 781402 053191

MIX
Papier aus verantwortungsvollen Quellen
Paper from responsible sources
FSC® C105338

If you have any concerns about our products,
you can contact us on
ProductSafety@springernature.com

In case Publisher is established outside the EU,
the EU authorized representative is:
Springer Nature Customer Service Center GmbH
Europaplatz 3, 69115 Heidelberg, Germany

Printed by Libri Plureos GmbH
in Hamburg, Germany